CHARLEY'S WAR

1 August 1916 – 17 October 1916

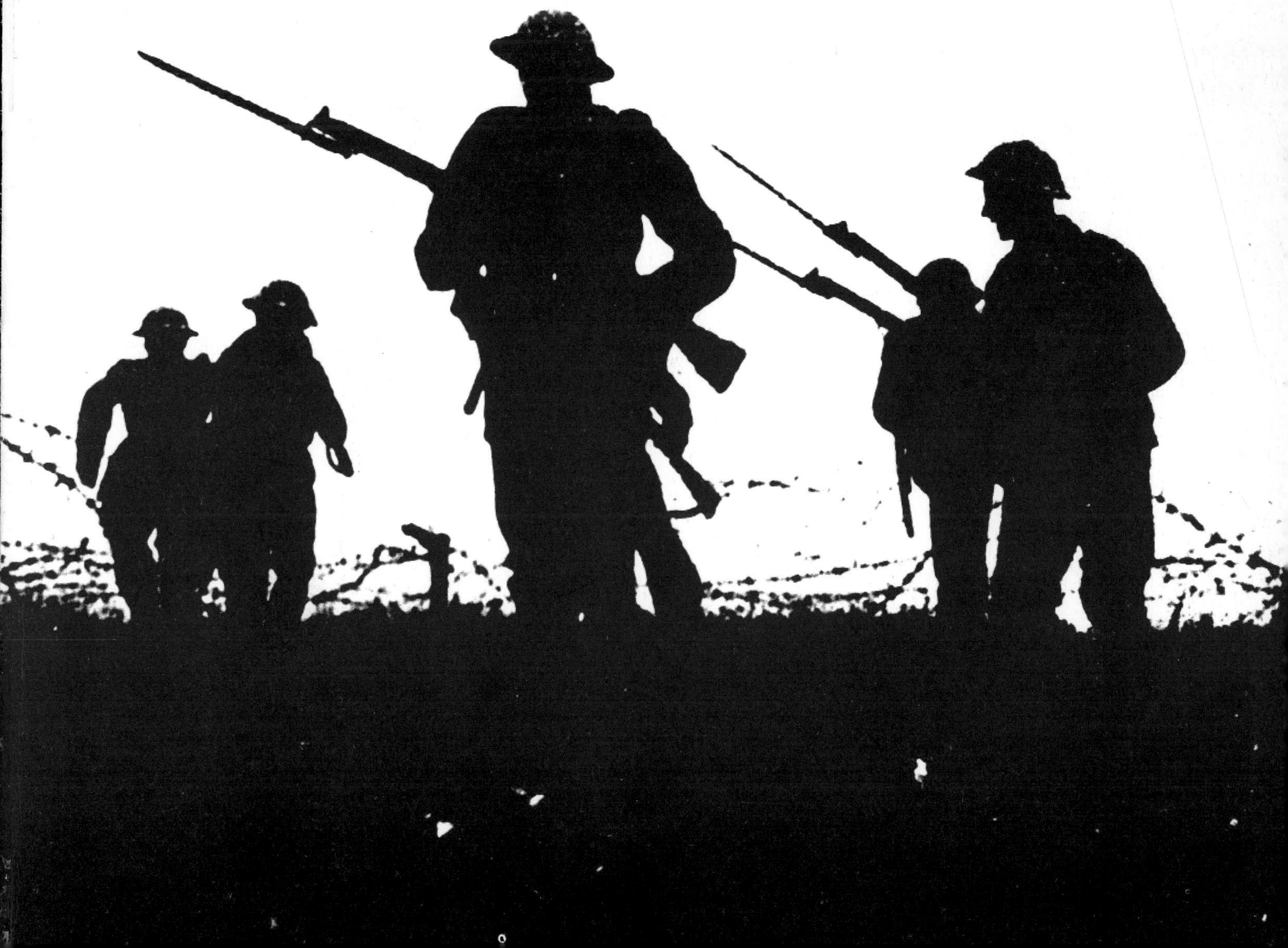

CHARLEY'S WAR: 1 August 1916 – 17 October 1916
ISBN 1 84023 929 8

Published by
Titan Books
A division of Titan Publishing Group Ltd
144 Southwark Street
London SE1 0UP

A CIP catalogue record for this title is available from the British Library.

This edition first published: October 2005
2 4 6 8 10 9 7 5 3 1

Printed in Italy.

Also available from Titan Books:
Charley's War: 2 June 1916 – 1 August 1916 (ISBN: 1 84023 627 2)

Grateful thanks to Pat Mills, Trucie Henderson, Alan Barnes, Garth Ennis, Steve White and
Michael Duffy for their help and support in the production of this book.

Cover photo used by permission of the Imperial War Museum, London (Q-70167).
Poppy artwork © 2005 Trucie Henderson.

'Landships' © 2005 Steve White.
Strip commentary © 2005 Pat Mills.
Afterword © 2005 Garth Ennis.

What did you think of this book? We love to hear from our readers.
Please email us at : readerfeedback@titanemail.com, or write to us
at the above address.

Much of the comic strip material used by Titan in this edition is exceedingly rare.
As such, we hope that readers appreciate that the quality of the materials can be variable.

www.titanbooks.com

CHARLEY'S WAR

1 August 1916 – 17 October 1916

PAT MILLS

JOE COLQUHOUN

Titan Books

LANDSHIPS

The Evolution of the Tank

by Steve White

Considering Pat Mills' zealous attention to detail and also that the Battle of the Somme provides the shattered backdrop to *Charley's War*, it was inevitable that young Charley would encounter tanks. An everyday occurrence on the modern battlefield, in September 1916, they were the British Army's soon-to-be-unleashed, war-ending secret weapon. It was therefore natural that Charley, never a mere observer of history within the story, would soon find himself at the helm of one of these steel monstrosities.

Armour is about as old as war itself – be it tightly thatched reeds, leather, iron, bronze or steel. But the idea of mechanised armour is somewhat newer, with the concept of a travelling fortress dating back to the invention of steam power and Stevenson's Rocket in the 18th Century. Even Leonardo da Vinci sketched a cannon-armed design. But it was in the First World War that the tank as it's generally now seen came into being.

The Battle of the Somme is remembered for many things. It immortalised forever the needless waste of young lives in the Great War and the notion of a high-society High Command squandering working class cannon fodder before German machine-guns. These sweeping generalisations have over-shadowed one important and unassailable fact: the latter stages of the battle saw the first combat use of the tank.

The early stages in the evolution of the modern tank concept extend back to the end of the 19th Century, when tractor builders in the USA developed a working caterpillar track. The American Civil War had seen the development of steam-powered, metal-armoured warships but it seemed something of a leap of faith and imagination to bring warships ashore.

It was down to another mechanical enthusiast to take the next step. Frederick Simms designed a 'motor-war car' armed with two of the new machine-guns, and powered by a Daimler engine. Simms offered it to the British Army but the Minister of War - Lord Kitchener - dismissed it, like the machine-gun before it, as having little practical use. This shouldn't have come as any real surprise to Simms. The British Army's officer corps found it hard to look beyond its horses and cavalry divisions. Lancers were still making charges at the outbreak of the First World War, even though these transpired to be the last huzzah of the cavalry, who now faced barbed wire and machine-guns.

However, the concept of the tank had a champion in Colonel Ernest Swinton. He had been an officer with the British Army during the Boer War when, on 13 June 1900, he had a revelation and realised that there was a need for

BELOW: The first landships roll into action.

THEN, THROUGH THE MORNING MIST, THE "MOTHERS" OF DESTRUCTION APPEARED!

NEIN! THE DEVIL IS COMING! THE DEVIL IS COMING!

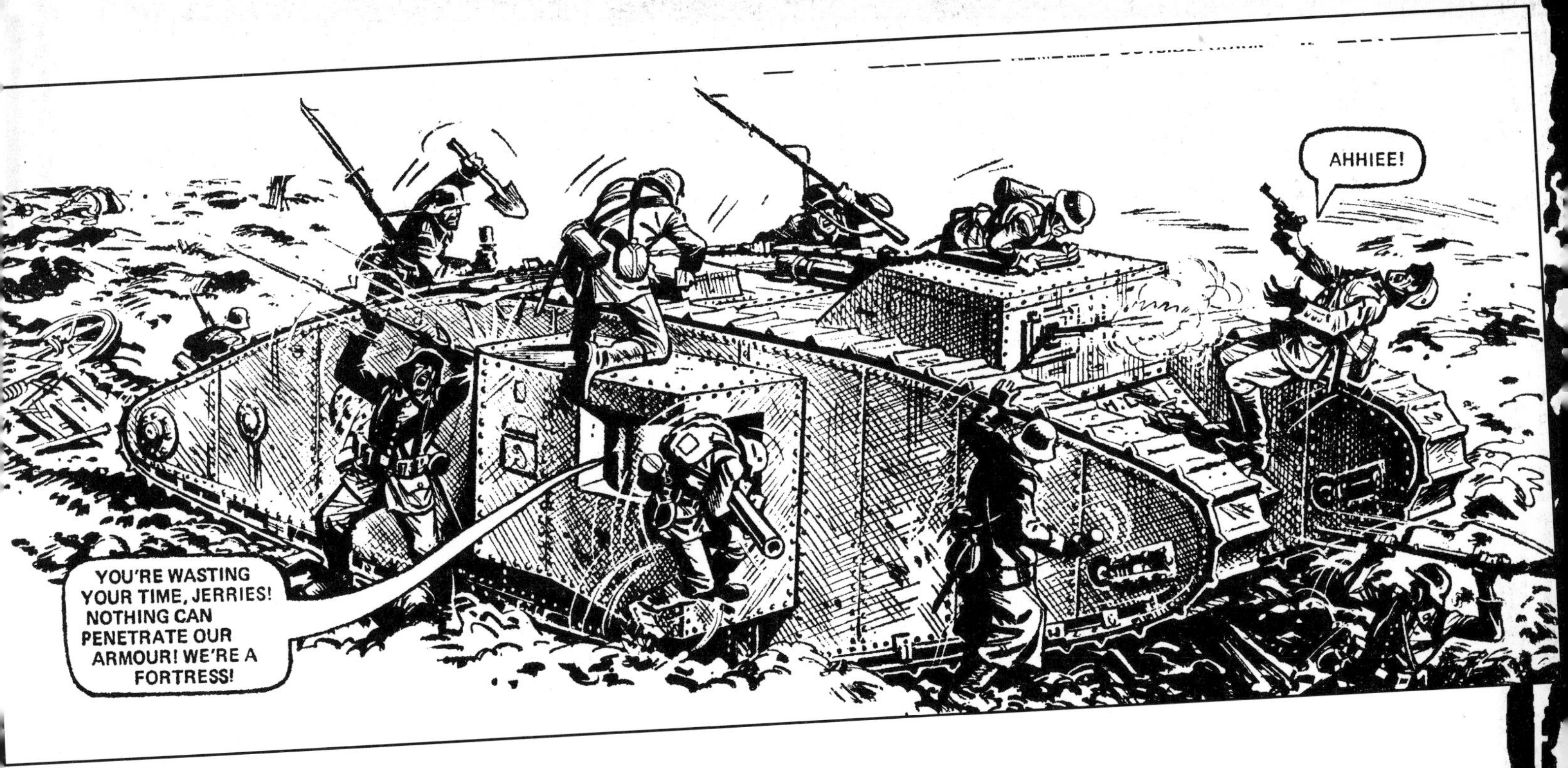
AHHIEE!
YOU'RE WASTING YOUR TIME, JERRIES! NOTHING CAN PENETRATE OUR ARMOUR! WE'RE A FORTRESS!

ABOVE: The tank crew enjoy the relative safety of their armour...

BELOW: ...But the protection of the armour also serves to trap the tank crew.

an armoured vehicle to withstand the growing power of artillery and the new automatic weapons.

He was joined in his enthusiasm by Maurice Hankey, Secretary of the Committee for Imperial Defence, and between them, they arranged a demonstration of a Killen-Strait tractor in June 1915. The audience included David Lloyd George – at the time the Minister of Munitions but, by the end of the First World War, Prime Minister – and Winston Churchill, the First Lord of the Admiralty whose stock was at a low ebb after the disastrous landing at Gallipoli, which he had overseen.

Still, the demonstration went well. The vehicle cut a barbed wire fence and both men were enthusiastic. Churchill went so far as to sponsor a study of the potential of what were known as 'landships' – a reflection of the belief that these armoured vehicles were just battleships on land.

This study led to an agreement to begin the design and construction of the first landships. Swinton was to work alongside Lieutenant Walter Wilson of the Naval Air Service and William Tritton of William Foster & Co. Whilst it may seem a little incongruous to have a member of the Royal Navy working on an ostensibly Army project, the Navy were regular users of armoured cars, a popular vehicle on the Western Front in 1915, when the War was still one of mobility and firepower and yet to be supplanted by the stultifying stagnation of trench warfare. The Navy had been pioneers in the deployment of armoured cars, and in 1914 the Naval Brigade and the Royal Naval Air Squadron had sent theirs to Antwerp, in Belgium, to defend Allied airstrips. It was only natural therefore, given the perceived nature of the tank, that the Navy be involved from the start.

Due to the secret nature of the project, the vehicle was given a codename. Because it looked like tracked water tanks, it became known, as of December 1915, as a 'tank' and whilst landship may be

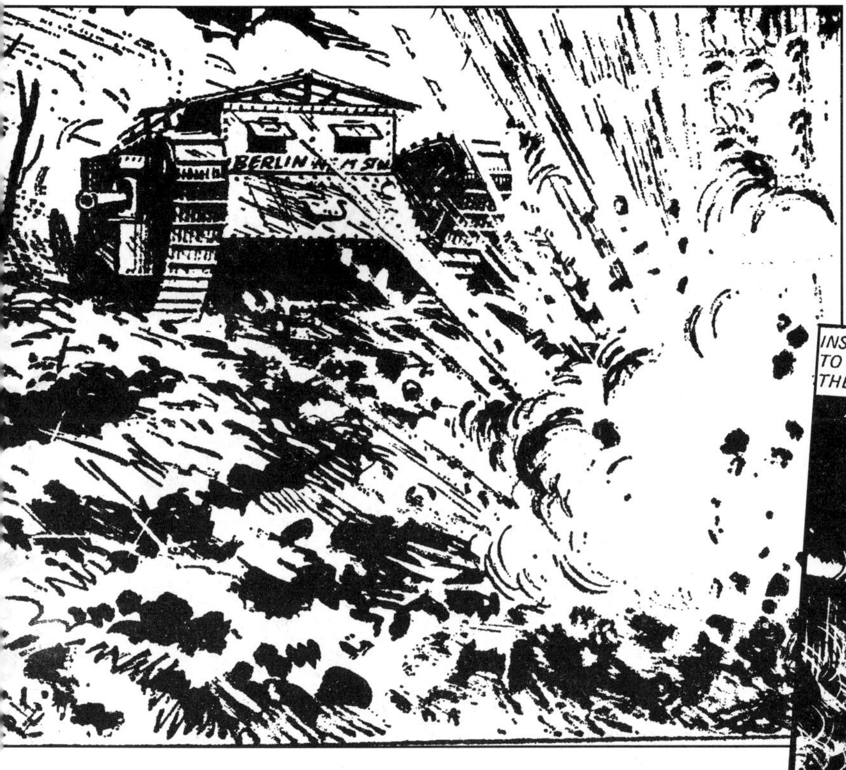

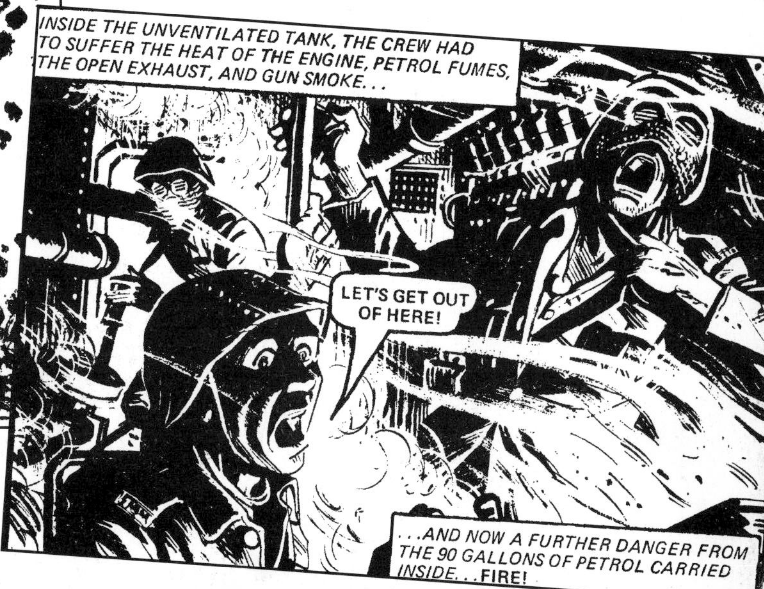
INSIDE THE UNVENTILATED TANK, THE CREW HAD TO SUFFER THE HEAT OF THE ENGINE, PETROL FUMES, THE OPEN EXHAUST, AND GUN SMOKE...
LET'S GET OUT OF HERE!
...AND NOW A FURTHER DANGER FROM THE 90 GALLONS OF PETROL CARRIED INSIDE... FIRE!

BELOW: Theoretically safer than footsoldiers, the tank crews were still in great danger from flying shrapnel and debris.

more evocative, the nickname stuck.

Swinton gave the builders several design criteria he felt had to be met. It had to be able to climb a five-foot obstacle; cross a five foot-wide trench; have a top speed of four miles an hour on a flat surface, two in battlefield conditions; withstand machine-gun bullets, and have a crew of ten men, who were to man the two machine-guns mounted on board.

Things got off to a bad start. The first prototype shed its tracks two days after leaving the production line on 8 September, then again on the 19th. Also, the first version, 'Little Willie', weighing fourteen tons and powered by a Daimler engine, did not meet the tough specifications laid down. It was not able to cross trenches and carried a crew of only three in very cramped conditions.

Fortunately, these were seen as mere teething troubles and progress was such that, by January 1916, a top-secret demonstration was arranged to put 'Big Willie' through its paces. The new tank was considerably larger, carried 10mm armour on the front and 8mm armour on its sides, had a crew of eight and was to be armed with 57mm naval guns in side turrets. In front on an audience of politicians and high-ranking military commanders, the tank was put through its paces. Lord Kitchener was amongst those watching and seemed unimpressed. He called it a "pretty mechanical toy", but it's possible, according to those close to him, that he said this to goad the 'tank team' to greater effort in proving the worth of their creation.

More impressed was Lloyd George, who ordered 100 of the tanks, now known as the heavy Mark I, into production.

Driven by the enthusiasm and tenacity of Swinton, Wilson and Tritton, the teething troubles were beaten out of the prototypes and tactics were developed for their use. Swinton saw the tanks and infantry operating in symphony, but knew the reality to be that the tanks would actually be supporting the soldiers on the ground as they attempted to break German defences.

In April, Sir Douglas Haig, Commander-in-Chief of the British Army in Europe, told Swinton he wanted tanks and their crews ready by 1 June in the hope they would be ready to participate in the forthcoming battle of the Somme. Easier said than done. There were no crews available and no tanks to train any on. It should be remembered as well that very few, except the very wealthy, had any experience in operating a mechanical vehicle. Horses were still the transport of choice.

In the end, crews were drawn from the Motor Machine Gun Service and Naval Armoured Car Squadrons. Also enlisted were civilians with experience in mechanical vehicles.

In an effort to disguise its true nature, the six companies formed were called the Armoured Car Section of the Motor Machine Gun Service. Despite the efforts of Swinton and his team, the tanks were not available to take part in the 'big push' on 1 July. The impact, if any, they would have had on the slaughter that took place that day can only really be speculated on.

The tanks didn't get into action until 15 September. On that day, in a historical first, Captain H. W. Mortimore drove his tank into battle at the infamous Bois d'Elville (known as 'Devil's Wood' by the troops), where South African infantry had fought a gruelling battle against German defenders in what would be their most costly action on the Western Front. One tank made little difference and the South Africans were never able to overcome the Germans.

The tanks had a more positive impact in the fighting around the villages of Flers and Courcelette. In a subsidiary attack of the Somme offensive, the first massed tank assault took place when forty-nine tanks – every one available to the British Army – went into action on the same day, 15 September.

Conditions for the tank crews were at best uncomfortable, at worst infernal. They were stiflingly hot, cramped,

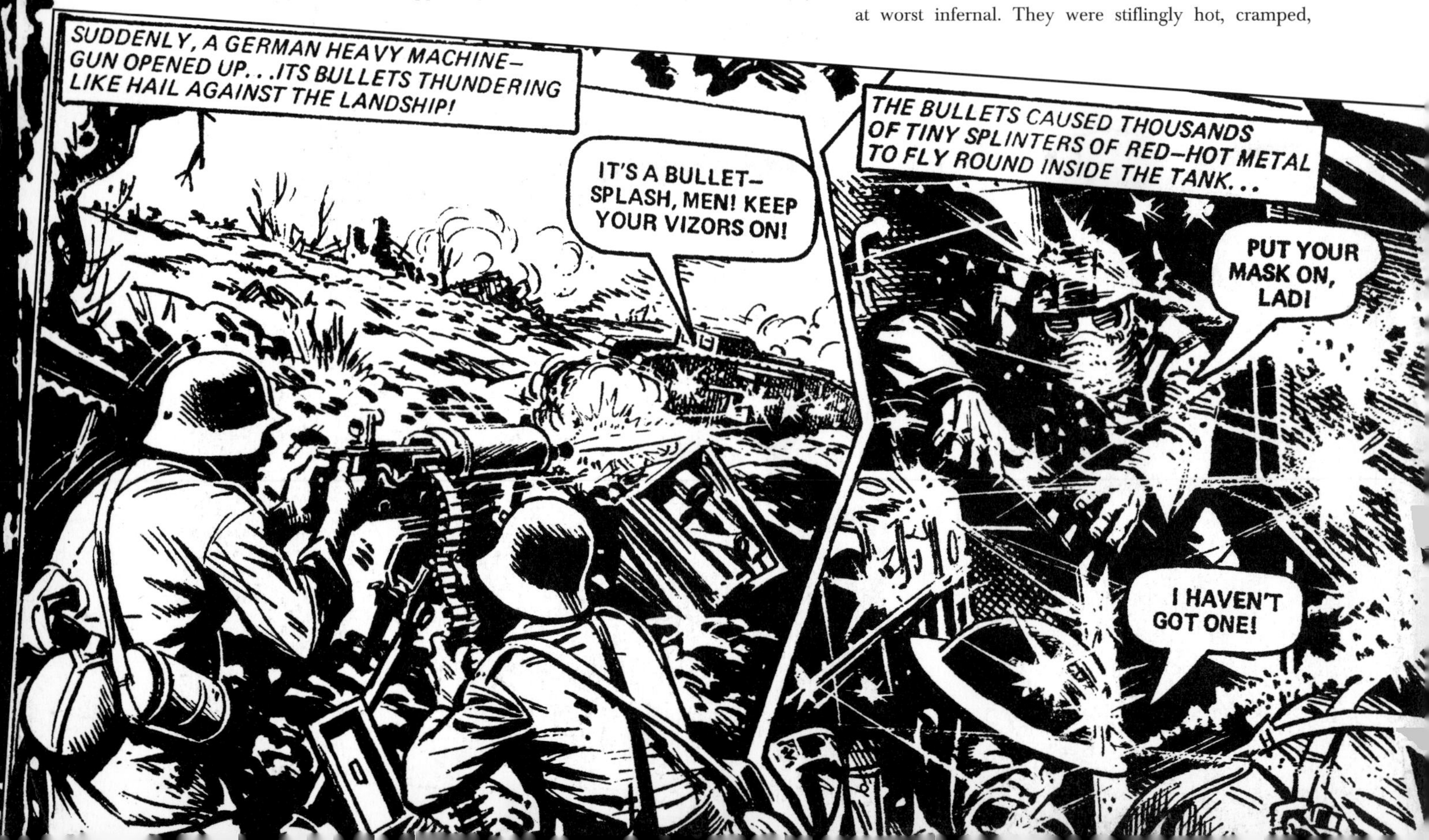
SUDDENLY, A GERMAN HEAVY MACHINE-GUN OPENED UP...ITS BULLETS THUNDERING LIKE HAIL AGAINST THE LANDSHIP!
IT'S A BULLET-SPLASH, MEN! KEEP YOUR VIZORS ON!
THE BULLETS CAUSED THOUSANDS OF TINY SPLINTERS OF RED-HOT METAL TO FLY ROUND INSIDE THE TANK...
PUT YOUR MASK ON, LAD!
I HAVEN'T GOT ONE!

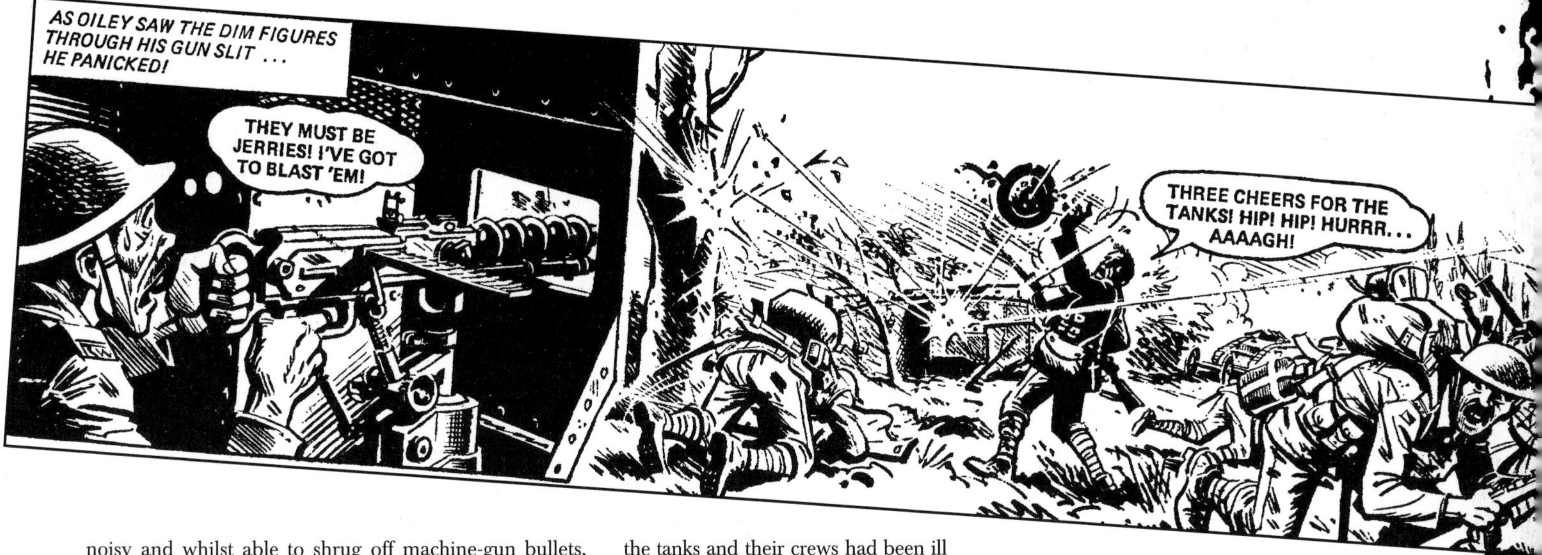
AS OILEY SAW THE DIM FIGURES THROUGH HIS GUN SLIT . . . HE PANICKED!
THEY MUST BE JERRIES! I'VE GOT TO BLAST 'EM!
THREE CHEERS FOR THE TANKS! HIP! HIP! HURRR. . . AAAAGH!

noisy and whilst able to shrug off machine-gun bullets, the impact of rounds would often send metal chips flying around the cabin. As protection, crews were expected to wear chain mail visors, but in the blistering heat, these were uncomfortable and seldom used.

There were other problems: visibility was poor, making navigation difficult and on occasion leading to friendly fire incidents. The tanks were also reliability nightmares, breaking down with monotonous regularity. Of the forty-nine tanks that were scheduled to attack, seventeen failed to make the start line. Seven more broke down before the attack began, leaving just fifteen to actually go into action.

Despite these problems, any misgivings about their impact on the battlefield were soon dispelled when the Germans in the villages fled at the approach of these mechanical monstrosities. The tanks' entry into Flers was witnessed by an aircraft overhead. The crew reported, "A tank is walking down the main street of Flers with the British Army cheering behind it."

It was a shaky start. Haig had had high hopes for the tanks, envisaging them breaking the deadlock gripping the Western Front. But the tanks and their crews had been ill prepared for the battle, and they had been too few in number to make a decisive difference. Stalwart supporter Winston Churchill feared that "my poor little 'land battleships' have been let off prematurely on a petty scale."

Even so the signs were all there, albeit on a local level, that the tank was going to have a bright future on the battlefield. In 1940, it was the Germans – who ironically had thought very little of tanks in 1916 – who proved just how far use of armour had come when the First World War battlefields rumbled once again to the approach of tanks as the *Blitzkrieg* thundered into France and Belgium. ✢

ABOVE: 'Oiley' discovers the dangers of limited visibility when he accidentally fires on British troops.

BELOW: A British tank strikes terror into the hearts of the German army.

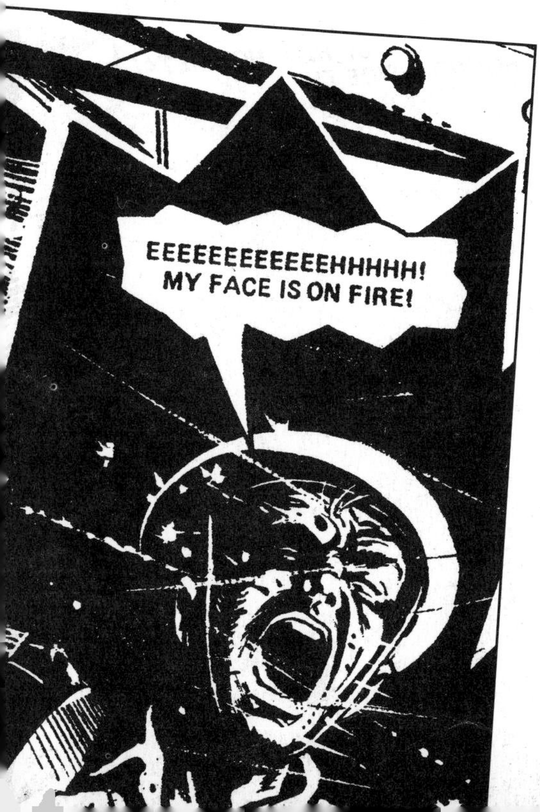
EEEEEEEEEEEEHHHHH! MY FACE IS ON FIRE!

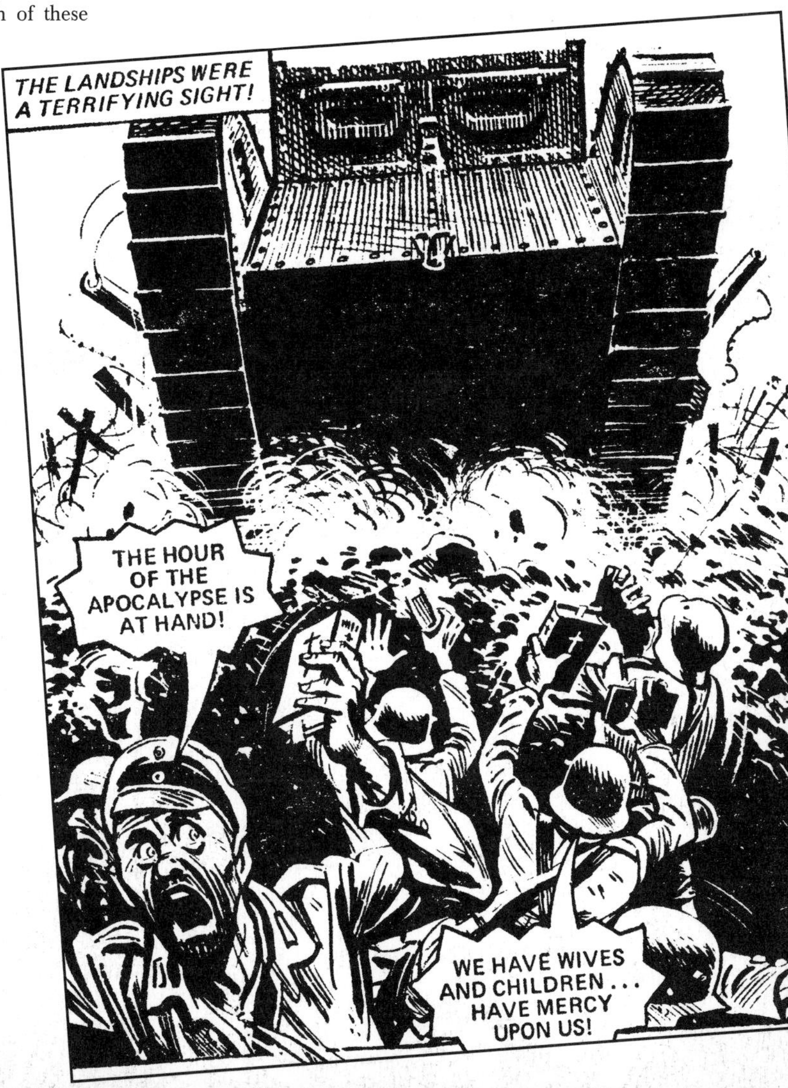
THE LANDSHIPS WERE A TERRIFYING SIGHT!
THE HOUR OF THE APOCALYPSE IS AT HAND!
WE HAVE WIVES AND CHILDREN . . . HAVE MERCY UPON US!

PREVIOUSLY IN *CHARLEY'S WAR*

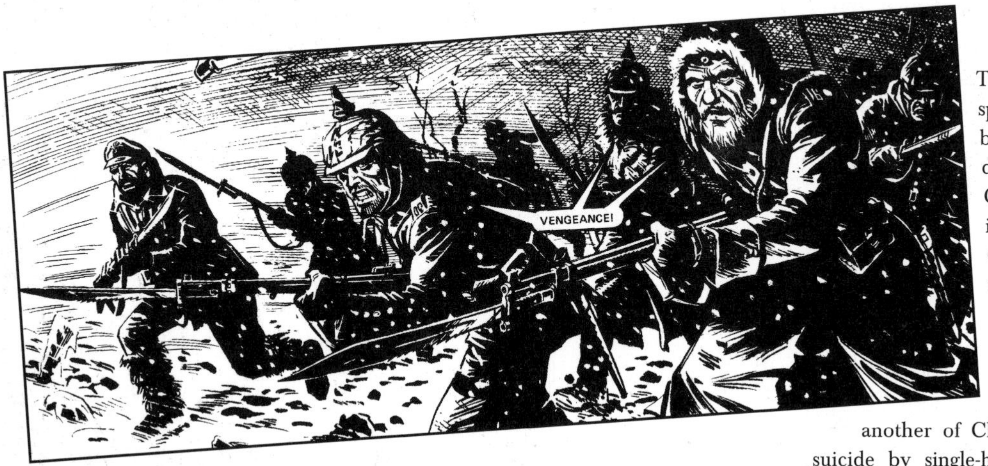
VENGEANCE!

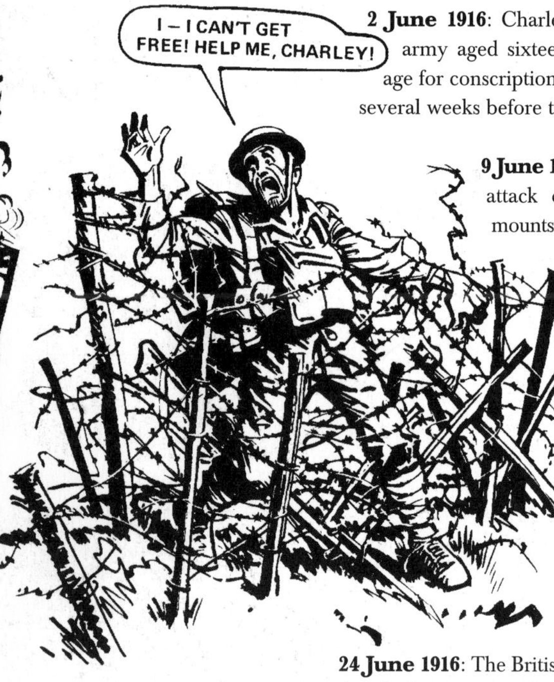
I – I CAN'T GET FREE! HELP ME, CHARLEY!

2 June 1916: Charley Bourne, who has joined the army aged sixteen (two years under the official age for conscription), is sent with his unit to France, several weeks before the Battle of the Somme.

9 June 1916: Following a sustained sniper attack on his trench, Charley's unit mounts a night-time raid on the German lines. Charley kills his first man by chance as much as skill – a German sniper.

16 June 1916: Charley persuades a fellow soldier, "Lucky", not to self-inflict a wound that would ensure his return to England. Later, "Lucky" is wounded by German shelling, losing a leg, but returns to England honourably.

24 June 1916: The British guns begin a sustained, seven-day shelling campaign on the German trenches, prior to the 'big push' of soldiers directly attacking the German lines. Charley's Lieutenant, Thomas, knows that the shelling will be ineffectual, having seen the depth of the German dug-outs, but he does not communicate the information for fear of lowering morale.

1 July 1916: The Battle of the Somme begins. Charley's unit discover a lone German soldier in an abandoned trench, chained to his machine-gun. Though Charley and his comrades spare the soldier, he is shot in cold blood by Lieutenant Snell. Later that day, Charley's unit assaults a fortified German village. "Mad Mick" O'Riley is killed single-handedly stopping a German counter-attack. By the end of the day, four of the group have been killed; Williams, the last to die, is shot by a sniper during roll-call.

2 July – 14 July 1916: "Lonely", another of Charley's unit, attempts to commit suicide by single-handedly charging into No Man's Land. During their attempt to rescue him, Charley, "Ginger" Jones and "Lonely" are captured. "Lonely" reveals the secret of the lost platoon, his old unit. When "Big Rudi", the brother of a man "Lonely" killed tries to execute all three prisoners, they manage to escape. However, during the escape, Charley inhales poison gas and becomes gravely ill.

14 July 1916: Charley, Ginger and "Lonely" meet a group of British cavalrymen, but they are all threatened by a group of German machine-gunners concealed out of spotter-plane range. "Lonely" bravely sacrifices himself to give away the German position. During the cavalry charge, Charley kills "Big Rudi". Eventually Charley and Ginger find their way back to their Sergeant Tozer, who punches them both for temporarily going absent without leave.

1 August 1916: On Charley's seventeenth birthday, the British forces accidentally begin shelling their own side, including Charley's unit. "Pops" is killed a day before he was due to be taken out of the trenches. After twelve communications runners are killed before they can pass the message to stop shelling, Charley volunteers to be the thirteenth runner… ✛

TOP: The Germans take their revenge after Snell's cowardly 'joke', as told by 'Lonely'.

ABOVE: 'Toots' is trapped on the wire in No-Man's-Land.

RIGHT: 'Ginger' takes desperate measures to stop Charley from charging to his doom.

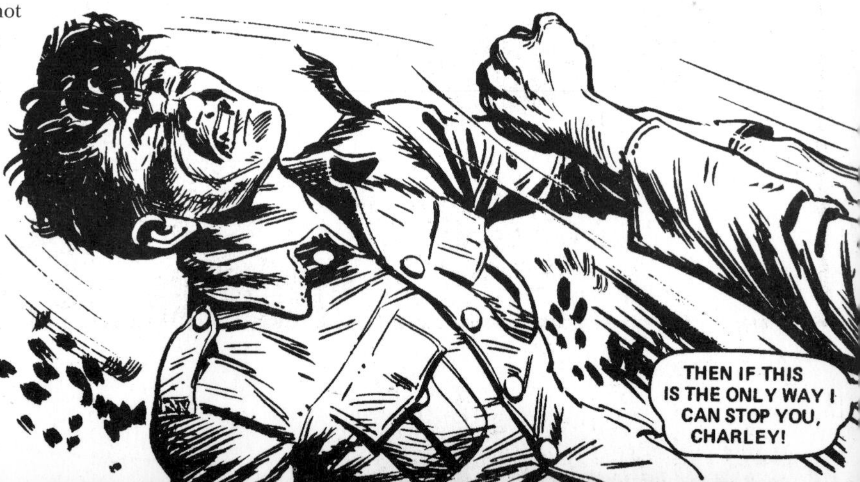
THEN IF THIS IS THE ONLY WAY I CAN STOP YOU, CHARLEY!

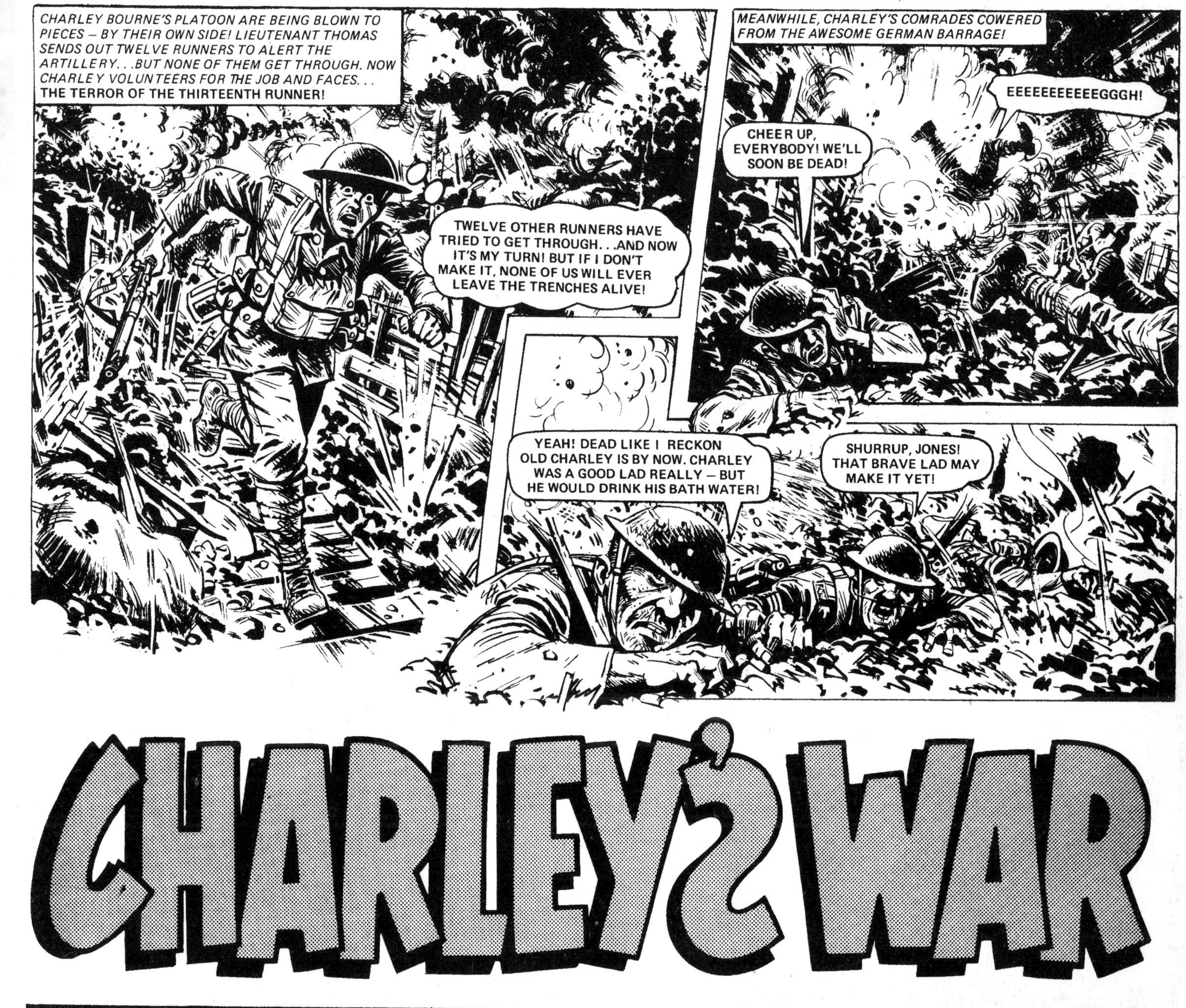
CHARLEY BOURNE'S PLATOON ARE BEING BLOWN TO PIECES – BY THEIR OWN SIDE! LIEUTENANT THOMAS SENDS OUT TWELVE RUNNERS TO ALERT THE ARTILLERY. . .BUT NONE OF THEM GET THROUGH. NOW CHARLEY VOLUNTEERS FOR THE JOB AND FACES. . .
THE TERROR OF THE THIRTEENTH RUNNER!
TWELVE OTHER RUNNERS HAVE TRIED TO GET THROUGH. . .AND NOW IT'S MY TURN! BUT IF I DON'T MAKE IT, NONE OF US WILL EVER LEAVE THE TRENCHES ALIVE!
MEANWHILE, CHARLEY'S COMRADES COWERED FROM THE AWESOME GERMAN BARRAGE!
EEEEEEEEEEEGGGH!
CHEER UP, EVERYBODY! WE'LL SOON BE DEAD!
YEAH! DEAD LIKE I RECKON OLD CHARLEY IS BY NOW. CHARLEY WAS A GOOD LAD REALLY – BUT HE WOULD DRINK HIS BATH WATER!
SHURRUP, JONES! THAT BRAVE LAD MAY MAKE IT YET!

CHARLEY'S WAR

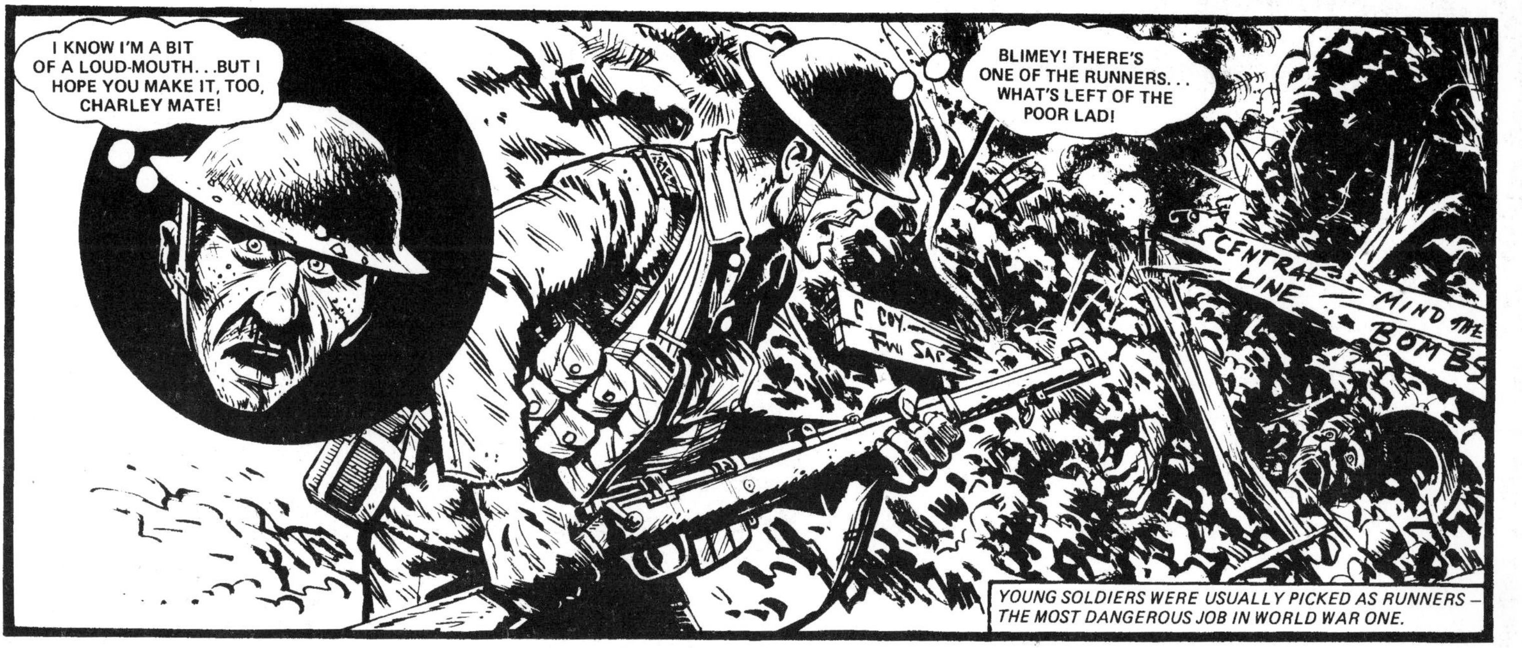
I KNOW I'M A BIT OF A LOUD-MOUTH. . .BUT I HOPE YOU MAKE IT, TOO, CHARLEY MATE!
BLIMEY! THERE'S ONE OF THE RUNNERS. . . WHAT'S LEFT OF THE POOR LAD!
C COY.
CENTRAL LINE
MIND THE BOMBS
YOUNG SOLDIERS WERE USUALLY PICKED AS RUNNERS – THE MOST DANGEROUS JOB IN WORLD WAR ONE.

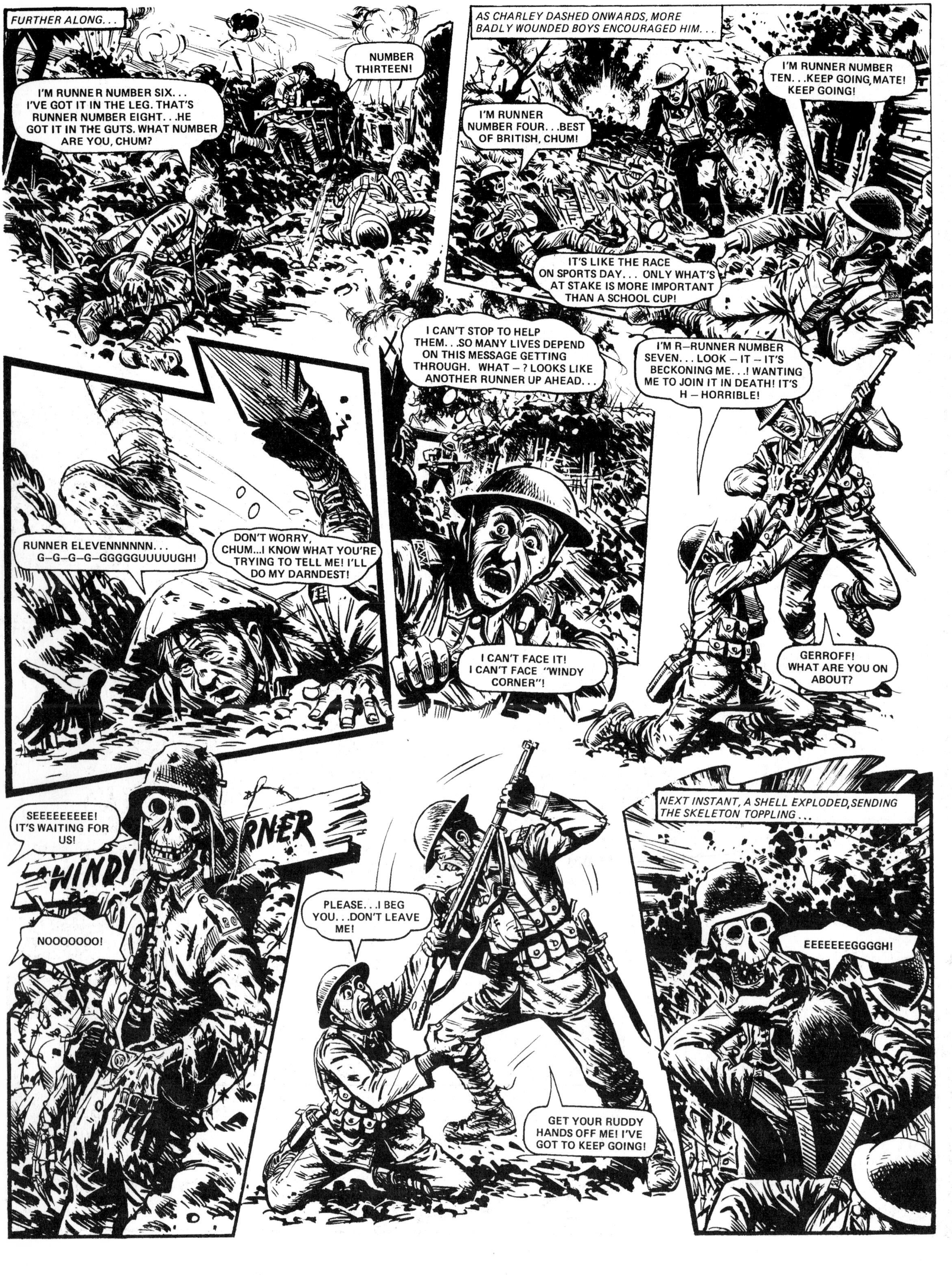

FURTHER ALONG...
NUMBER THIRTEEN!
I'M RUNNER NUMBER SIX... I'VE GOT IT IN THE LEG. THAT'S RUNNER NUMBER EIGHT...HE GOT IT IN THE GUTS. WHAT NUMBER ARE YOU, CHUM?
AS CHARLEY DASHED ONWARDS, MORE BADLY WOUNDED BOYS ENCOURAGED HIM...
I'M RUNNER NUMBER TEN...KEEP GOING, MATE! KEEP GOING!
I'M RUNNER NUMBER FOUR...BEST OF BRITISH, CHUM!
IT'S LIKE THE RACE ON SPORTS DAY... ONLY WHAT'S AT STAKE IS MORE IMPORTANT THAN A SCHOOL CUP!
RUNNER ELEVENNNNNN... G–G–G–G–GGGGGUUUUUGH!
DON'T WORRY, CHUM...I KNOW WHAT YOU'RE TRYING TO TELL ME! I'LL DO MY DARNDEST!
I CAN'T STOP TO HELP THEM...SO MANY LIVES DEPEND ON THIS MESSAGE GETTING THROUGH. WHAT–? LOOKS LIKE ANOTHER RUNNER UP AHEAD...
I CAN'T FACE IT! I CAN'T FACE "WINDY CORNER"!
I'M R–RUNNER NUMBER SEVEN... LOOK – IT – IT'S BECKONING ME...! WANTING ME TO JOIN IT IN DEATH! IT'S H – HORRIBLE!
GERROFF! WHAT ARE YOU ON ABOUT?
SEEEEEEEEE! IT'S WAITING FOR US!
WINDY ... RNER
NOOOOOOO!
PLEASE...I BEG YOU...DON'T LEAVE ME!
GET YOUR RUDDY HANDS OFF ME! I'VE GOT TO KEEP GOING!
NEXT INSTANT, A SHELL EXPLODED, SENDING THE SKELETON TOPPLING...
EEEEEEEGGGGH!

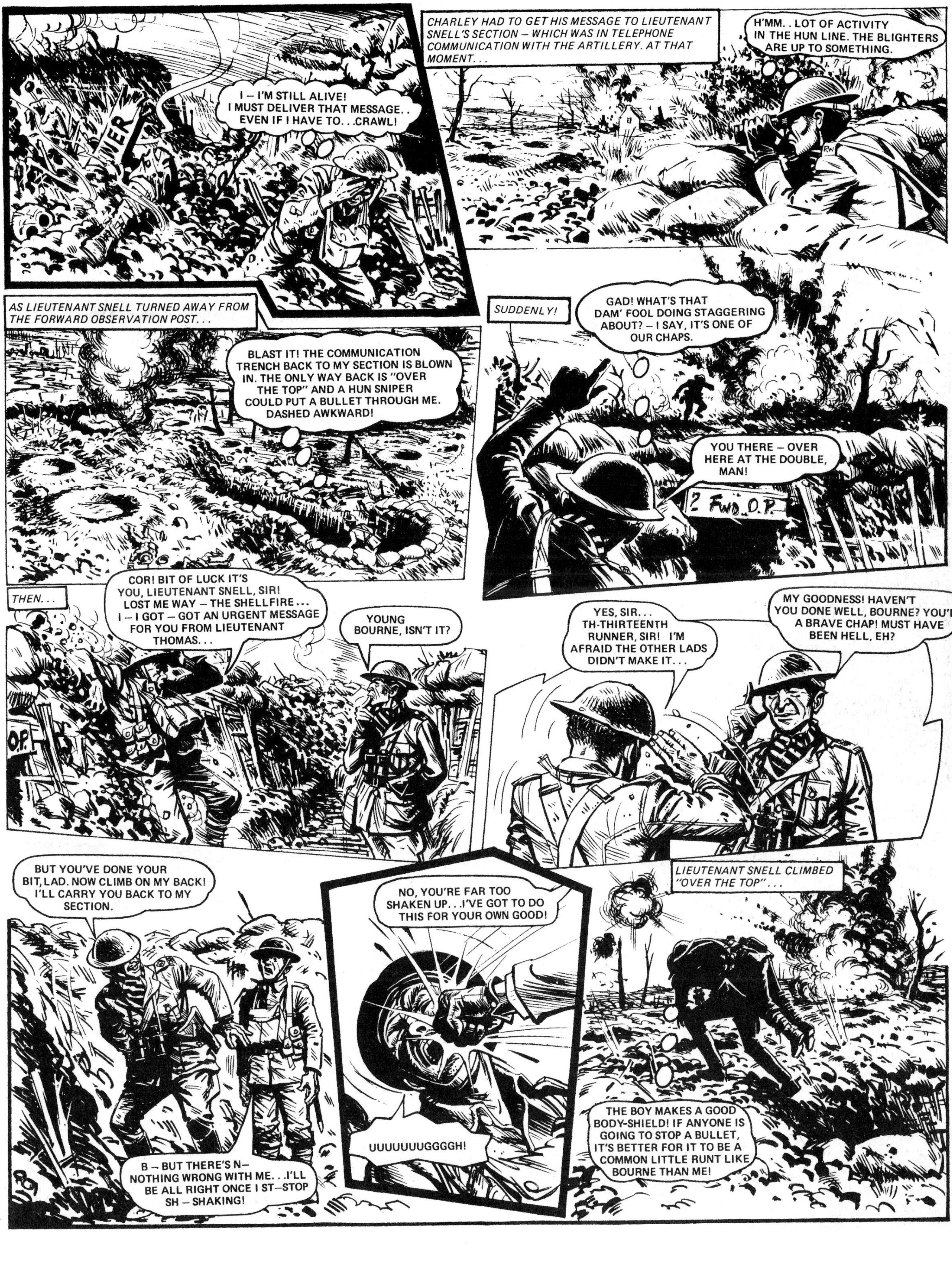

I – I'M STILL ALIVE! I MUST DELIVER THAT MESSAGE.. EVEN IF I HAVE TO...CRAWL!
CHARLEY HAD TO GET HIS MESSAGE TO LIEUTENANT SNELL'S SECTION – WHICH WAS IN TELEPHONE COMMUNICATION WITH THE ARTILLERY. AT THAT MOMENT...
H'MM.. LOT OF ACTIVITY IN THE HUN LINE. THE BLIGHTERS ARE UP TO SOMETHING.
AS LIEUTENANT SNELL TURNED AWAY FROM THE FORWARD OBSERVATION POST...
BLAST IT! THE COMMUNICATION TRENCH BACK TO MY SECTION IS BLOWN IN. THE ONLY WAY BACK IS "OVER THE TOP" AND A HUN SNIPER COULD PUT A BULLET THROUGH ME. DASHED AWKWARD!
SUDDENLY!
GAD! WHAT'S THAT DAM' FOOL DOING STAGGERING ABOUT? – I SAY, IT'S ONE OF OUR CHAPS.
YOU THERE – OVER HERE AT THE DOUBLE, MAN!
? FWD O.P.
THEN...
COR! BIT OF LUCK IT'S YOU, LIEUTENANT SNELL, SIR! LOST ME WAY – THE SHELLFIRE... I – I GOT – GOT AN URGENT MESSAGE FOR YOU FROM LIEUTENANT THOMAS...
YOUNG BOURNE, ISN'T IT?
YES, SIR... TH-THIRTEENTH RUNNER, SIR! I'M AFRAID THE OTHER LADS DIDN'T MAKE IT...
MY GOODNESS! HAVEN'T YOU DONE WELL, BOURNE? YOU'RE A BRAVE CHAP! MUST HAVE BEEN HELL, EH?
BUT YOU'VE DONE YOUR BIT, LAD. NOW CLIMB ON MY BACK! I'LL CARRY YOU BACK TO MY SECTION.
B – BUT THERE'S N–NOTHING WRONG WITH ME...I'LL BE ALL RIGHT ONCE I ST–STOP SH – SHAKING!
NO, YOU'RE FAR TOO SHAKEN UP...I'VE GOT TO DO THIS FOR YOUR OWN GOOD!
UUUUUUUGGGGH!
LIEUTENANT SNELL CLIMBED "OVER THE TOP"...
THE BOY MAKES A GOOD BODY-SHIELD! IF ANYONE IS GOING TO STOP A BULLET, IT'S BETTER FOR IT TO BE A COMMON LITTLE RUNT LIKE BOURNE THAN ME!

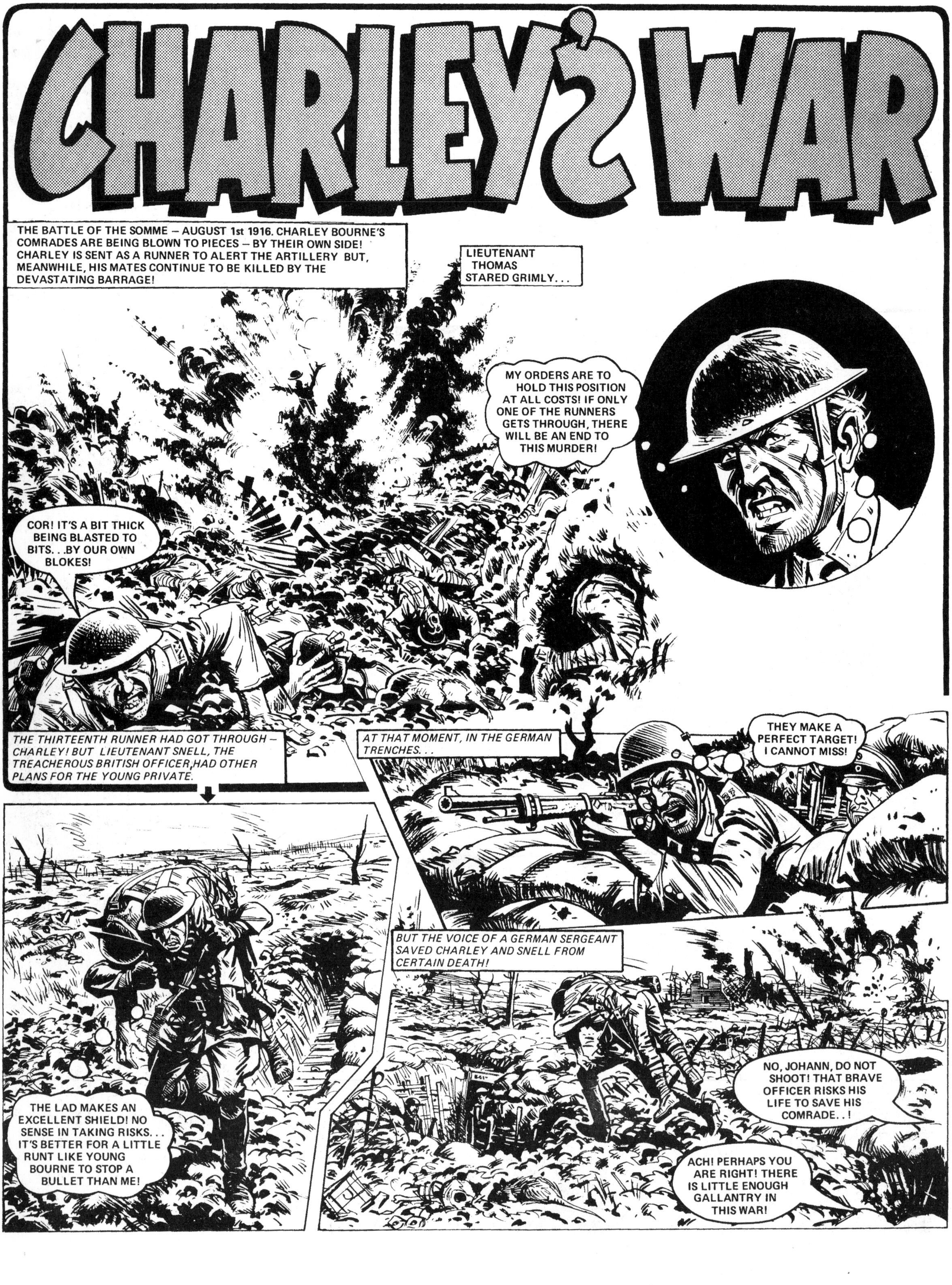
CHARLEY'S WAR
THE BATTLE OF THE SOMME – AUGUST 1st 1916. CHARLEY BOURNE'S COMRADES ARE BEING BLOWN TO PIECES – BY THEIR OWN SIDE! CHARLEY IS SENT AS A RUNNER TO ALERT THE ARTILLERY BUT, MEANWHILE, HIS MATES CONTINUE TO BE KILLED BY THE DEVASTATING BARRAGE!
COR! IT'S A BIT THICK BEING BLASTED TO BITS. . .BY OUR OWN BLOKES!
LIEUTENANT THOMAS STARED GRIMLY. . .
MY ORDERS ARE TO HOLD THIS POSITION AT ALL COSTS! IF ONLY ONE OF THE RUNNERS GETS THROUGH, THERE WILL BE AN END TO THIS MURDER!
THE THIRTEENTH RUNNER HAD GOT THROUGH – CHARLEY! BUT LIEUTENANT SNELL, THE TREACHEROUS BRITISH OFFICER,HAD OTHER PLANS FOR THE YOUNG PRIVATE.
THE LAD MAKES AN EXCELLENT SHIELD! NO SENSE IN TAKING RISKS. . . IT'S BETTER FOR A LITTLE RUNT LIKE YOUNG BOURNE TO STOP A BULLET THAN ME!
AT THAT MOMENT, IN THE GERMAN TRENCHES. . .
THEY MAKE A PERFECT TARGET! I CANNOT MISS!
BUT THE VOICE OF A GERMAN SERGEANT SAVED CHARLEY AND SNELL FROM CERTAIN DEATH!
NO, JOHANN, DO NOT SHOOT! THAT BRAVE OFFICER RISKS HIS LIFE TO SAVE HIS COMRADE. . !
ACH! PERHAPS YOU ARE RIGHT! THERE IS LITTLE ENOUGH GALLANTRY IN THIS WAR!

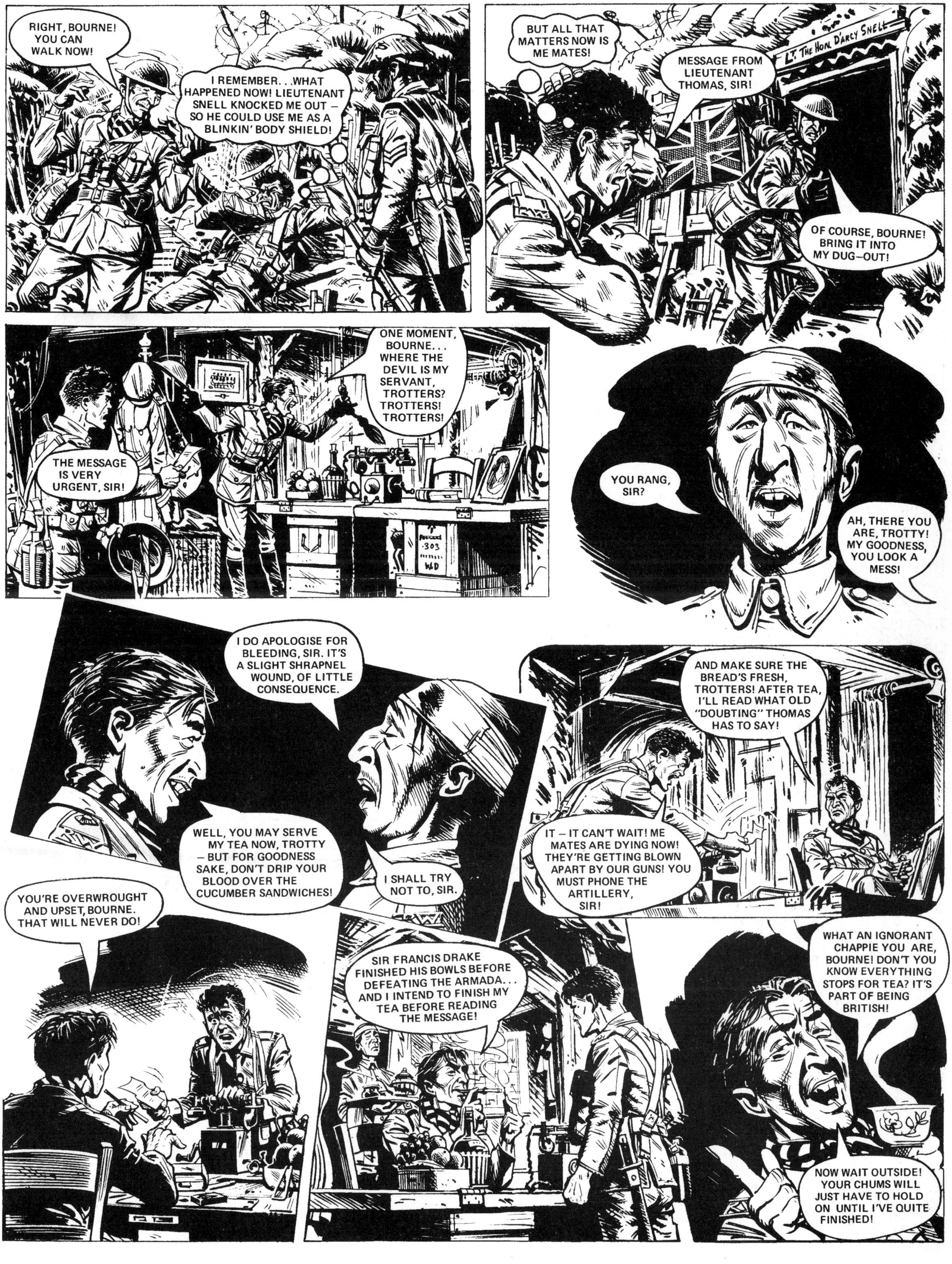
RIGHT, BOURNE! YOU CAN WALK NOW!
I REMEMBER. . .WHAT HAPPENED NOW! LIEUTENANT SNELL KNOCKED ME OUT – SO HE COULD USE ME AS A BLINKIN' BODY SHIELD!
BUT ALL THAT MATTERS NOW IS ME MATES!
LT. THE HON. D'ARCY SNELL
MESSAGE FROM LIEUTENANT THOMAS, SIR!
OF COURSE, BOURNE! BRING IT INTO MY DUG-OUT!
ONE MOMENT, BOURNE. . . WHERE THE DEVIL IS MY SERVANT, TROTTERS? TROTTERS! TROTTERS!
THE MESSAGE IS VERY URGENT, SIR!
YOU RANG, SIR?
AH, THERE YOU ARE, TROTTY! MY GOODNESS, YOU LOOK A MESS!
I DO APOLOGISE FOR BLEEDING, SIR. IT'S A SLIGHT SHRAPNEL WOUND, OF LITTLE CONSEQUENCE.
WELL, YOU MAY SERVE MY TEA NOW, TROTTY – BUT FOR GOODNESS SAKE, DON'T DRIP YOUR BLOOD OVER THE CUCUMBER SANDWICHES!
I SHALL TRY NOT TO, SIR.
AND MAKE SURE THE BREAD'S FRESH, TROTTERS! AFTER TEA, I'LL READ WHAT OLD "DOUBTING" THOMAS HAS TO SAY!
IT – IT CAN'T WAIT! ME MATES ARE DYING NOW! THEY'RE GETTING BLOWN APART BY OUR GUNS! YOU MUST PHONE THE ARTILLERY, SIR!
YOU'RE OVERWROUGHT AND UPSET, BOURNE. THAT WILL NEVER DO!
SIR FRANCIS DRAKE FINISHED HIS BOWLS BEFORE DEFEATING THE ARMADA. . . AND I INTEND TO FINISH MY TEA BEFORE READING THE MESSAGE!
WHAT AN IGNORANT CHAPPIE YOU ARE, BOURNE! DON'T YOU KNOW EVERYTHING STOPS FOR TEA? IT'S PART OF BEING BRITISH!
NOW WAIT OUTSIDE! YOUR CHUMS WILL JUST HAVE TO HOLD ON UNTIL I'VE QUITE FINISHED!

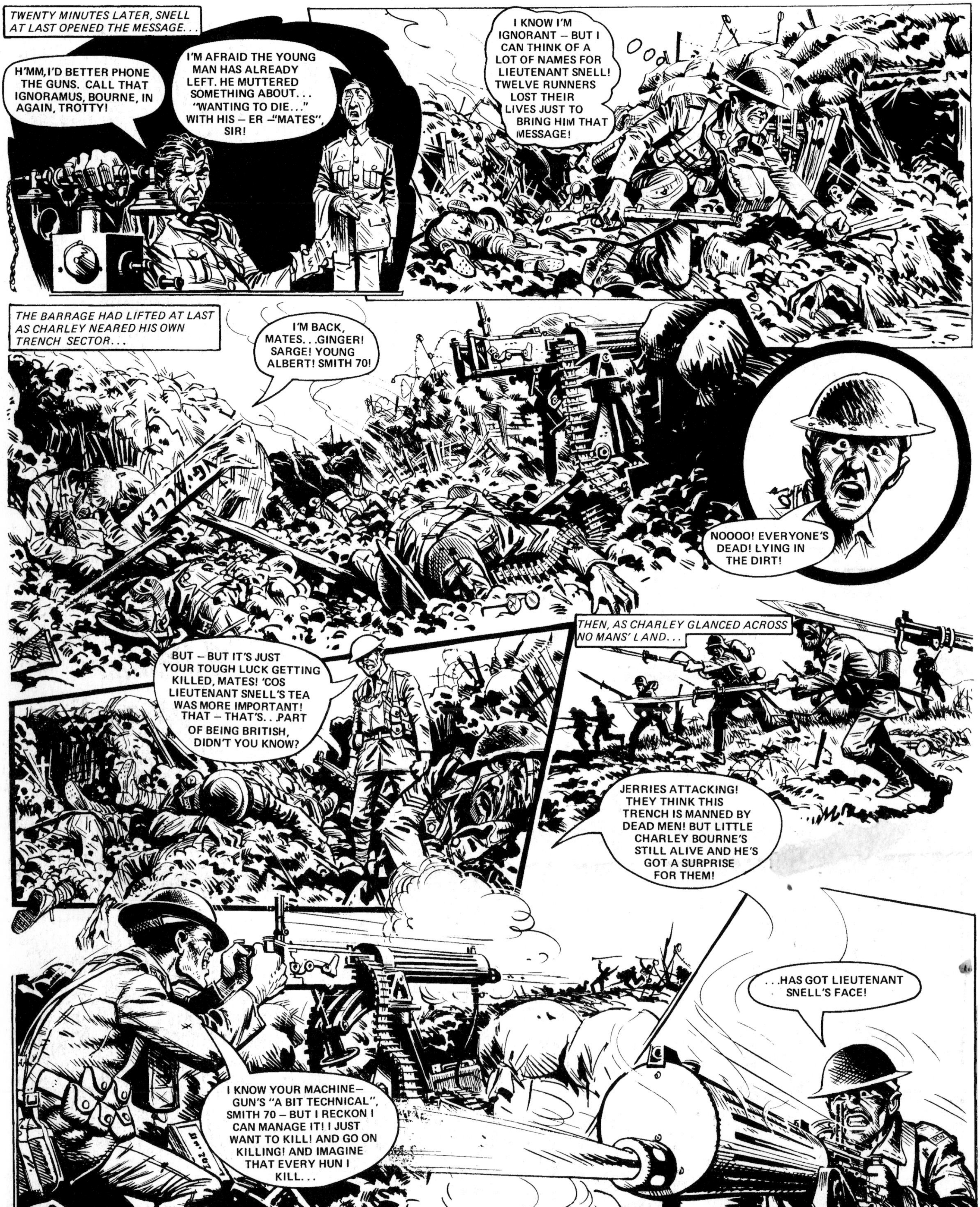
TWENTY MINUTES LATER, SNELL AT LAST OPENED THE MESSAGE...
H'MM, I'D BETTER PHONE THE GUNS. CALL THAT IGNORAMUS, BOURNE, IN AGAIN, TROTTY!
I'M AFRAID THE YOUNG MAN HAS ALREADY LEFT. HE MUTTERED SOMETHING ABOUT... "WANTING TO DIE..." WITH HIS – ER –"MATES", SIR!
I KNOW I'M IGNORANT – BUT I CAN THINK OF A LOT OF NAMES FOR LIEUTENANT SNELL! TWELVE RUNNERS LOST THEIR LIVES JUST TO BRING HIM THAT MESSAGE!
THE BARRAGE HAD LIFTED AT LAST AS CHARLEY NEARED HIS OWN TRENCH SECTOR...
I'M BACK, MATES... GINGER! SARGE! YOUNG ALBERT! SMITH 70!
NOOOO! EVERYONE'S DEAD! LYING IN THE DIRT!
BUT – BUT IT'S JUST YOUR TOUGH LUCK GETTING KILLED, MATES! 'COS LIEUTENANT SNELL'S TEA WAS MORE IMPORTANT! THAT – THAT'S... PART OF BEING BRITISH, DIDN'T YOU KNOW?
THEN, AS CHARLEY GLANCED ACROSS NO MANS' LAND...
JERRIES ATTACKING! THEY THINK THIS TRENCH IS MANNED BY DEAD MEN! BUT LITTLE CHARLEY BOURNE'S STILL ALIVE AND HE'S GOT A SURPRISE FOR THEM!
I KNOW YOUR MACHINE-GUN'S "A BIT TECHNICAL", SMITH 70 – BUT I RECKON I CAN MANAGE IT! I JUST WANT TO KILL! AND GO ON KILLING! AND IMAGINE THAT EVERY HUN I KILL...
...HAS GOT LIEUTENANT SNELL'S FACE!

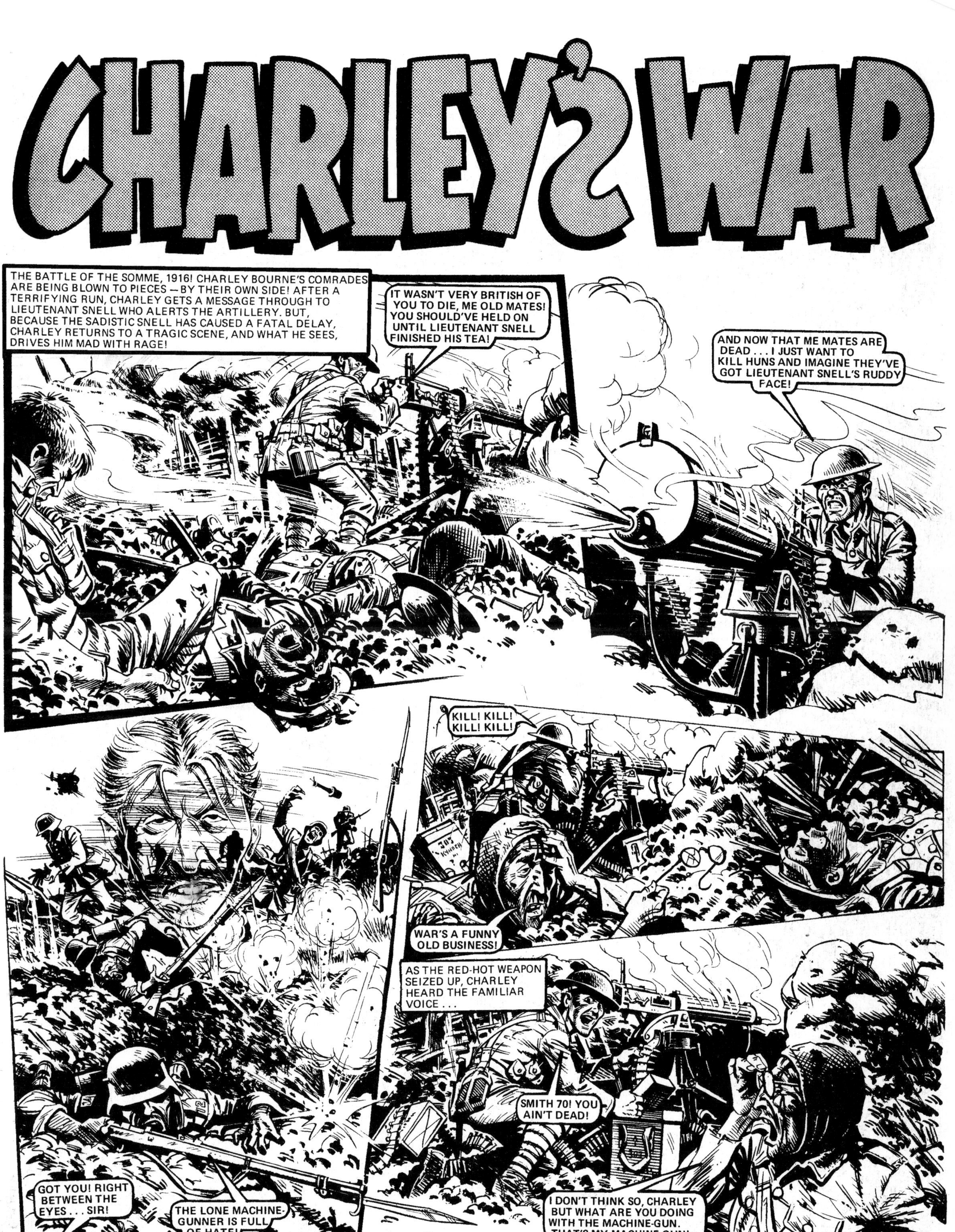
CHARLEY'S WAR
THE BATTLE OF THE SOMME, 1916! CHARLEY BOURNE'S COMRADES ARE BEING BLOWN TO PIECES — BY THEIR OWN SIDE! AFTER A TERRIFYING RUN, CHARLEY GETS A MESSAGE THROUGH TO LIEUTENANT SNELL WHO ALERTS THE ARTILLERY. BUT, BECAUSE THE SADISTIC SNELL HAS CAUSED A FATAL DELAY, CHARLEY RETURNS TO A TRAGIC SCENE, AND WHAT HE SEES, DRIVES HIM MAD WITH RAGE!
IT WASN'T VERY BRITISH OF YOU TO DIE, ME OLD MATES! YOU SHOULD'VE HELD ON UNTIL LIEUTENANT SNELL FINISHED HIS TEA!
AND NOW THAT ME MATES ARE DEAD . . . I JUST WANT TO KILL HUNS AND IMAGINE THEY'VE GOT LIEUTENANT SNELL'S RUDDY FACE!
GOT YOU! RIGHT BETWEEN THE EYES . . . SIR!
THE LONE MACHINE-GUNNER IS FULL OF HATE!
KILL! KILL! KILL! KILL!
WAR'S A FUNNY OLD BUSINESS!
AS THE RED-HOT WEAPON SEIZED UP, CHARLEY HEARD THE FAMILIAR VOICE . . .
SMITH 70! YOU AIN'T DEAD!
I DON'T THINK SO, CHARLEY BUT WHAT ARE YOU DOING WITH THE MACHINE-GUN. THAT'S MY MACHINE-GUN!

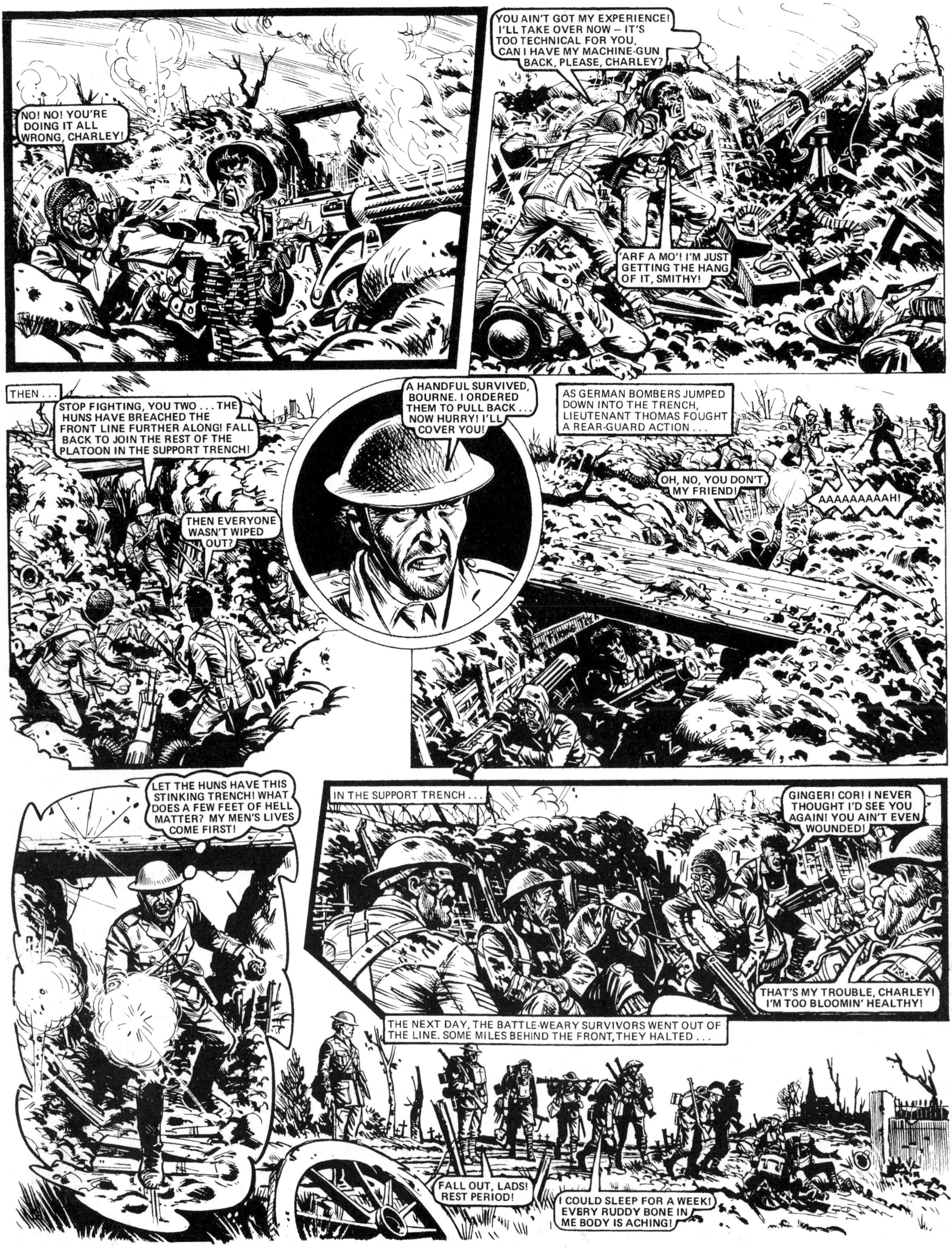
NO! NO! YOU'RE DOING IT ALL WRONG, CHARLEY!
YOU AIN'T GOT MY EXPERIENCE! I'LL TAKE OVER NOW – IT'S TOO TECHNICAL FOR YOU, CAN I HAVE MY MACHINE-GUN BACK, PLEASE, CHARLEY?
'ARF A MO'! I'M JUST GETTING THE HANG OF IT, SMITHY!
THEN . . .
STOP FIGHTING, YOU TWO . . . THE HUNS HAVE BREACHED THE FRONT LINE FURTHER ALONG! FALL BACK TO JOIN THE REST OF THE PLATOON IN THE SUPPORT TRENCH!
THEN EVERYONE WASN'T WIPED OUT?
A HANDFUL SURVIVED, BOURNE. I ORDERED THEM TO PULL BACK . . . NOW HURRY! I'LL COVER YOU!
AS GERMAN BOMBERS JUMPED DOWN INTO THE TRENCH, LIEUTENANT THOMAS FOUGHT A REAR-GUARD ACTION . . .
OH, NO, YOU DON'T, MY FRIEND!
AAAAAAAAAH!
LET THE HUNS HAVE THIS STINKING TRENCH! WHAT DOES A FEW FEET OF HELL MATTER? MY MEN'S LIVES COME FIRST!
IN THE SUPPORT TRENCH . . .
GINGER! COR! I NEVER THOUGHT I'D SEE YOU AGAIN! YOU AIN'T EVEN WOUNDED!
THAT'S MY TROUBLE, CHARLEY! I'M TOO BLOOMIN' HEALTHY!
THE NEXT DAY, THE BATTLE-WEARY SURVIVORS WENT OUT OF THE LINE. SOME MILES BEHIND THE FRONT, THEY HALTED . . .
FALL OUT, LADS! REST PERIOD!
I COULD SLEEP FOR A WEEK! EVERY RUDDY BONE IN ME BODY IS ACHING!

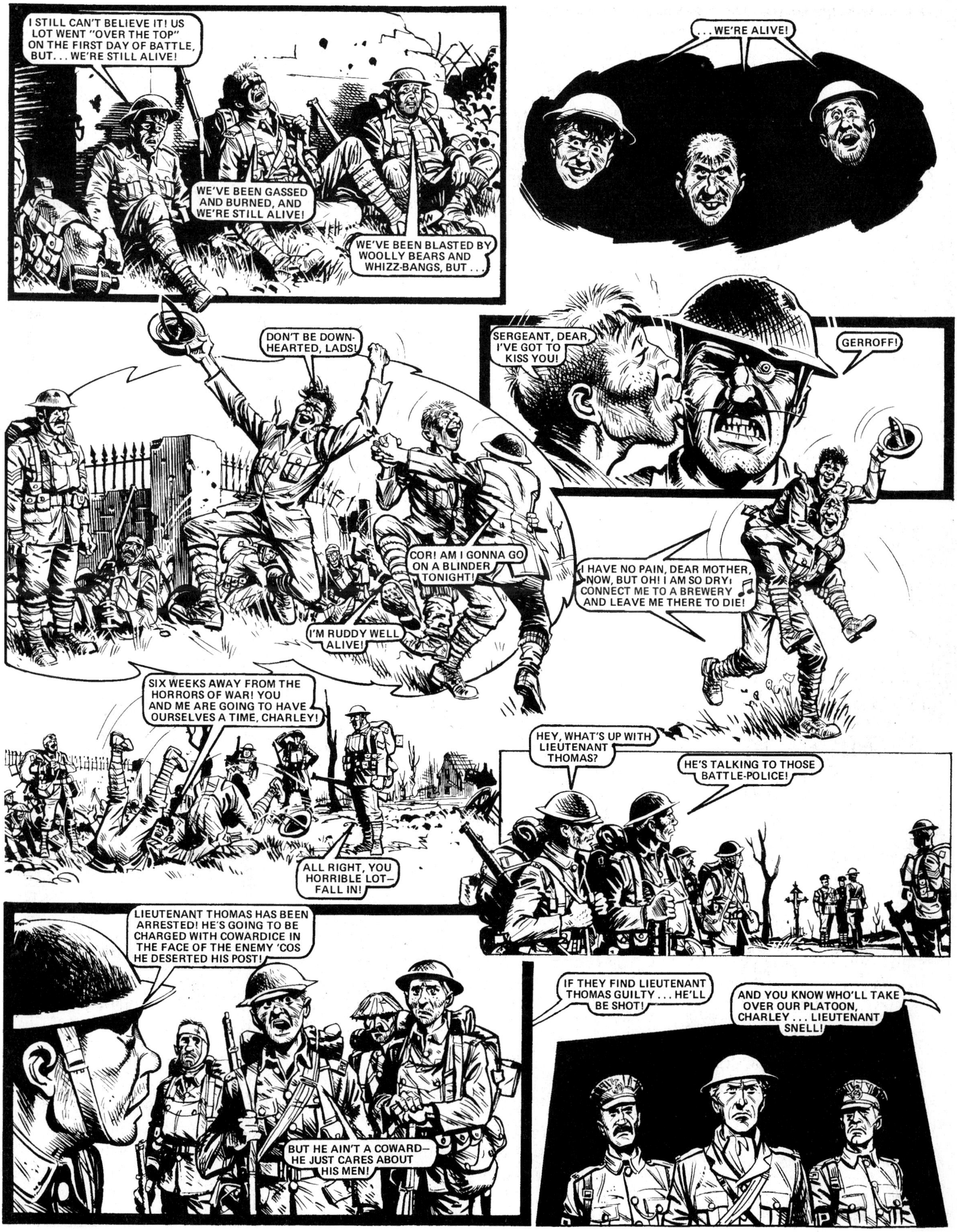
I STILL CAN'T BELIEVE IT! US LOT WENT "OVER THE TOP" ON THE FIRST DAY OF BATTLE, BUT. . . WE'RE STILL ALIVE!
WE'VE BEEN GASSED AND BURNED, AND WE'RE STILL ALIVE!
WE'VE BEEN BLASTED BY WOOLLY BEARS AND WHIZZ-BANGS, BUT . . .
. . . WE'RE ALIVE!
DON'T BE DOWN-HEARTED, LADS!
COR! AM I GONNA GO ON A BLINDER TONIGHT!
I'M RUDDY WELL ALIVE!
SERGEANT, DEAR, I'VE GOT TO KISS YOU!
GERROFF!
I HAVE NO PAIN, DEAR MOTHER, NOW, BUT OH! I AM SO DRY; CONNECT ME TO A BREWERY AND LEAVE ME THERE TO DIE!
SIX WEEKS AWAY FROM THE HORRORS OF WAR! YOU AND ME ARE GOING TO HAVE OURSELVES A TIME, CHARLEY!
ALL RIGHT, YOU HORRIBLE LOT— FALL IN!
HEY, WHAT'S UP WITH LIEUTENANT THOMAS?
HE'S TALKING TO THOSE BATTLE-POLICE!
LIEUTENANT THOMAS HAS BEEN ARRESTED! HE'S GOING TO BE CHARGED WITH COWARDICE IN THE FACE OF THE ENEMY 'COS HE DESERTED HIS POST!
BUT HE AIN'T A COWARD— HE JUST CARES ABOUT HIS MEN!
IF THEY FIND LIEUTENANT THOMAS GUILTY . . . HE'LL BE SHOT!
AND YOU KNOW WHO'LL TAKE OVER OUR PLATOON, CHARLEY . . . LIEUTENANT SNELL!

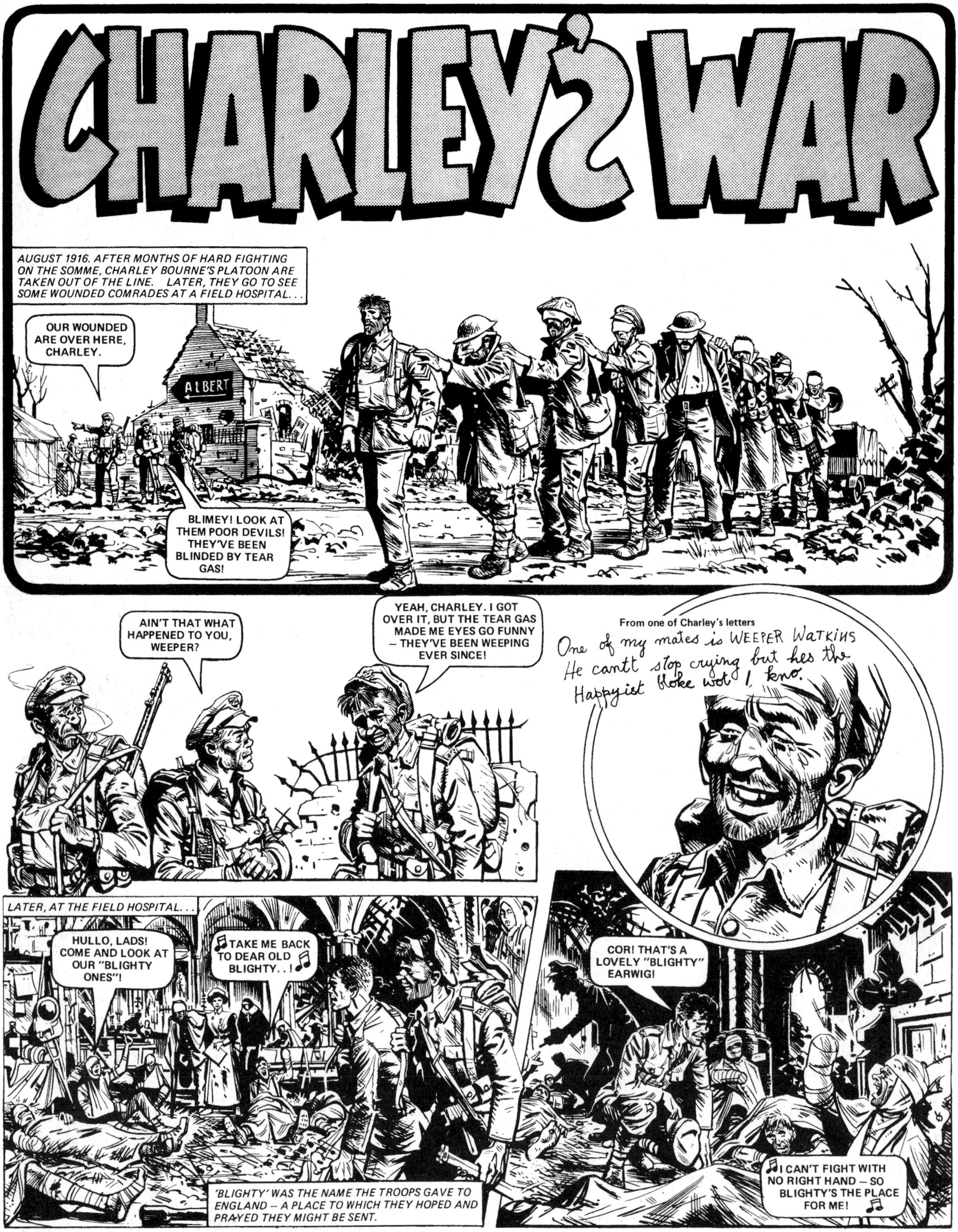
CHARLEY'S WAR
AUGUST 1916. AFTER MONTHS OF HARD FIGHTING ON THE SOMME, CHARLEY BOURNE'S PLATOON ARE TAKEN OUT OF THE LINE. LATER, THEY GO TO SEE SOME WOUNDED COMRADES AT A FIELD HOSPITAL. . .
OUR WOUNDED ARE OVER HERE, CHARLEY.
ALBERT
BLIMEY! LOOK AT THEM POOR DEVILS! THEY'VE BEEN BLINDED BY TEAR GAS!
AIN'T THAT WHAT HAPPENED TO YOU, WEEPER?
YEAH, CHARLEY. I GOT OVER IT, BUT THE TEAR GAS MADE ME EYES GO FUNNY – THEY'VE BEEN WEEPING EVER SINCE!
From one of Charley's letters
One of my mates is WEEPER WATKINS He cantt stop crying but hes the Happyist bloke wot I kno.
LATER, AT THE FIELD HOSPITAL. . .
HULLO, LADS! COME AND LOOK AT OUR "BLIGHTY ONES"!
♪ TAKE ME BACK TO DEAR OLD BLIGHTY. . ! ♪
'BLIGHTY' WAS THE NAME THE TROOPS GAVE TO ENGLAND – A PLACE TO WHICH THEY HOPED AND PRAYED THEY MIGHT BE SENT.
COR! THAT'S A LOVELY "BLIGHTY" EARWIG!
♪ I CAN'T FIGHT WITH NO RIGHT HAND – SO BLIGHTY'S THE PLACE FOR ME! ♪

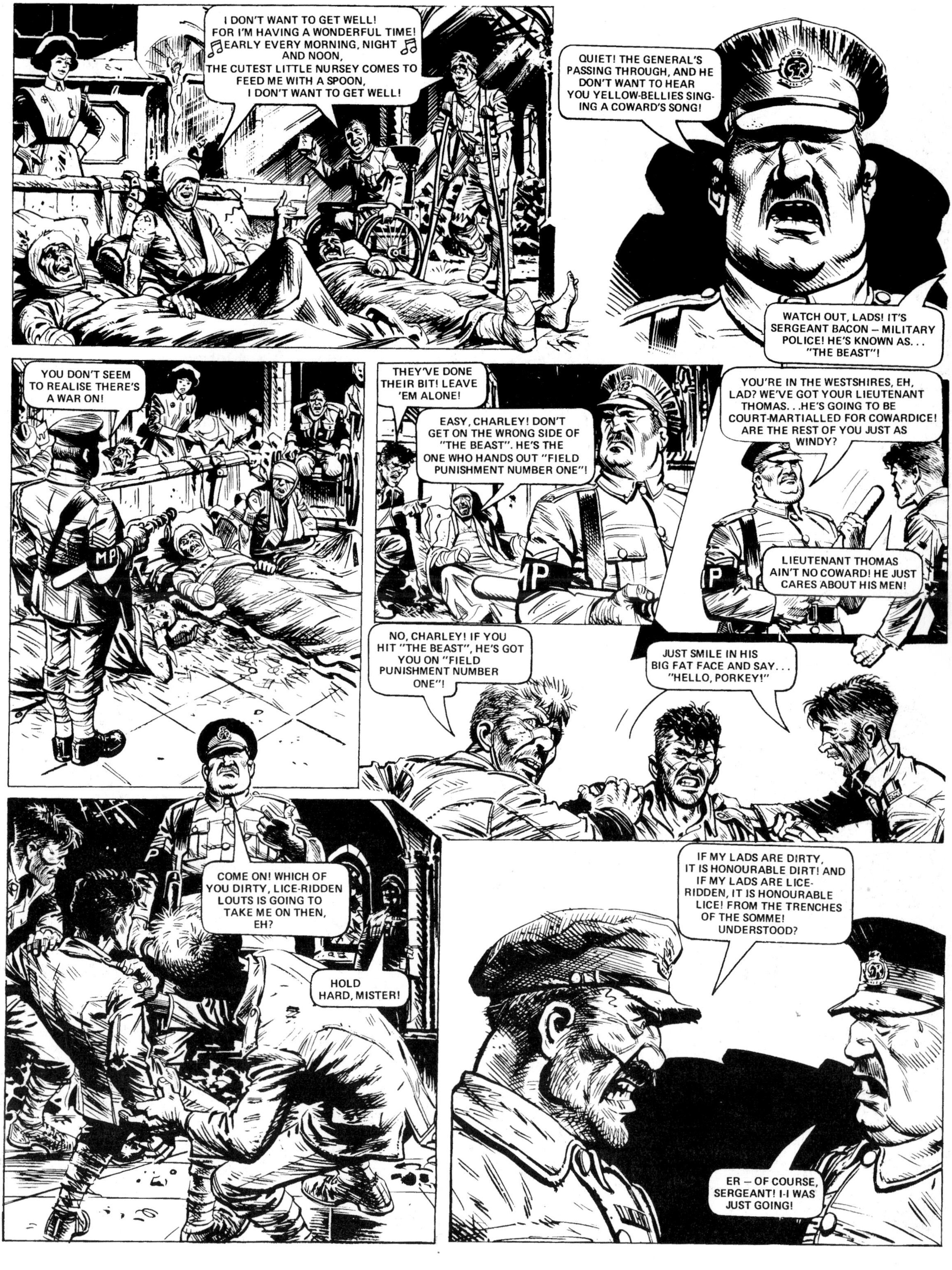
I DON'T WANT TO GET WELL! FOR I'M HAVING A WONDERFUL TIME! EARLY EVERY MORNING, NIGHT AND NOON, THE CUTEST LITTLE NURSEY COMES TO FEED ME WITH A SPOON, I DON'T WANT TO GET WELL!
QUIET! THE GENERAL'S PASSING THROUGH, AND HE DON'T WANT TO HEAR YOU YELLOW-BELLIES SINGING A COWARD'S SONG!
WATCH OUT, LADS! IT'S SERGEANT BACON – MILITARY POLICE! HE'S KNOWN AS. . . "THE BEAST"!
YOU DON'T SEEM TO REALISE THERE'S A WAR ON!
MP
THEY'VE DONE THEIR BIT! LEAVE 'EM ALONE!
EASY, CHARLEY! DON'T GET ON THE WRONG SIDE OF "THE BEAST". HE'S THE ONE WHO HANDS OUT "FIELD PUNISHMENT NUMBER ONE"!
MP
YOU'RE IN THE WESTSHIRES, EH, LAD? WE'VE GOT YOUR LIEUTENANT THOMAS. . .HE'S GOING TO BE COURT-MARTIALLED FOR COWARDICE! ARE THE REST OF YOU JUST AS WINDY?
LIEUTENANT THOMAS AIN'T NO COWARD! HE JUST CARES ABOUT HIS MEN!
NO, CHARLEY! IF YOU HIT "THE BEAST", HE'S GOT YOU ON "FIELD PUNISHMENT NUMBER ONE"!
JUST SMILE IN HIS BIG FAT FACE AND SAY. . . "HELLO, PORKEY!"
COME ON! WHICH OF YOU DIRTY, LICE-RIDDEN LOUTS IS GOING TO TAKE ME ON THEN, EH?
HOLD HARD, MISTER!
IF MY LADS ARE DIRTY, IT IS HONOURABLE DIRT! AND IF MY LADS ARE LICE-RIDDEN, IT IS HONOURABLE LICE! FROM THE TRENCHES OF THE SOMME! UNDERSTOOD?
ER – OF COURSE, SERGEANT! I-I WAS JUST GOING!

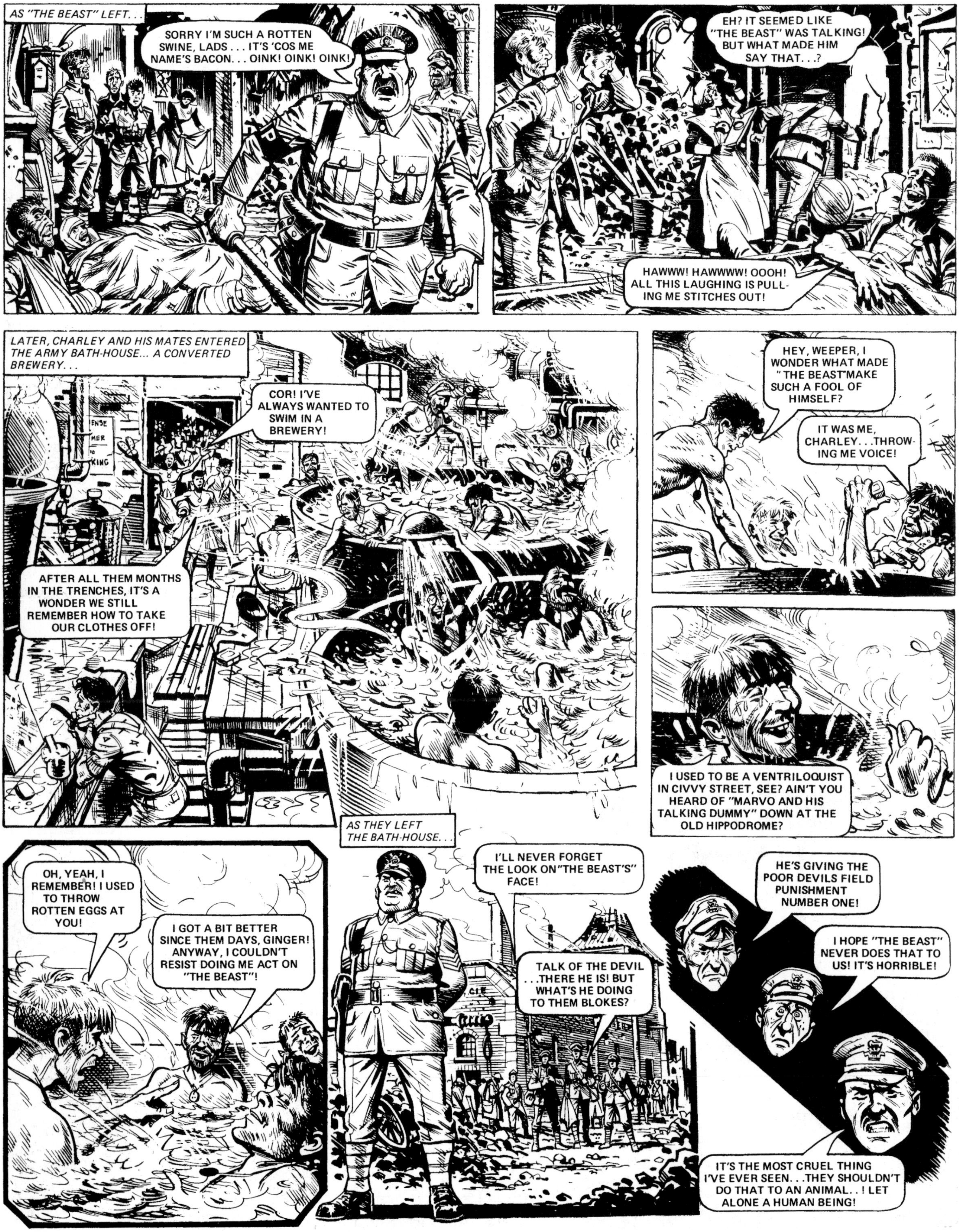
AS "THE BEAST" LEFT...
SORRY I'M SUCH A ROTTEN SWINE, LADS . . . IT'S 'COS ME NAME'S BACON . . . OINK! OINK! OINK!
EH? IT SEEMED LIKE "THE BEAST" WAS TALKING! BUT WHAT MADE HIM SAY THAT. . .?
HAWWW! HAWWWW! OOOH! ALL THIS LAUGHING IS PULL-ING ME STITCHES OUT!
LATER, CHARLEY AND HIS MATES ENTERED THE ARMY BATH-HOUSE... A CONVERTED BREWERY...
COR! I'VE ALWAYS WANTED TO SWIM IN A BREWERY!
AFTER ALL THEM MONTHS IN THE TRENCHES, IT'S A WONDER WE STILL REMEMBER HOW TO TAKE OUR CLOTHES OFF!
HEY, WEEPER, I WONDER WHAT MADE "THE BEAST" MAKE SUCH A FOOL OF HIMSELF?
IT WAS ME, CHARLEY. . .THROW-ING ME VOICE!
I USED TO BE A VENTRILOQUIST IN CIVVY STREET, SEE? AIN'T YOU HEARD OF "MARVO AND HIS TALKING DUMMY" DOWN AT THE OLD HIPPODROME?
OH, YEAH, I REMEMBER! I USED TO THROW ROTTEN EGGS AT YOU!
I GOT A BIT BETTER SINCE THEM DAYS, GINGER! ANYWAY, I COULDN'T RESIST DOING ME ACT ON "THE BEAST"!
AS THEY LEFT THE BATH-HOUSE. . .
I'LL NEVER FORGET THE LOOK ON "THE BEAST'S" FACE!
TALK OF THE DEVIL . . .THERE HE IS! BUT WHAT'S HE DOING TO THEM BLOKES?
HE'S GIVING THE POOR DEVILS FIELD PUNISHMENT NUMBER ONE!
I HOPE "THE BEAST" NEVER DOES THAT TO US! IT'S HORRIBLE!
IT'S THE MOST CRUEL THING I'VE EVER SEEN. . .THEY SHOULDN'T DO THAT TO AN ANIMAL. . ! LET ALONE A HUMAN BEING!

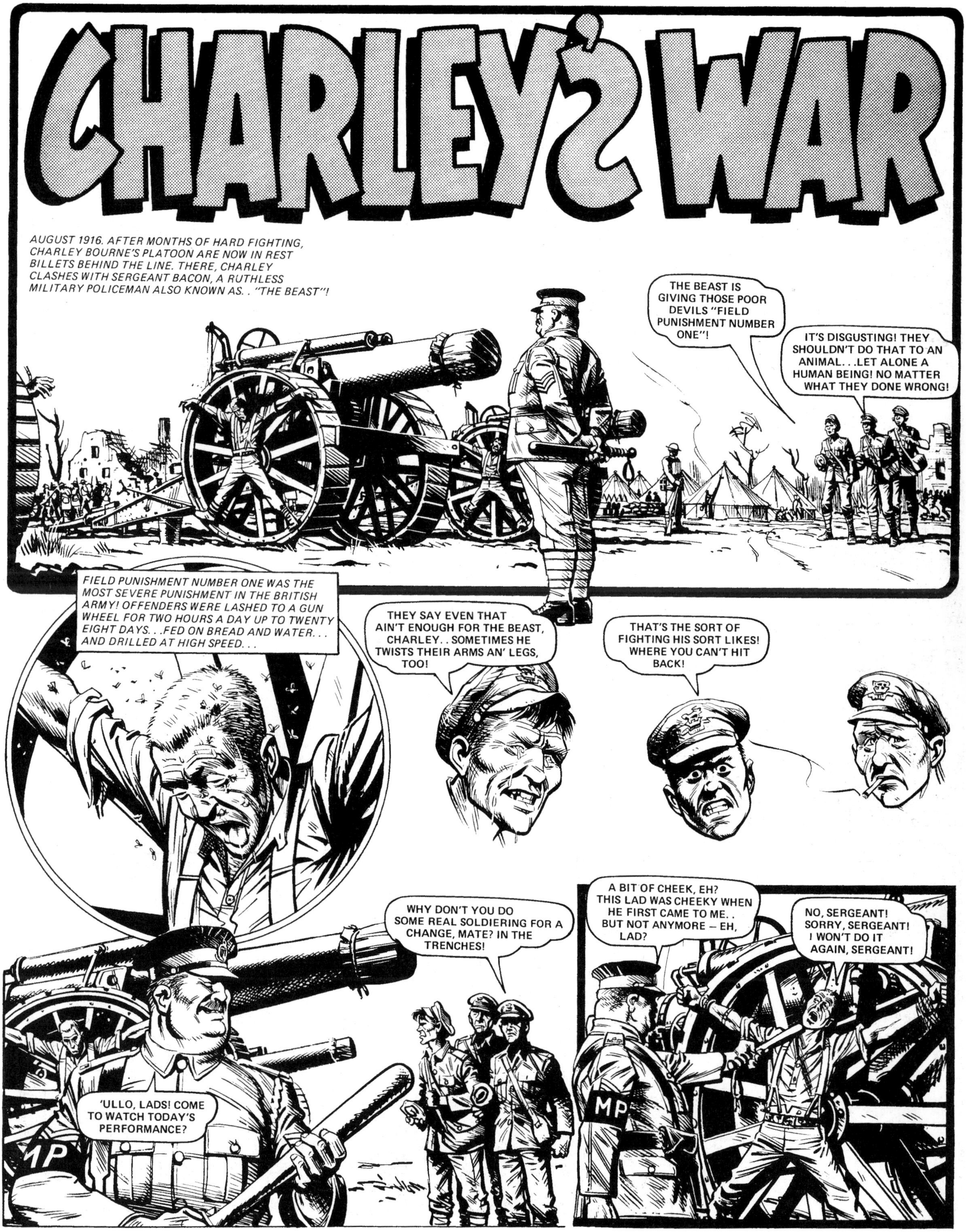
CHARLEY'S WAR
AUGUST 1916. AFTER MONTHS OF HARD FIGHTING, CHARLEY BOURNE'S PLATOON ARE NOW IN REST BILLETS BEHIND THE LINE. THERE, CHARLEY CLASHES WITH SERGEANT BACON, A RUTHLESS MILITARY POLICEMAN ALSO KNOWN AS. . "THE BEAST"!
THE BEAST IS GIVING THOSE POOR DEVILS "FIELD PUNISHMENT NUMBER ONE"!
IT'S DISGUSTING! THEY SHOULDN'T DO THAT TO AN ANIMAL. . .LET ALONE A HUMAN BEING! NO MATTER WHAT THEY DONE WRONG!
FIELD PUNISHMENT NUMBER ONE WAS THE MOST SEVERE PUNISHMENT IN THE BRITISH ARMY! OFFENDERS WERE LASHED TO A GUN WHEEL FOR TWO HOURS A DAY UP TO TWENTY EIGHT DAYS. . .FED ON BREAD AND WATER. . . AND DRILLED AT HIGH SPEED. . .
THEY SAY EVEN THAT AIN'T ENOUGH FOR THE BEAST, CHARLEY. . SOMETIMES HE TWISTS THEIR ARMS AN' LEGS, TOO!
THAT'S THE SORT OF FIGHTING HIS SORT LIKES! WHERE YOU CAN'T HIT BACK!
'ULLO, LADS! COME TO WATCH TODAY'S PERFORMANCE?
MP
WHY DON'T YOU DO SOME REAL SOLDIERING FOR A CHANGE, MATE? IN THE TRENCHES!
A BIT OF CHEEK, EH? THIS LAD WAS CHEEKY WHEN HE FIRST CAME TO ME. . BUT NOT ANYMORE – EH, LAD?
NO, SERGEANT! SORRY, SERGEANT! I WON'T DO IT AGAIN, SERGEANT!
MP

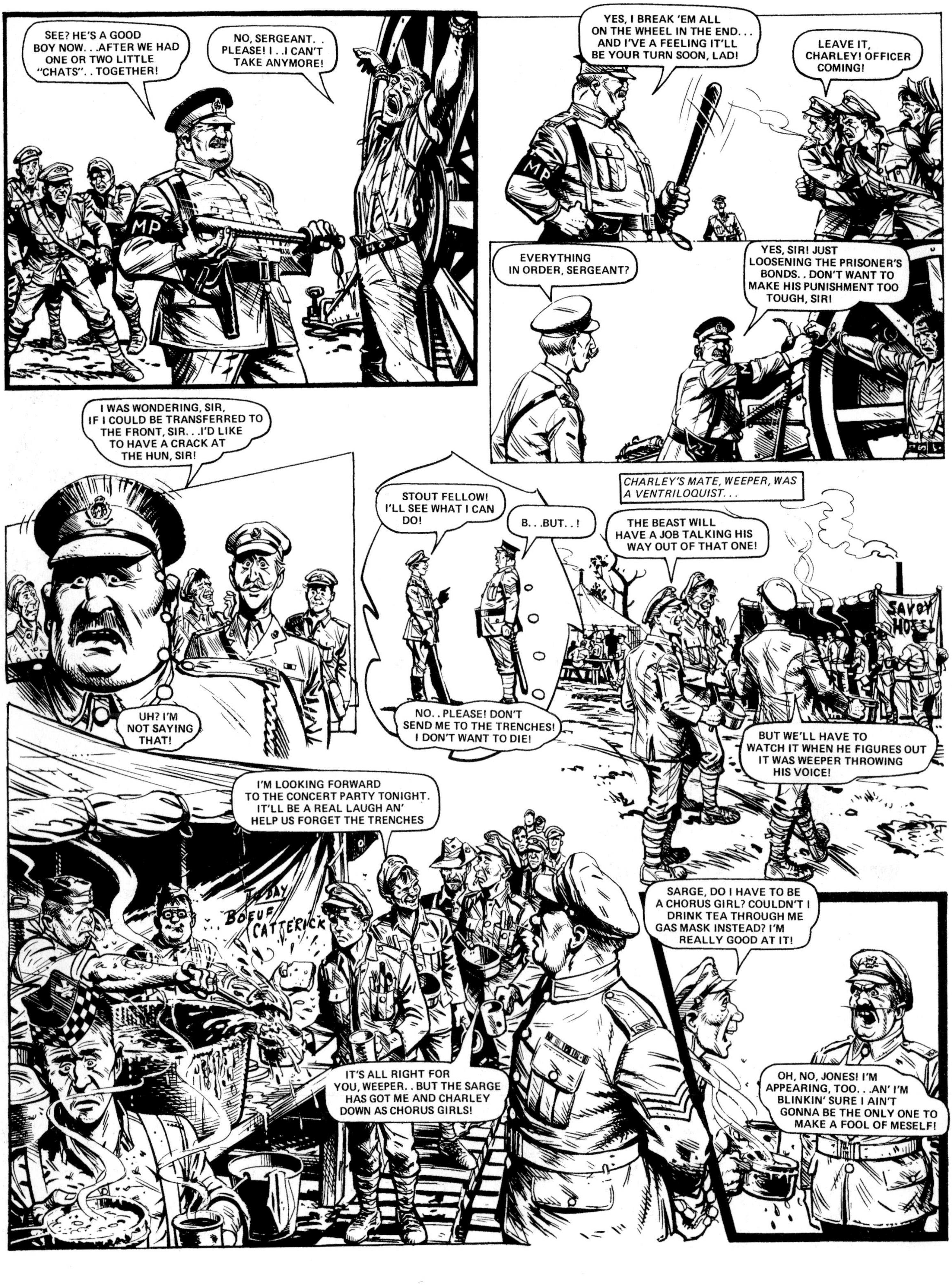
SEE? HE'S A GOOD BOY NOW. . .AFTER WE HAD ONE OR TWO LITTLE "CHATS". . TOGETHER!
NO, SERGEANT. . PLEASE! I . .I CAN'T TAKE ANYMORE!
YES, I BREAK 'EM ALL ON THE WHEEL IN THE END. . . AND I'VE A FEELING IT'LL BE YOUR TURN SOON, LAD!
LEAVE IT, CHARLEY! OFFICER COMING!
EVERYTHING IN ORDER, SERGEANT?
YES, SIR! JUST LOOSENING THE PRISONER'S BONDS. . DON'T WANT TO MAKE HIS PUNISHMENT TOO TOUGH, SIR!
I WAS WONDERING, SIR, IF I COULD BE TRANSFERRED TO THE FRONT, SIR. . .I'D LIKE TO HAVE A CRACK AT THE HUN, SIR!
UH? I'M NOT SAYING THAT!
STOUT FELLOW! I'LL SEE WHAT I CAN DO!
B. . .BUT. . !
NO. . PLEASE! DON'T SEND ME TO THE TRENCHES! I DON'T WANT TO DIE!
CHARLEY'S MATE, WEEPER, WAS A VENTRILOQUIST. . .
THE BEAST WILL HAVE A JOB TALKING HIS WAY OUT OF THAT ONE!
BUT WE'LL HAVE TO WATCH IT WHEN HE FIGURES OUT IT WAS WEEPER THROWING HIS VOICE!
SAVOY HOTEL
I'M LOOKING FORWARD TO THE CONCERT PARTY TONIGHT. IT'LL BE A REAL LAUGH AN' HELP US FORGET THE TRENCHES
BOFUF CATTERICK
IT'S ALL RIGHT FOR YOU, WEEPER. . BUT THE SARGE HAS GOT ME AND CHARLEY DOWN AS CHORUS GIRLS!
SARGE, DO I HAVE TO BE A CHORUS GIRL? COULDN'T I DRINK TEA THROUGH ME GAS MASK INSTEAD? I'M REALLY GOOD AT IT!
OH, NO, JONES! I'M APPEARING, TOO. . .AN' I'M BLINKIN' SURE I AIN'T GONNA BE THE ONLY ONE TO MAKE A FOOL OF MESELF!

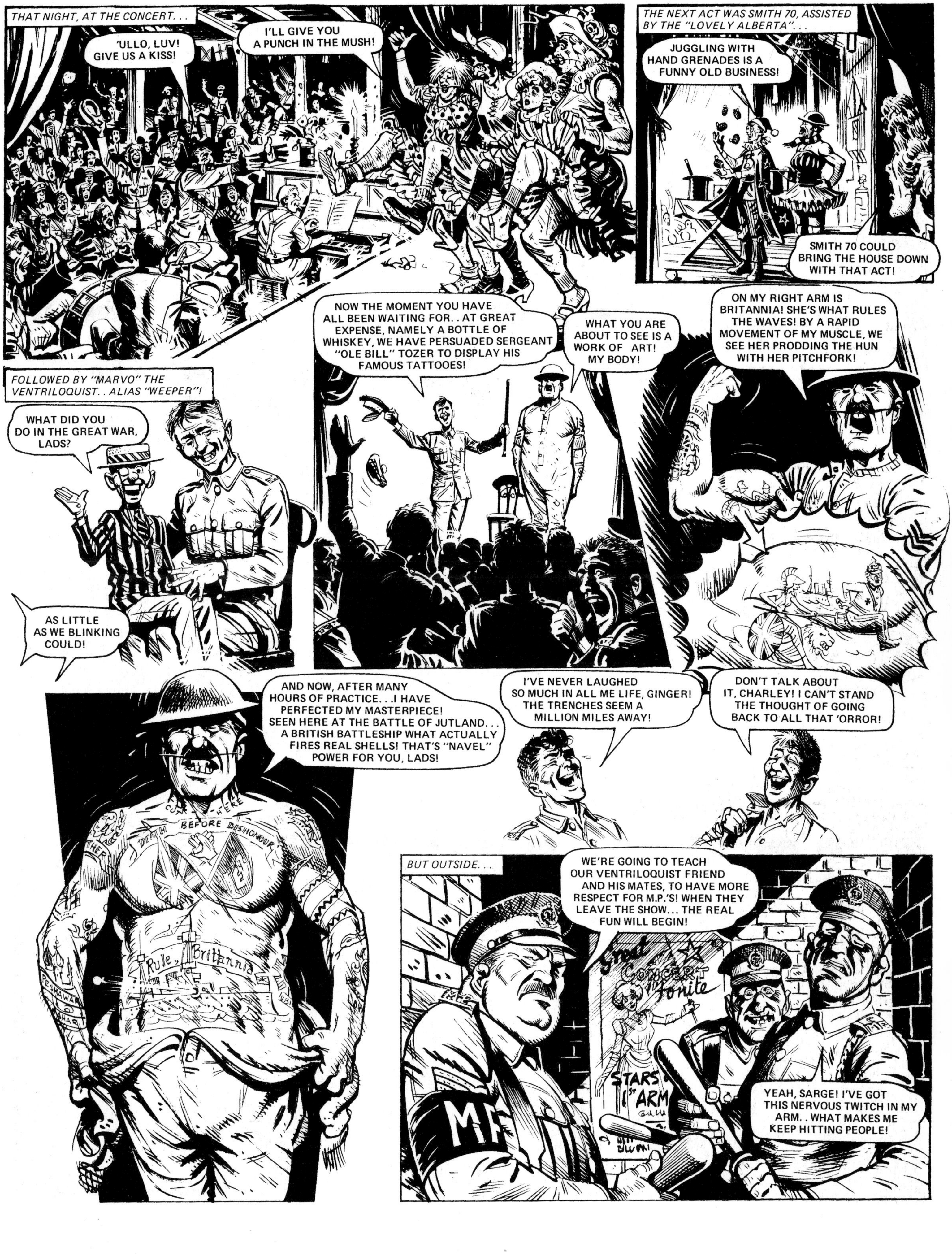
THAT NIGHT, AT THE CONCERT. . .
'ULLO, LUV! GIVE US A KISS!
I'LL GIVE YOU A PUNCH IN THE MUSH!
THE NEXT ACT WAS SMITH 70, ASSISTED BY THE "LOVELY ALBERTA". . .
JUGGLING WITH HAND GRENADES IS A FUNNY OLD BUSINESS!
SMITH 70 COULD BRING THE HOUSE DOWN WITH THAT ACT!
FOLLOWED BY "MARVO" THE VENTRILOQUIST. . ALIAS "WEEPER"!
WHAT DID YOU DO IN THE GREAT WAR, LADS?
AS LITTLE AS WE BLINKING COULD!
NOW THE MOMENT YOU HAVE ALL BEEN WAITING FOR. . AT GREAT EXPENSE, NAMELY A BOTTLE OF WHISKEY, WE HAVE PERSUADED SERGEANT "OLE BILL" TOZER TO DISPLAY HIS FAMOUS TATTOOES!
WHAT YOU ARE ABOUT TO SEE IS A WORK OF ART! MY BODY!
ON MY RIGHT ARM IS BRITANNIA! SHE'S WHAT RULES THE WAVES! BY A RAPID MOVEMENT OF MY MUSCLE, WE SEE HER PRODDING THE HUN WITH HER PITCHFORK!
AND NOW, AFTER MANY HOURS OF PRACTICE. . .I HAVE PERFECTED MY MASTERPIECE! SEEN HERE AT THE BATTLE OF JUTLAND. . . A BRITISH BATTLESHIP WHAT ACTUALLY FIRES REAL SHELLS! THAT'S "NAVEL" POWER FOR YOU, LADS!
BEFORE DISHONOUR
Rule, Brittannia
I'VE NEVER LAUGHED SO MUCH IN ALL ME LIFE, GINGER! THE TRENCHES SEEM A MILLION MILES AWAY!
DON'T TALK ABOUT IT, CHARLEY! I CAN'T STAND THE THOUGHT OF GOING BACK TO ALL THAT 'ORROR!
BUT OUTSIDE. . .
WE'RE GOING TO TEACH OUR VENTRILOQUIST FRIEND AND HIS MATES, TO HAVE MORE RESPECT FOR M.P.'S! WHEN THEY LEAVE THE SHOW. . . THE REAL FUN WILL BEGIN!
Great Concert Tonite
STARS 1st ARM
MP
YEAH, SARGE! I'VE GOT THIS NERVOUS TWITCH IN MY ARM. . WHAT MAKES ME KEEP HITTING PEOPLE!

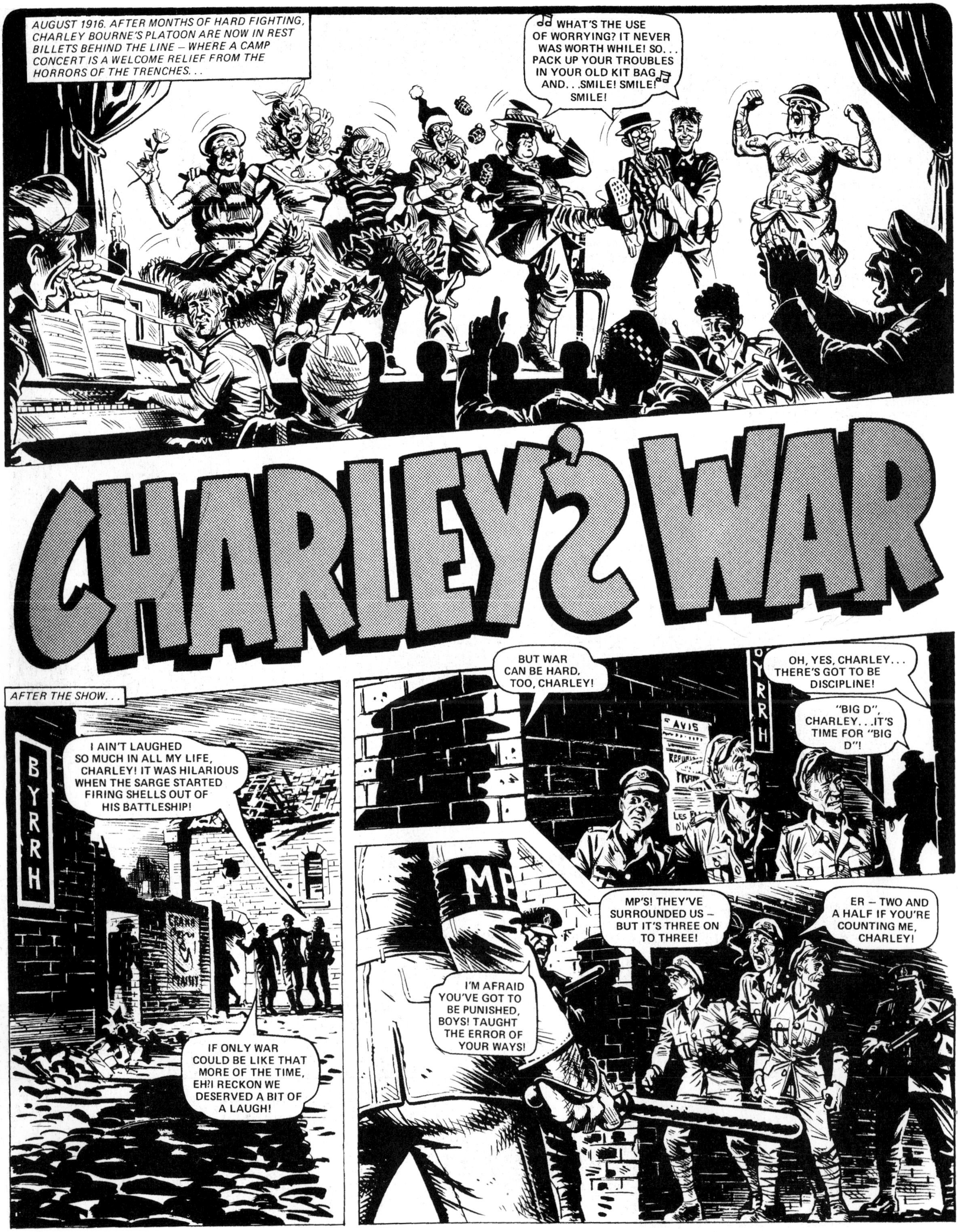

AUGUST 1916. AFTER MONTHS OF HARD FIGHTING, CHARLEY BOURNE'S PLATOON ARE NOW IN REST BILLETS BEHIND THE LINE – WHERE A CAMP CONCERT IS A WELCOME RELIEF FROM THE HORRORS OF THE TRENCHES. . .
WHAT'S THE USE OF WORRYING? IT NEVER WAS WORTH WHILE! SO. . . PACK UP YOUR TROUBLES IN YOUR OLD KIT BAG AND. . .SMILE! SMILE! SMILE!
CHARLEY'S WAR
AFTER THE SHOW. . .
I AIN'T LAUGHED SO MUCH IN ALL MY LIFE, CHARLEY! IT WAS HILARIOUS WHEN THE SARGE STARTED FIRING SHELLS OUT OF HIS BATTLESHIP!
BYRRH
IF ONLY WAR COULD BE LIKE THAT MORE OF THE TIME, EH?I RECKON WE DESERVED A BIT OF A LAUGH!
BUT WAR CAN BE HARD, TOO, CHARLEY!
OH, YES, CHARLEY. . . THERE'S GOT TO BE DISCIPLINE!
"BIG D", CHARLEY. . .IT'S TIME FOR "BIG D"!
AVIS
MP
MP'S! THEY'VE SURROUNDED US – BUT IT'S THREE ON TO THREE!
ER – TWO AND A HALF IF YOU'RE COUNTING ME, CHARLEY!
I'M AFRAID YOU'VE GOT TO BE PUNISHED, BOYS! TAUGHT THE ERROR OF YOUR WAYS!

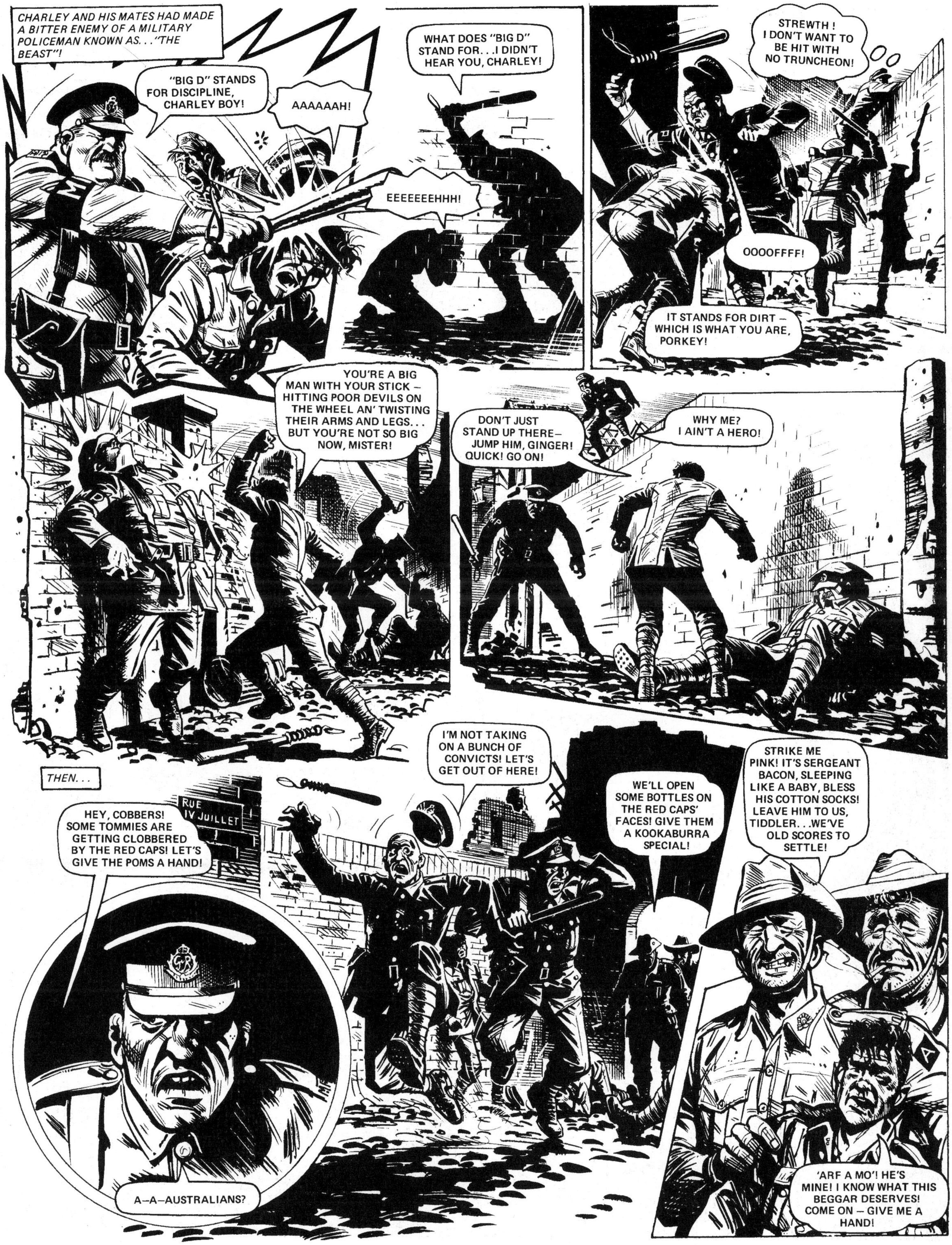
CHARLEY AND HIS MATES HAD MADE A BITTER ENEMY OF A MILITARY POLICEMAN KNOWN AS. . . "THE BEAST"!
"BIG D" STANDS FOR DISCIPLINE, CHARLEY BOY!
AAAAAAH!
WHAT DOES "BIG D" STAND FOR. . . I DIDN'T HEAR YOU, CHARLEY!
EEEEEEEHHH!
STREWTH ! I DON'T WANT TO BE HIT WITH NO TRUNCHEON!
OOOOFFFF!
IT STANDS FOR DIRT – WHICH IS WHAT YOU ARE, PORKEY!
YOU'RE A BIG MAN WITH YOUR STICK – HITTING POOR DEVILS ON THE WHEEL AN' TWISTING THEIR ARMS AND LEGS. . . BUT YOU'RE NOT SO BIG NOW, MISTER!
DON'T JUST STAND UP THERE– JUMP HIM, GINGER! QUICK! GO ON!
WHY ME? I AIN'T A HERO!
THEN. . .
RUE IV JUILLET
HEY, COBBERS! SOME TOMMIES ARE GETTING CLOBBERED BY THE RED CAPS! LET'S GIVE THE POMS A HAND!
A–A–AUSTRALIANS?
I'M NOT TAKING ON A BUNCH OF CONVICTS! LET'S GET OUT OF HERE!
WE'LL OPEN SOME BOTTLES ON THE RED CAPS' FACES! GIVE THEM A KOOKABURRA SPECIAL!
STRIKE ME PINK! IT'S SERGEANT BACON, SLEEPING LIKE A BABY, BLESS HIS COTTON SOCKS! LEAVE HIM TO US, TIDDLER. . . WE'VE OLD SCORES TO SETTLE!
'ARF A MO'! HE'S MINE! I KNOW WHAT THIS BEGGAR DESERVES! COME ON – GIVE ME A HAND!

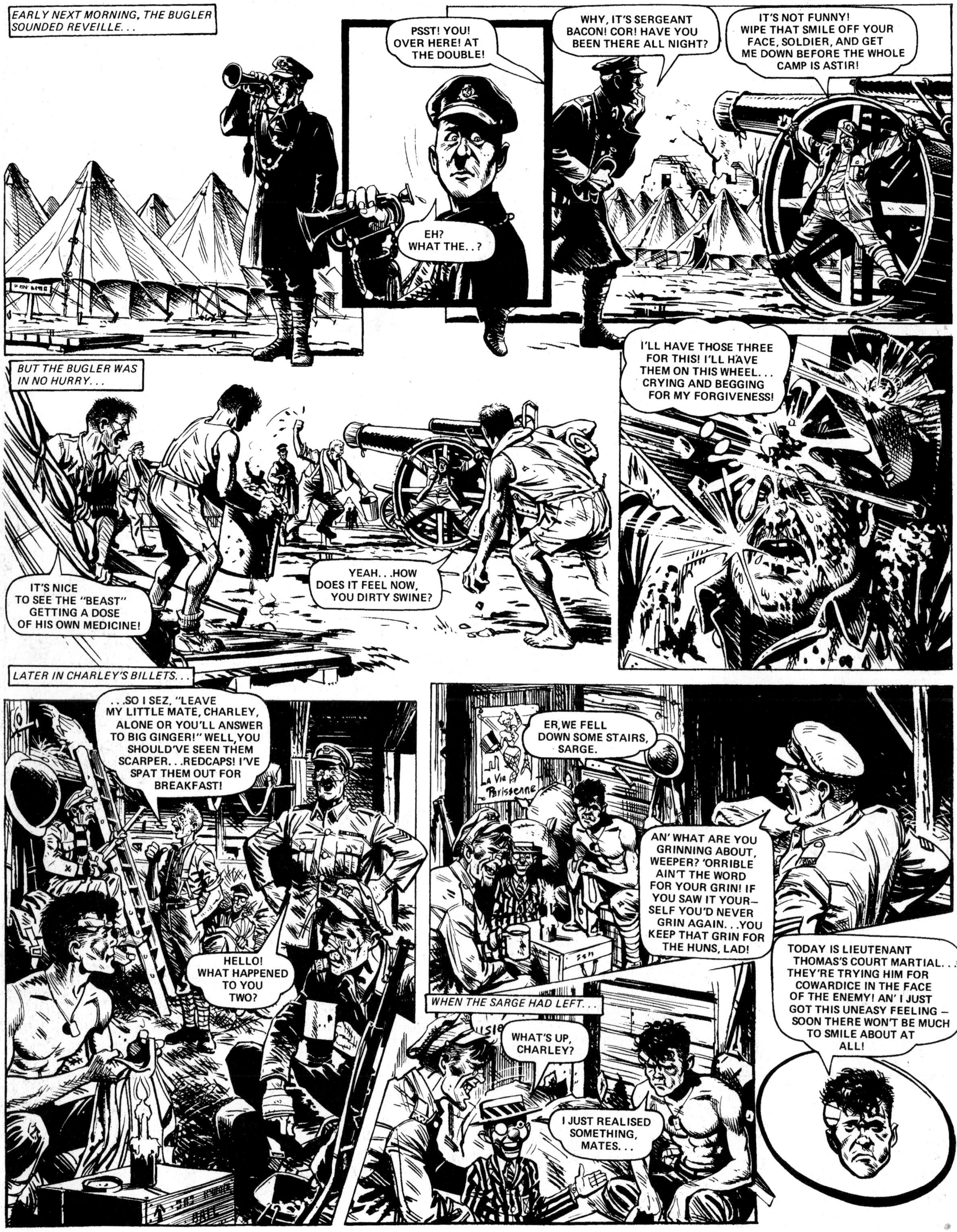

EARLY NEXT MORNING, THE BUGLER SOUNDED REVEILLE...
PSST! YOU! OVER HERE! AT THE DOUBLE!
EH? WHAT THE..?
WHY, IT'S SERGEANT BACON! COR! HAVE YOU BEEN THERE ALL NIGHT?
IT'S NOT FUNNY! WIPE THAT SMILE OFF YOUR FACE, SOLDIER, AND GET ME DOWN BEFORE THE WHOLE CAMP IS ASTIR!
BUT THE BUGLER WAS IN NO HURRY...
IT'S NICE TO SEE THE "BEAST" GETTING A DOSE OF HIS OWN MEDICINE!
YEAH...HOW DOES IT FEEL NOW, YOU DIRTY SWINE?
I'LL HAVE THOSE THREE FOR THIS! I'LL HAVE THEM ON THIS WHEEL... CRYING AND BEGGING FOR MY FORGIVENESS!
LATER IN CHARLEY'S BILLETS...
...SO I SEZ, "LEAVE MY LITTLE MATE, CHARLEY, ALONE OR YOU'LL ANSWER TO BIG GINGER!" WELL, YOU SHOULD'VE SEEN THEM SCARPER...REDCAPS! I'VE SPAT THEM OUT FOR BREAKFAST!
HELLO! WHAT HAPPENED TO YOU TWO?
ER, WE FELL DOWN SOME STAIRS, SARGE.
La Vie Parisienne
AN' WHAT ARE YOU GRINNING ABOUT, WEEPER? 'ORRIBLE AIN'T THE WORD FOR YOUR GRIN! IF YOU SAW IT YOUR-SELF YOU'D NEVER GRIN AGAIN...YOU KEEP THAT GRIN FOR THE HUNS, LAD!
WHEN THE SARGE HAD LEFT...
WHAT'S UP, CHARLEY?
I JUST REALISED SOMETHING, MATES...
TODAY IS LIEUTENANT THOMAS'S COURT MARTIAL... THEY'RE TRYING HIM FOR COWARDICE IN THE FACE OF THE ENEMY! AN' I JUST GOT THIS UNEASY FEELING – SOON THERE WON'T BE MUCH TO SMILE ABOUT AT ALL!

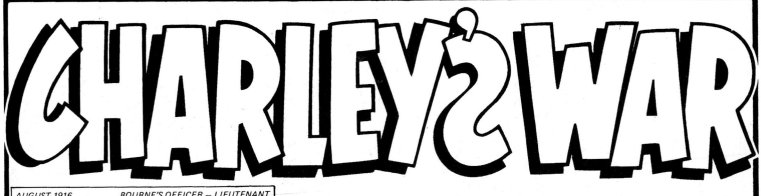

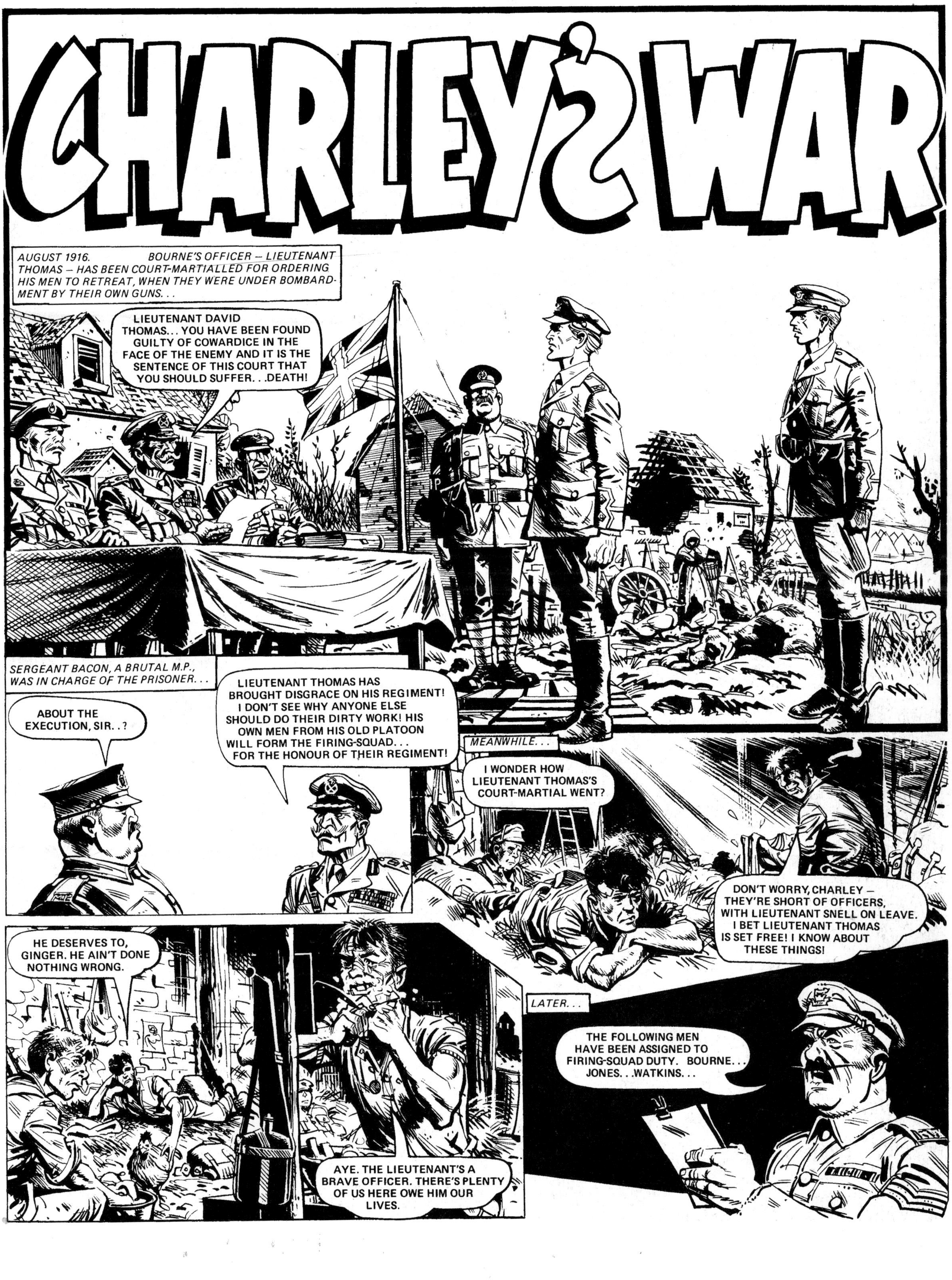

CHARLEY'S WAR

AUGUST 1916. BOURNE'S OFFICER – LIEUTENANT THOMAS – HAS BEEN COURT-MARTIALLED FOR ORDERING HIS MEN TO RETREAT, WHEN THEY WERE UNDER BOMBARD-MENT BY THEIR OWN GUNS. . .

LIEUTENANT DAVID THOMAS. . . YOU HAVE BEEN FOUND GUILTY OF COWARDICE IN THE FACE OF THE ENEMY AND IT IS THE SENTENCE OF THIS COURT THAT YOU SHOULD SUFFER. . .DEATH!

SERGEANT BACON, A BRUTAL M.P., WAS IN CHARGE OF THE PRISONER. . .

ABOUT THE EXECUTION, SIR. . ?

LIEUTENANT THOMAS HAS BROUGHT DISGRACE ON HIS REGIMENT! I DON'T SEE WHY ANYONE ELSE SHOULD DO THEIR DIRTY WORK! HIS OWN MEN FROM HIS OLD PLATOON WILL FORM THE FIRING-SQUAD. . . FOR THE HONOUR OF THEIR REGIMENT!

MEANWHILE. . .

I WONDER HOW LIEUTENANT THOMAS'S COURT-MARTIAL WENT?

DON'T WORRY, CHARLEY – THEY'RE SHORT OF OFFICERS, WITH LIEUTENANT SNELL ON LEAVE. I BET LIEUTENANT THOMAS IS SET FREE! I KNOW ABOUT THESE THINGS!

HE DESERVES TO, GINGER. HE AIN'T DONE NOTHING WRONG.

AYE. THE LIEUTENANT'S A BRAVE OFFICER. THERE'S PLENTY OF US HERE OWE HIM OUR LIVES.

LATER. . .

THE FOLLOWING MEN HAVE BEEN ASSIGNED TO FIRING-SQUAD DUTY. BOURNE. . . JONES. . .WATKINS. . .

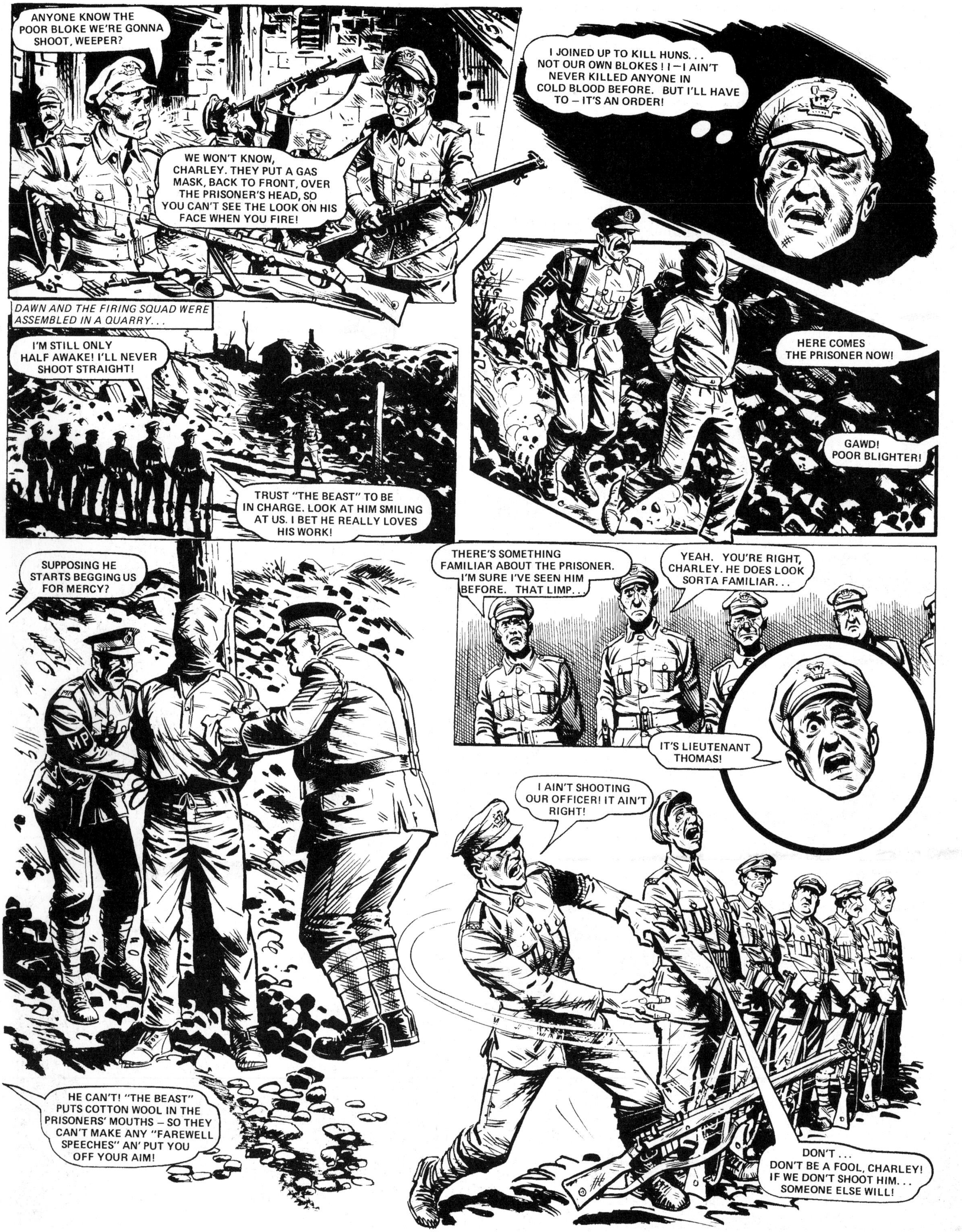
ANYONE KNOW THE POOR BLOKE WE'RE GONNA SHOOT, WEEPER?
WE WON'T KNOW, CHARLEY. THEY PUT A GAS MASK, BACK TO FRONT, OVER THE PRISONER'S HEAD, SO YOU CAN'T SEE THE LOOK ON HIS FACE WHEN YOU FIRE!
I JOINED UP TO KILL HUNS. . . NOT OUR OWN BLOKES! I – I AIN'T NEVER KILLED ANYONE IN COLD BLOOD BEFORE. BUT I'LL HAVE TO – IT'S AN ORDER!
DAWN AND THE FIRING SQUAD WERE ASSEMBLED IN A QUARRY. . .
I'M STILL ONLY HALF AWAKE! I'LL NEVER SHOOT STRAIGHT!
TRUST "THE BEAST" TO BE IN CHARGE. LOOK AT HIM SMILING AT US. I BET HE REALLY LOVES HIS WORK!
HERE COMES THE PRISONER NOW!
GAWD! POOR BLIGHTER!
SUPPOSING HE STARTS BEGGING US FOR MERCY?
HE CAN'T! "THE BEAST" PUTS COTTON WOOL IN THE PRISONERS' MOUTHS – SO THEY CAN'T MAKE ANY "FAREWELL SPEECHES" AN' PUT YOU OFF YOUR AIM!
THERE'S SOMETHING FAMILIAR ABOUT THE PRISONER. I'M SURE I'VE SEEN HIM BEFORE. THAT LIMP. . .
YEAH. YOU'RE RIGHT, CHARLEY. HE DOES LOOK SORTA FAMILIAR. . .
IT'S LIEUTENANT THOMAS!
I AIN'T SHOOTING OUR OFFICER! IT AIN'T RIGHT!
DON'T . . . DON'T BE A FOOL, CHARLEY! IF WE DON'T SHOOT HIM. . . SOMEONE ELSE WILL!

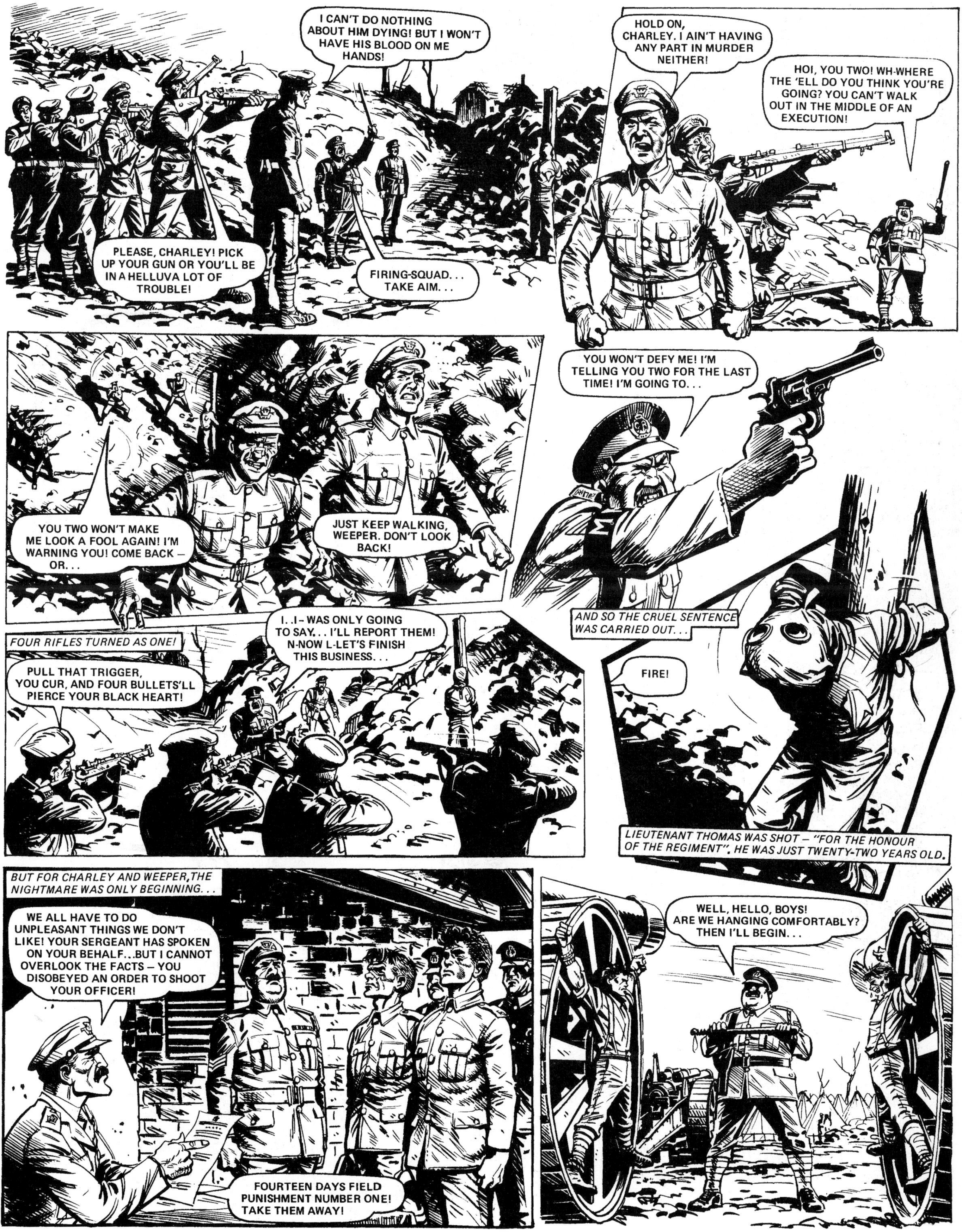
I CAN'T DO NOTHING ABOUT HIM DYING! BUT I WON'T HAVE HIS BLOOD ON ME HANDS!
PLEASE, CHARLEY! PICK UP YOUR GUN OR YOU'LL BE IN A HELLUVA LOT OF TROUBLE!
FIRING-SQUAD... TAKE AIM...
HOLD ON, CHARLEY. I AIN'T HAVING ANY PART IN MURDER NEITHER!
HOI, YOU TWO! WH-WHERE THE 'ELL DO YOU THINK YOU'RE GOING? YOU CAN'T WALK OUT IN THE MIDDLE OF AN EXECUTION!
YOU TWO WON'T MAKE ME LOOK A FOOL AGAIN! I'M WARNING YOU! COME BACK — OR...
JUST KEEP WALKING, WEEPER. DON'T LOOK BACK!
YOU WON'T DEFY ME! I'M TELLING YOU TWO FOR THE LAST TIME! I'M GOING TO...
FOUR RIFLES TURNED AS ONE!
PULL THAT TRIGGER, YOU CUR, AND FOUR BULLETS'LL PIERCE YOUR BLACK HEART!
I..I- WAS ONLY GOING TO SAY... I'LL REPORT THEM! N-NOW L-LET'S FINISH THIS BUSINESS...
AND SO THE CRUEL SENTENCE WAS CARRIED OUT...
FIRE!
LIEUTENANT THOMAS WAS SHOT — "FOR THE HONOUR OF THE REGIMENT". HE WAS JUST TWENTY-TWO YEARS OLD.
BUT FOR CHARLEY AND WEEPER, THE NIGHTMARE WAS ONLY BEGINNING...
WE ALL HAVE TO DO UNPLEASANT THINGS WE DON'T LIKE! YOUR SERGEANT HAS SPOKEN ON YOUR BEHALF...BUT I CANNOT OVERLOOK THE FACTS — YOU DISOBEYED AN ORDER TO SHOOT YOUR OFFICER!
FOURTEEN DAYS FIELD PUNISHMENT NUMBER ONE! TAKE THEM AWAY!
WELL, HELLO, BOYS! ARE WE HANGING COMFORTABLY? THEN I'LL BEGIN...

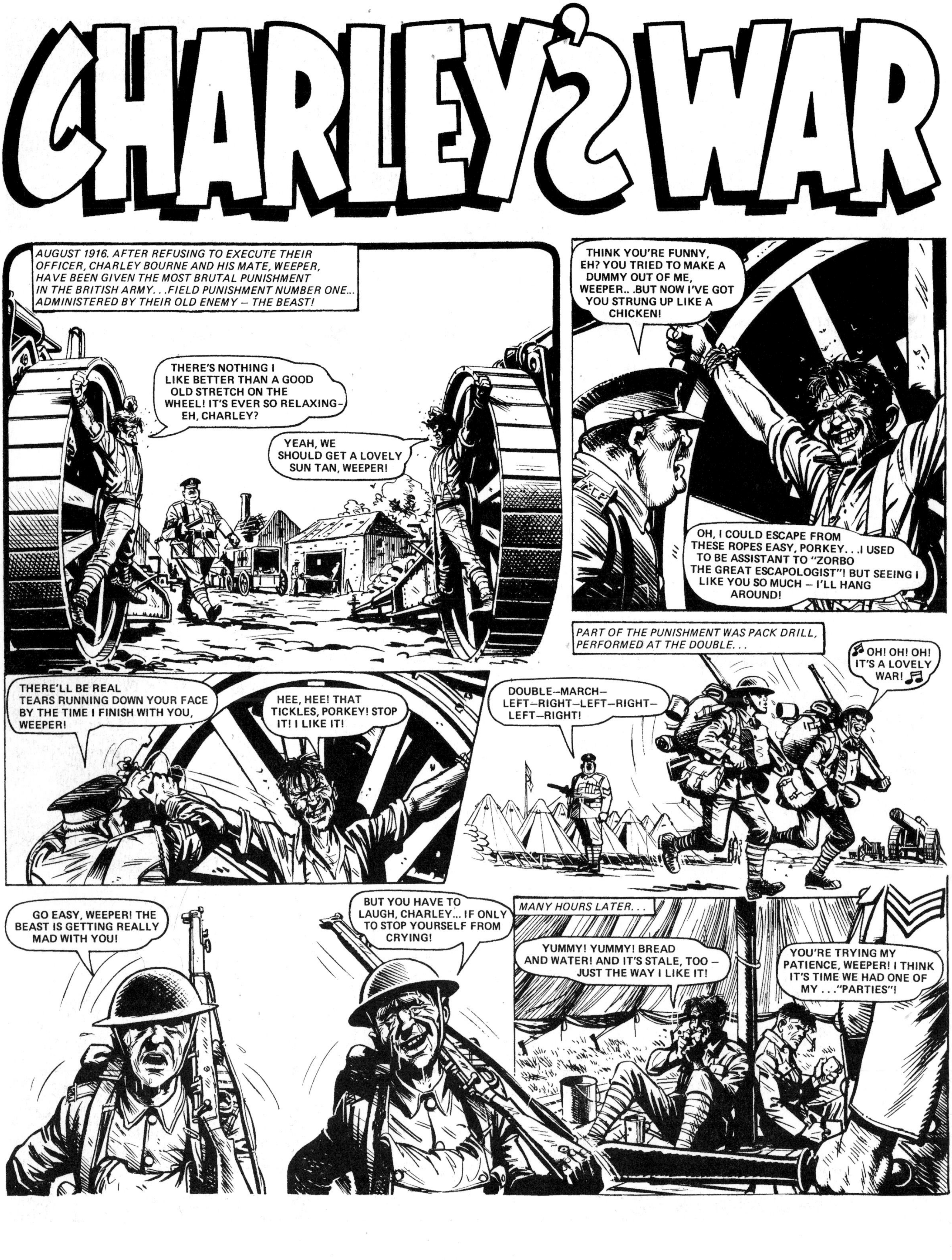
CHARLEY'S WAR
AUGUST 1916. AFTER REFUSING TO EXECUTE THEIR OFFICER, CHARLEY BOURNE AND HIS MATE, WEEPER, HAVE BEEN GIVEN THE MOST BRUTAL PUNISHMENT IN THE BRITISH ARMY. . . FIELD PUNISHMENT NUMBER ONE. . . ADMINISTERED BY THEIR OLD ENEMY — THE BEAST!
THERE'S NOTHING I LIKE BETTER THAN A GOOD OLD STRETCH ON THE WHEEL! IT'S EVER SO RELAXING—EH, CHARLEY?
YEAH, WE SHOULD GET A LOVELY SUN TAN, WEEPER!
THINK YOU'RE FUNNY, EH? YOU TRIED TO MAKE A DUMMY OUT OF ME, WEEPER.. .BUT NOW I'VE GOT YOU STRUNG UP LIKE A CHICKEN!
OH, I COULD ESCAPE FROM THESE ROPES EASY, PORKEY. . .I USED TO BE ASSISTANT TO "ZORBO THE GREAT ESCAPOLOGIST"! BUT SEEING I LIKE YOU SO MUCH — I'LL HANG AROUND!
THERE'LL BE REAL TEARS RUNNING DOWN YOUR FACE BY THE TIME I FINISH WITH YOU, WEEPER!
HEE, HEE! THAT TICKLES, PORKEY! STOP IT! I LIKE IT!
PART OF THE PUNISHMENT WAS PACK DRILL, PERFORMED AT THE DOUBLE. . .
DOUBLE—MARCH—LEFT—RIGHT—LEFT—RIGHT—LEFT—RIGHT!
OH! OH! OH! IT'S A LOVELY WAR!
GO EASY, WEEPER! THE BEAST IS GETTING REALLY MAD WITH YOU!
BUT YOU HAVE TO LAUGH, CHARLEY... IF ONLY TO STOP YOURSELF FROM CRYING!
MANY HOURS LATER. . .
YUMMY! YUMMY! BREAD AND WATER! AND IT'S STALE, TOO — JUST THE WAY I LIKE IT!
YOU'RE TRYING MY PATIENCE, WEEPER! I THINK IT'S TIME WE HAD ONE OF MY . . ."PARTIES"!

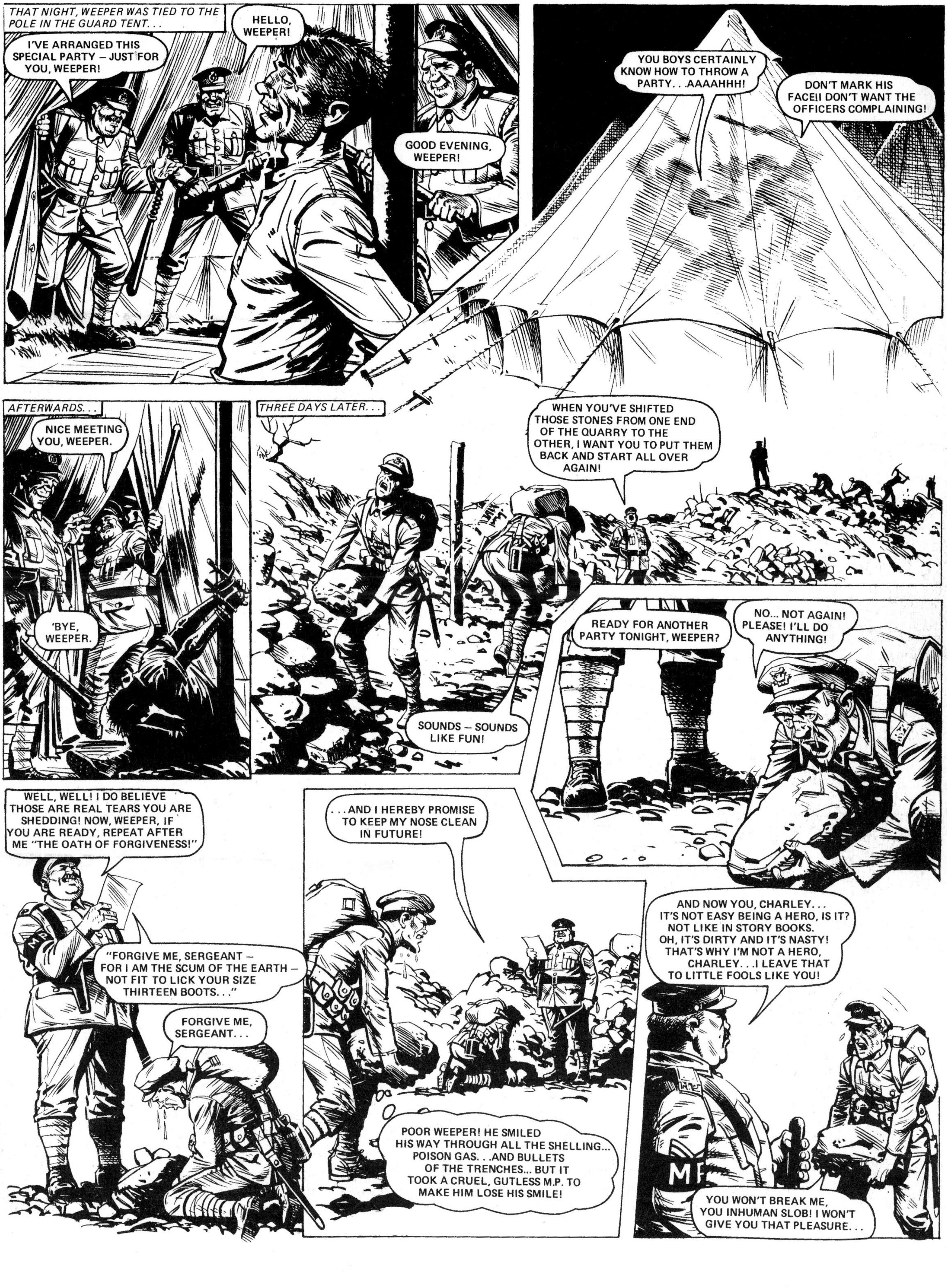

THAT NIGHT, WEEPER WAS TIED TO THE POLE IN THE GUARD TENT. . .
I'VE ARRANGED THIS SPECIAL PARTY – JUST FOR YOU, WEEPER!
HELLO, WEEPER!
GOOD EVENING, WEEPER!
YOU BOYS CERTAINLY KNOW HOW TO THROW A PARTY. . .AAAAHHH!
DON'T MARK HIS FACE!! DON'T WANT THE OFFICERS COMPLAINING!
AFTERWARDS. . .
NICE MEETING YOU, WEEPER.
'BYE, WEEPER.
THREE DAYS LATER. . .
WHEN YOU'VE SHIFTED THOSE STONES FROM ONE END OF THE QUARRY TO THE OTHER, I WANT YOU TO PUT THEM BACK AND START ALL OVER AGAIN!
SOUNDS – SOUNDS LIKE FUN!
READY FOR ANOTHER PARTY TONIGHT, WEEPER?
NO... NOT AGAIN! PLEASE! I'LL DO ANYTHING!
WELL, WELL! I DO BELIEVE THOSE ARE REAL TEARS YOU ARE SHEDDING! NOW, WEEPER, IF YOU ARE READY, REPEAT AFTER ME "THE OATH OF FORGIVENESS!"
"FORGIVE ME, SERGEANT – FOR I AM THE SCUM OF THE EARTH – NOT FIT TO LICK YOUR SIZE THIRTEEN BOOTS. . ."
FORGIVE ME, SERGEANT. . .
. . .AND I HEREBY PROMISE TO KEEP MY NOSE CLEAN IN FUTURE!
POOR WEEPER! HE SMILED HIS WAY THROUGH ALL THE SHELLING... POISON GAS. . .AND BULLETS OF THE TRENCHES... BUT IT TOOK A CRUEL, GUTLESS M.P. TO MAKE HIM LOSE HIS SMILE!
AND NOW YOU, CHARLEY. . . IT'S NOT EASY BEING A HERO, IS IT? NOT LIKE IN STORY BOOKS. OH, IT'S DIRTY AND IT'S NASTY! THAT'S WHY I'M NOT A HERO, CHARLEY. . .I LEAVE THAT TO LITTLE FOOLS LIKE YOU!
YOU WON'T BREAK ME, YOU INHUMAN SLOB! I WON'T GIVE YOU THAT PLEASURE. . .

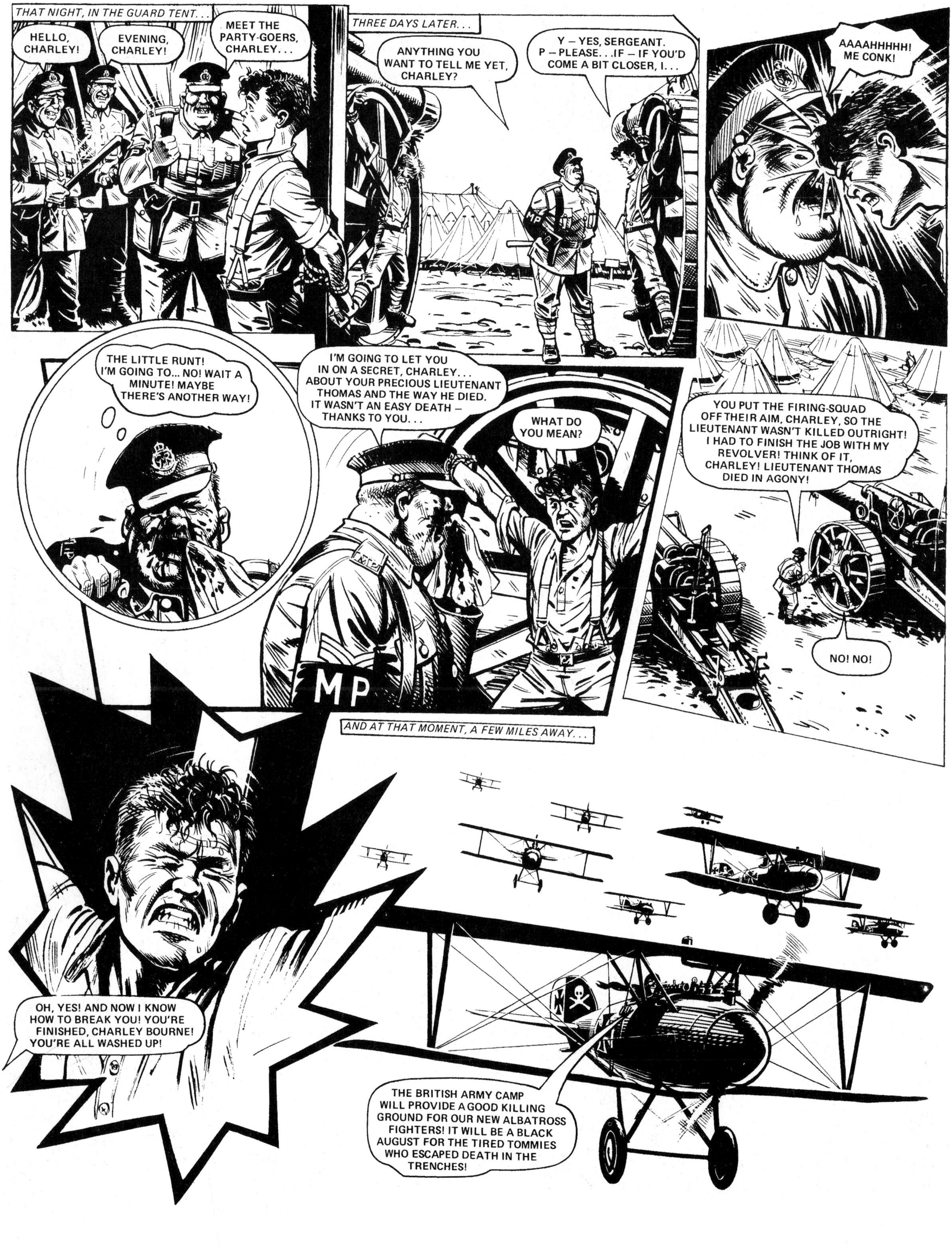
THAT NIGHT, IN THE GUARD TENT...
HELLO, CHARLEY!
EVENING, CHARLEY!
MEET THE PARTY-GOERS, CHARLEY...
THREE DAYS LATER...
ANYTHING YOU WANT TO TELL ME YET, CHARLEY?
Y – YES, SERGEANT. P – PLEASE...IF – IF YOU'D COME A BIT CLOSER, I...
AAAAHHHHH! ME CONK!
THE LITTLE RUNT! I'M GOING TO... NO! WAIT A MINUTE! MAYBE THERE'S ANOTHER WAY!
I'M GOING TO LET YOU IN ON A SECRET, CHARLEY... ABOUT YOUR PRECIOUS LIEUTENANT THOMAS AND THE WAY HE DIED. IT WASN'T AN EASY DEATH – THANKS TO YOU...
WHAT DO YOU MEAN?
MP
YOU PUT THE FIRING-SQUAD OFF THEIR AIM, CHARLEY, SO THE LIEUTENANT WASN'T KILLED OUTRIGHT! I HAD TO FINISH THE JOB WITH MY REVOLVER! THINK OF IT, CHARLEY! LIEUTENANT THOMAS DIED IN AGONY!
NO! NO!
AND AT THAT MOMENT, A FEW MILES AWAY...
OH, YES! AND NOW I KNOW HOW TO BREAK YOU! YOU'RE FINISHED, CHARLEY BOURNE! YOU'RE ALL WASHED UP!
THE BRITISH ARMY CAMP WILL PROVIDE A GOOD KILLING GROUND FOR OUR NEW ALBATROSS FIGHTERS! IT WILL BE A BLACK AUGUST FOR THE TIRED TOMMIES WHO ESCAPED DEATH IN THE TRENCHES!

CHARLEY'S WAR

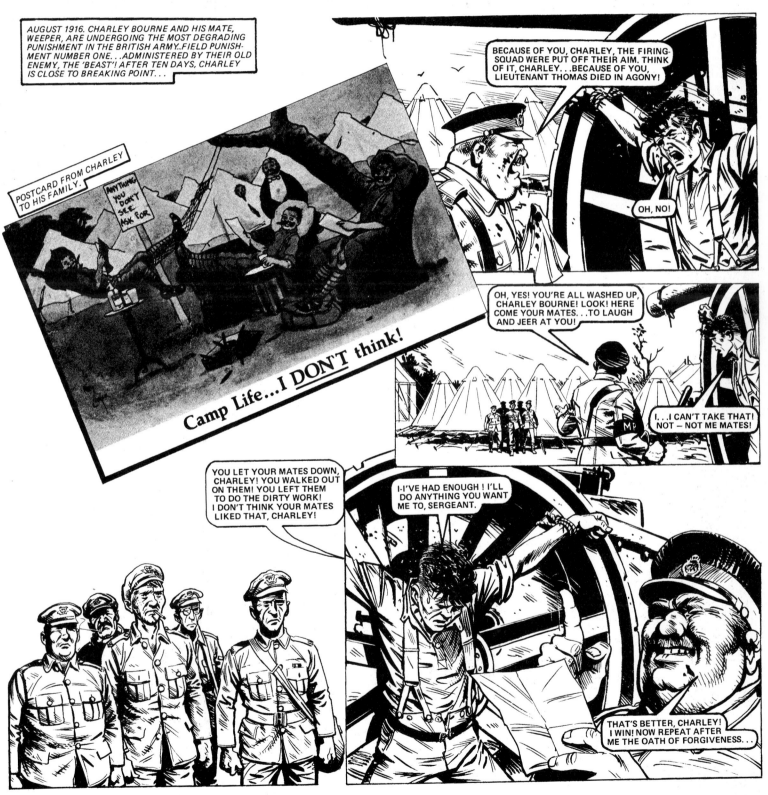

AUGUST 1916. CHARLEY BOURNE AND HIS MATE, WEEPER, ARE UNDERGOING THE MOST DEGRADING PUNISHMENT IN THE BRITISH ARMY...FIELD PUNISHMENT NUMBER ONE...ADMINISTERED BY THEIR OLD ENEMY, THE 'BEAST'! AFTER TEN DAYS, CHARLEY IS CLOSE TO BREAKING POINT...

POSTCARD FROM CHARLEY TO HIS FAMILY.

ANYTHING YOU DON'T SEE ASK FOR.

Camp Life...I DON'T think!

BECAUSE OF YOU, CHARLEY, THE FIRING-SQUAD WERE PUT OFF THEIR AIM. THINK OF IT, CHARLEY...BECAUSE OF YOU, LIEUTENANT THOMAS DIED IN AGONY!

OH, NO!

OH, YES! YOU'RE ALL WASHED UP, CHARLEY BOURNE! LOOK! HERE COME YOUR MATES...TO LAUGH AND JEER AT YOU!

I...I CAN'T TAKE THAT! NOT — NOT ME MATES!

YOU LET YOUR MATES DOWN, CHARLEY! YOU WALKED OUT ON THEM! YOU LEFT THEM TO DO THE DIRTY WORK! I DON'T THINK YOUR MATES LIKED THAT, CHARLEY!

I-I'VE HAD ENOUGH ! I'LL DO ANYTHING YOU WANT ME TO, SERGEANT.

THAT'S BETTER, CHARLEY! I WIN! NOW REPEAT AFTER ME THE OATH OF FORGIVENESS...

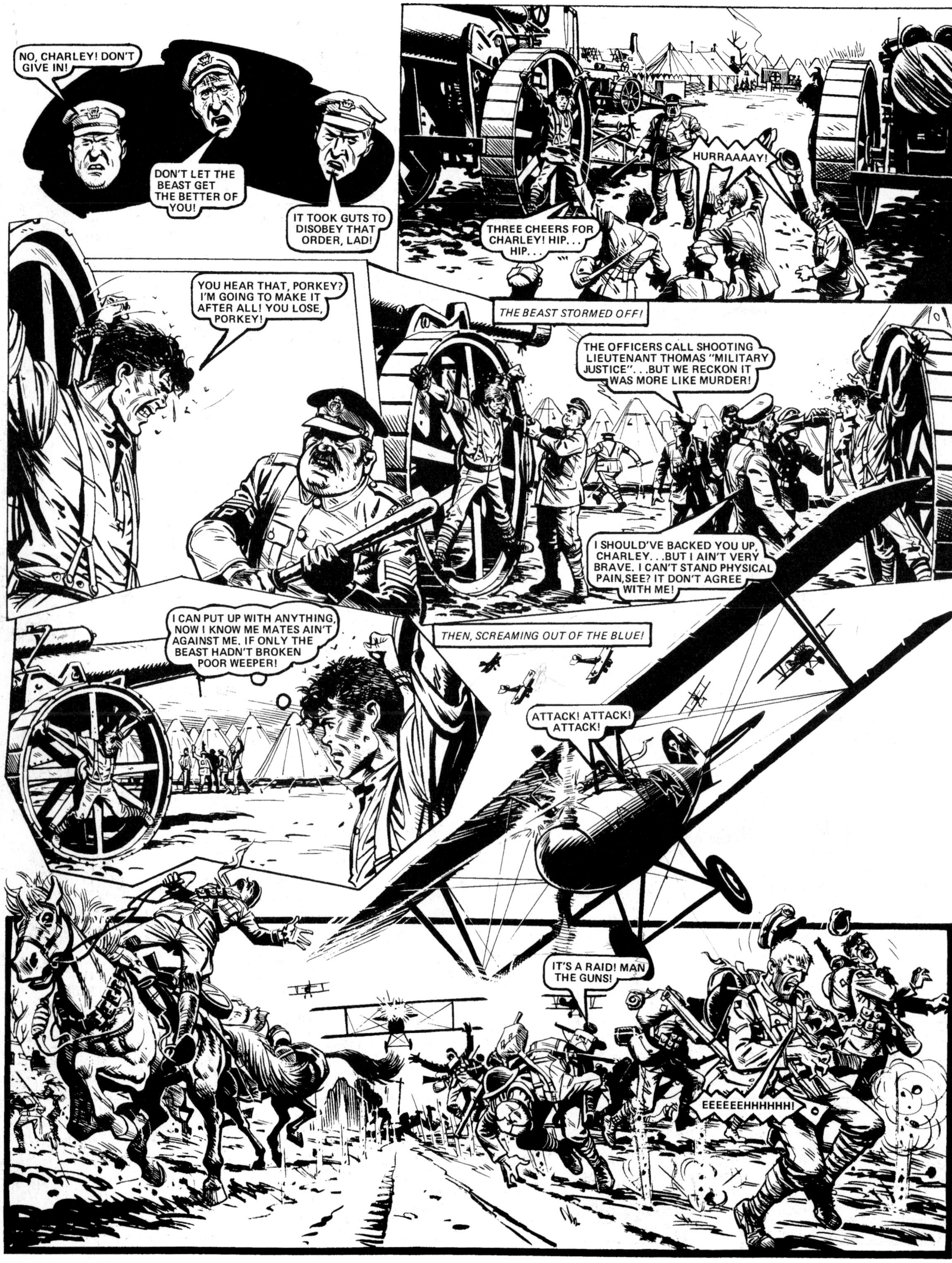
NO, CHARLEY! DON'T GIVE IN!
DON'T LET THE BEAST GET THE BETTER OF YOU!
IT TOOK GUTS TO DISOBEY THAT ORDER, LAD!
HURRAAAAY!
THREE CHEERS FOR CHARLEY! HIP... HIP...
YOU HEAR THAT, PORKEY? I'M GOING TO MAKE IT AFTER ALL! YOU LOSE, PORKEY!
THE BEAST STORMED OFF!
THE OFFICERS CALL SHOOTING LIEUTENANT THOMAS "MILITARY JUSTICE"...BUT WE RECKON IT WAS MORE LIKE MURDER!
I SHOULD'VE BACKED YOU UP, CHARLEY...BUT I AIN'T VERY BRAVE. I CAN'T STAND PHYSICAL PAIN,SEE? IT DON'T AGREE WITH ME!
I CAN PUT UP WITH ANYTHING, NOW I KNOW ME MATES AIN'T AGAINST ME. IF ONLY THE BEAST HADN'T BROKEN POOR WEEPER!
THEN, SCREAMING OUT OF THE BLUE!
ATTACK! ATTACK! ATTACK!
IT'S A RAID! MAN THE GUNS!
EEEEEEHHHHHH!

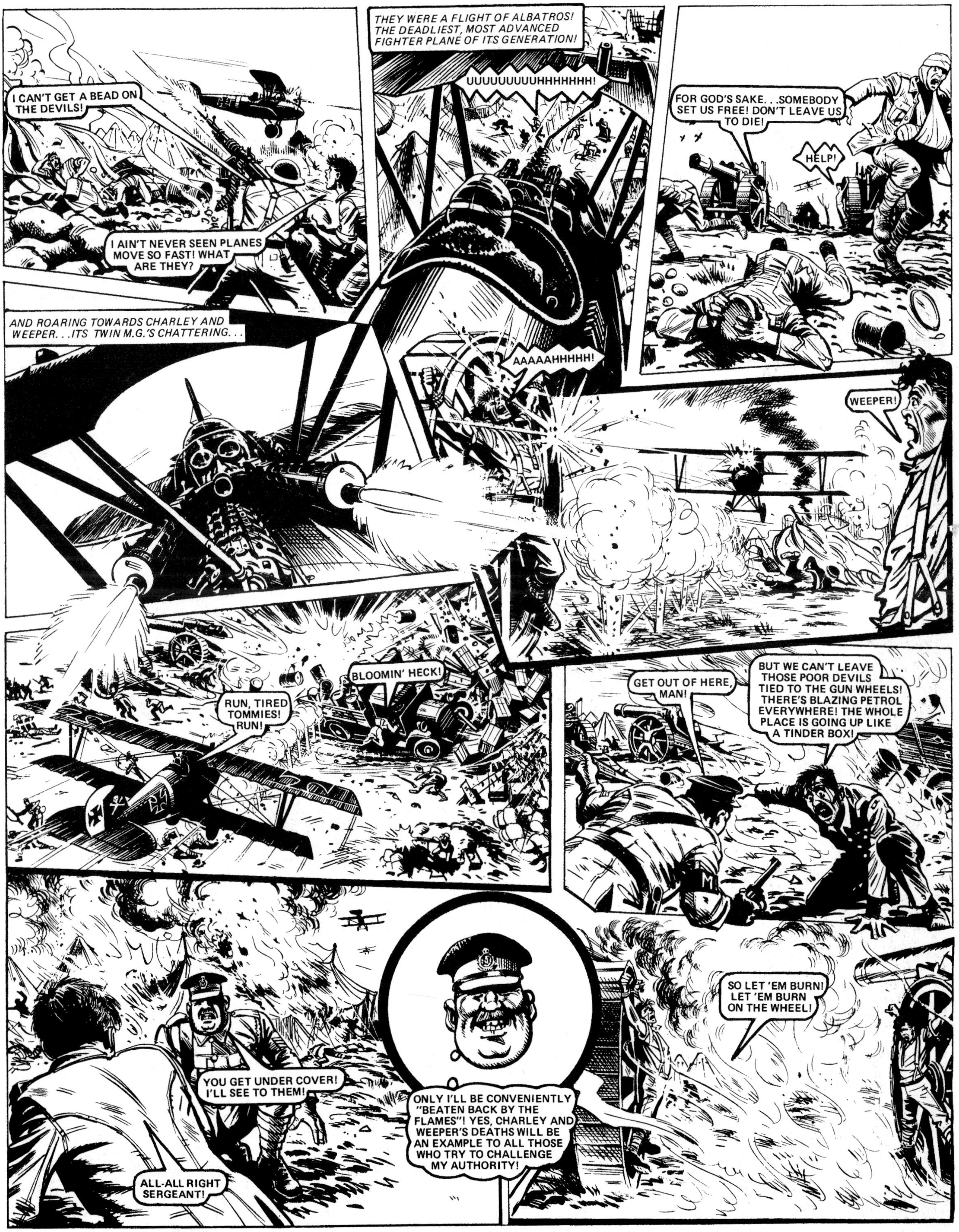
I CAN'T GET A BEAD ON THE DEVILS!
I AIN'T NEVER SEEN PLANES MOVE SO FAST! WHAT ARE THEY?
THEY WERE A FLIGHT OF ALBATROS! THE DEADLIEST, MOST ADVANCED FIGHTER PLANE OF ITS GENERATION!
UUUUUUUUUHHHHHHH!
FOR GOD'S SAKE. . .SOMEBODY SET US FREE! DON'T LEAVE US TO DIE!
HELP!
AND ROARING TOWARDS CHARLEY AND WEEPER. . .ITS TWIN M.G.'S CHATTERING. . .
AAAAAHHHHH!
WEEPER!
BLOOMIN' HECK!
RUN, TIRED TOMMIES! RUN!
GET OUT OF HERE, MAN!
BUT WE CAN'T LEAVE THOSE POOR DEVILS TIED TO THE GUN WHEELS! THERE'S BLAZING PETROL EVERYWHERE! THE WHOLE PLACE IS GOING UP LIKE A TINDER BOX!
YOU GET UNDER COVER! I'LL SEE TO THEM!
ALL-ALL RIGHT SERGEANT!
ONLY I'LL BE CONVENIENTLY "BEATEN BACK BY THE FLAMES"! YES, CHARLEY AND WEEPER'S DEATHS WILL BE AN EXAMPLE TO ALL THOSE WHO TRY TO CHALLENGE MY AUTHORITY!
SO LET 'EM BURN! LET 'EM BURN ON THE WHEEL!

CHARLEY'S WAR

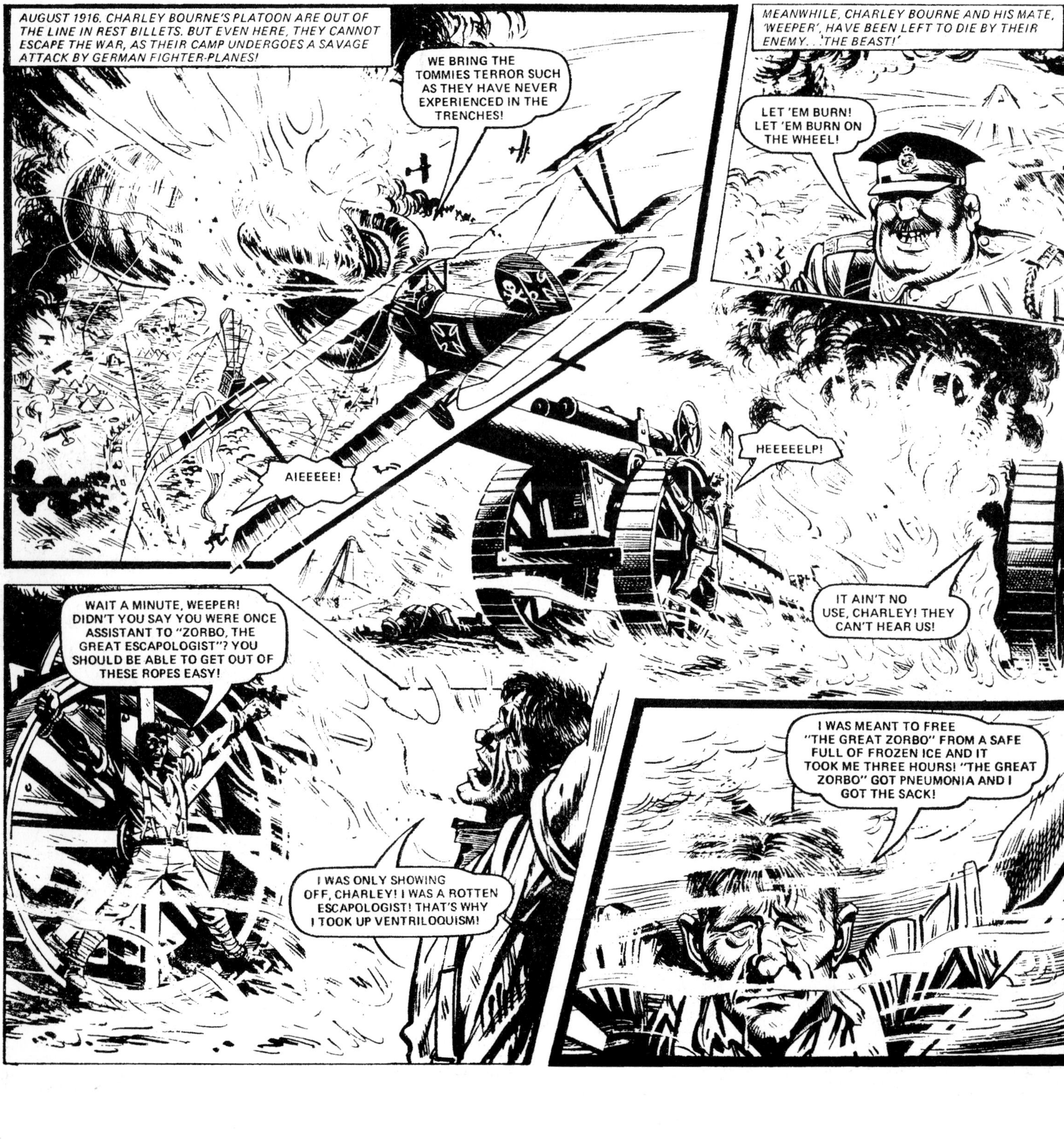

AUGUST 1916. CHARLEY BOURNE'S PLATOON ARE OUT OF THE LINE IN REST BILLETS. BUT EVEN HERE, THEY CANNOT ESCAPE THE WAR, AS THEIR CAMP UNDERGOES A SAVAGE ATTACK BY GERMAN FIGHTER-PLANES!
WE BRING THE TOMMIES TERROR SUCH AS THEY HAVE NEVER EXPERIENCED IN THE TRENCHES!
AIEEEEE!
MEANWHILE, CHARLEY BOURNE AND HIS MATE, 'WEEPER', HAVE BEEN LEFT TO DIE BY THEIR ENEMY. . .'THE BEAST!'
LET 'EM BURN! LET 'EM BURN ON THE WHEEL!
HEEEEELP!
IT AIN'T NO USE, CHARLEY! THEY CAN'T HEAR US!
WAIT A MINUTE, WEEPER! DIDN'T YOU SAY YOU WERE ONCE ASSISTANT TO "ZORBO, THE GREAT ESCAPOLOGIST"? YOU SHOULD BE ABLE TO GET OUT OF THESE ROPES EASY!
I WAS ONLY SHOWING OFF, CHARLEY! I WAS A ROTTEN ESCAPOLOGIST! THAT'S WHY I TOOK UP VENTRILOQUISM!
I WAS MEANT TO FREE "THE GREAT ZORBO" FROM A SAFE FULL OF FROZEN ICE AND IT TOOK ME THREE HOURS! "THE GREAT ZORBO" GOT PNEUMONIA AND I GOT THE SACK!

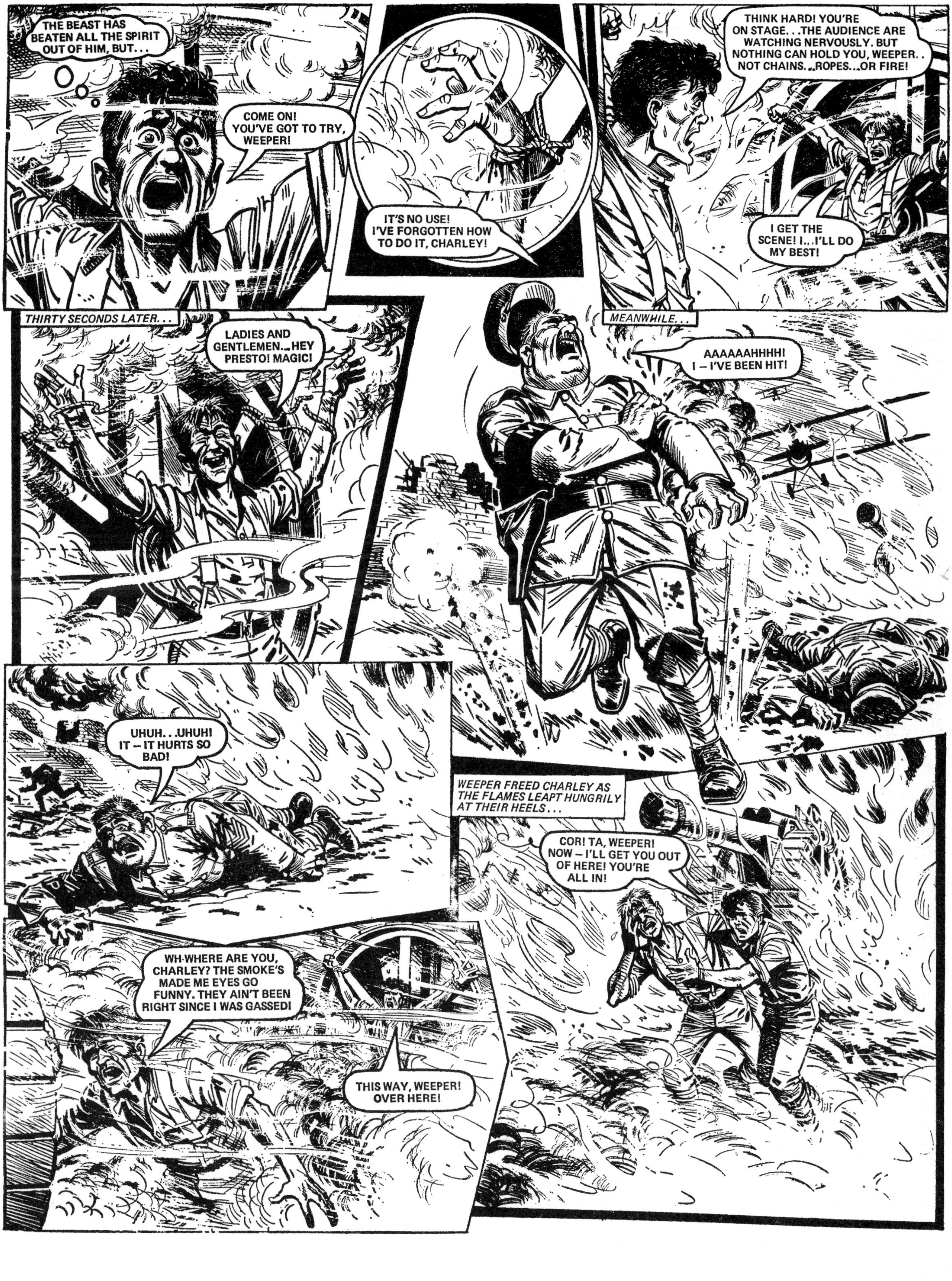
THE BEAST HAS BEATEN ALL THE SPIRIT OUT OF HIM, BUT...
COME ON! YOU'VE GOT TO TRY, WEEPER!
IT'S NO USE! I'VE FORGOTTEN HOW TO DO IT, CHARLEY!
THINK HARD! YOU'RE ON STAGE...THE AUDIENCE ARE WATCHING NERVOUSLY. BUT NOTHING CAN HOLD YOU, WEEPER.. NOT CHAINS...ROPES...OR FIRE!
I GET THE SCENE! I...I'LL DO MY BEST!
THIRTY SECONDS LATER...
LADIES AND GENTLEMEN...HEY PRESTO! MAGIC!
MEANWHILE...
AAAAAAHHHH! I – I'VE BEEN HIT!
UHUH...UHUH! IT – IT HURTS SO BAD!
WH-WHERE ARE YOU, CHARLEY? THE SMOKE'S MADE ME EYES GO FUNNY. THEY AIN'T BEEN RIGHT SINCE I WAS GASSED!
THIS WAY, WEEPER! OVER HERE!
WEEPER FREED CHARLEY AS THE FLAMES LEAPT HUNGRILY AT THEIR HEELS...
COR! TA, WEEPER! NOW – I'LL GET YOU OUT OF HERE! YOU'RE ALL IN!

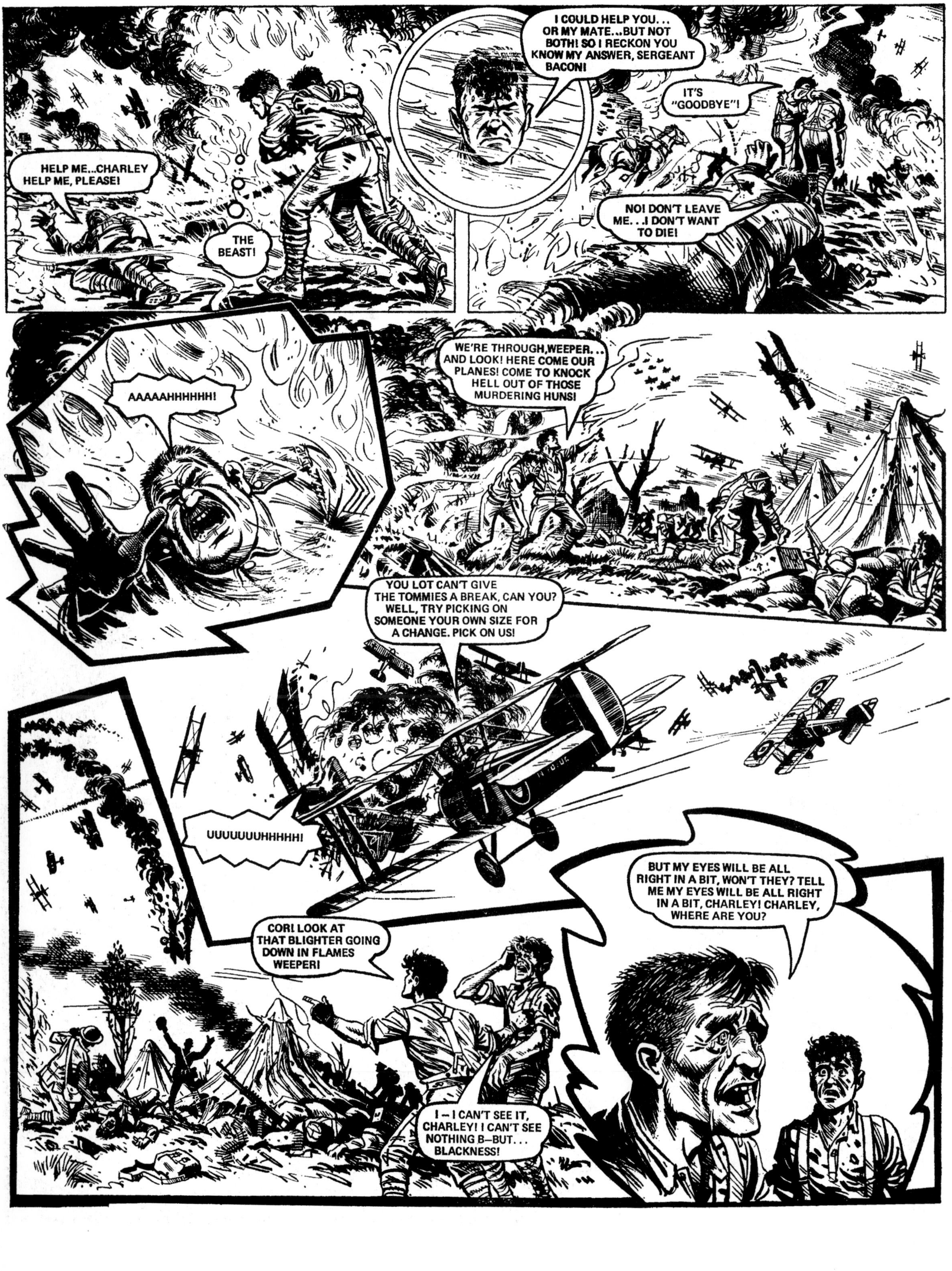
HELP ME...CHARLEY HELP ME, PLEASE!
THE BEAST!
I COULD HELP YOU... OR MY MATE...BUT NOT BOTH! SO I RECKON YOU KNOW MY ANSWER, SERGEANT BACON!
IT'S "GOODBYE"!
NO! DON'T LEAVE ME...I DON'T WANT TO DIE!
AAAAAHHHHHH!
WE'RE THROUGH, WEEPER... AND LOOK! HERE COME OUR PLANES! COME TO KNOCK HELL OUT OF THOSE MURDERING HUNS!
YOU LOT CAN'T GIVE THE TOMMIES A BREAK, CAN YOU? WELL, TRY PICKING ON SOMEONE YOUR OWN SIZE FOR A CHANGE. PICK ON US!
UUUUUUUHHHHHH!
COR! LOOK AT THAT BLIGHTER GOING DOWN IN FLAMES WEEPER!
I—I CAN'T SEE IT, CHARLEY! I CAN'T SEE NOTHING B—BUT... BLACKNESS!
BUT MY EYES WILL BE ALL RIGHT IN A BIT, WON'T THEY? TELL ME MY EYES WILL BE ALL RIGHT IN A BIT, CHARLEY! CHARLEY, WHERE ARE YOU?

CHARLEY'S WAR

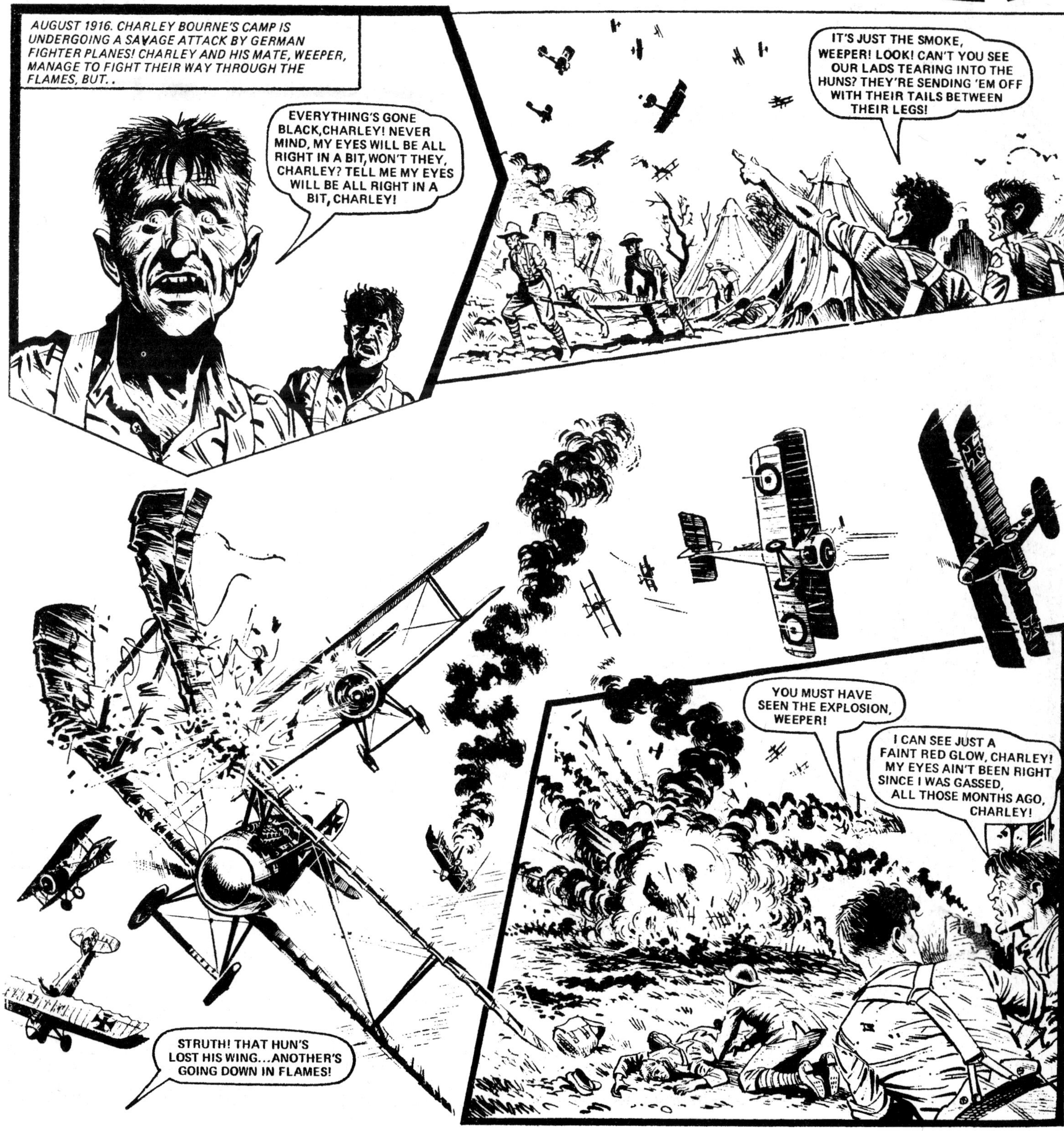

AUGUST 1916. CHARLEY BOURNE'S CAMP IS UNDERGOING A SAVAGE ATTACK BY GERMAN FIGHTER PLANES! CHARLEY AND HIS MATE, WEEPER, MANAGE TO FIGHT THEIR WAY THROUGH THE FLAMES, BUT. .
EVERYTHING'S GONE BLACK,CHARLEY! NEVER MIND, MY EYES WILL BE ALL RIGHT IN A BIT, WON'T THEY, CHARLEY? TELL ME MY EYES WILL BE ALL RIGHT IN A BIT, CHARLEY!
IT'S JUST THE SMOKE, WEEPER! LOOK! CAN'T YOU SEE OUR LADS TEARING INTO THE HUNS? THEY'RE SENDING 'EM OFF WITH THEIR TAILS BETWEEN THEIR LEGS!
STRUTH! THAT HUN'S LOST HIS WING...ANOTHER'S GOING DOWN IN FLAMES!
YOU MUST HAVE SEEN THE EXPLOSION, WEEPER!
I CAN SEE JUST A FAINT RED GLOW, CHARLEY! MY EYES AIN'T BEEN RIGHT SINCE I WAS GASSED, ALL THOSE MONTHS AGO, CHARLEY!

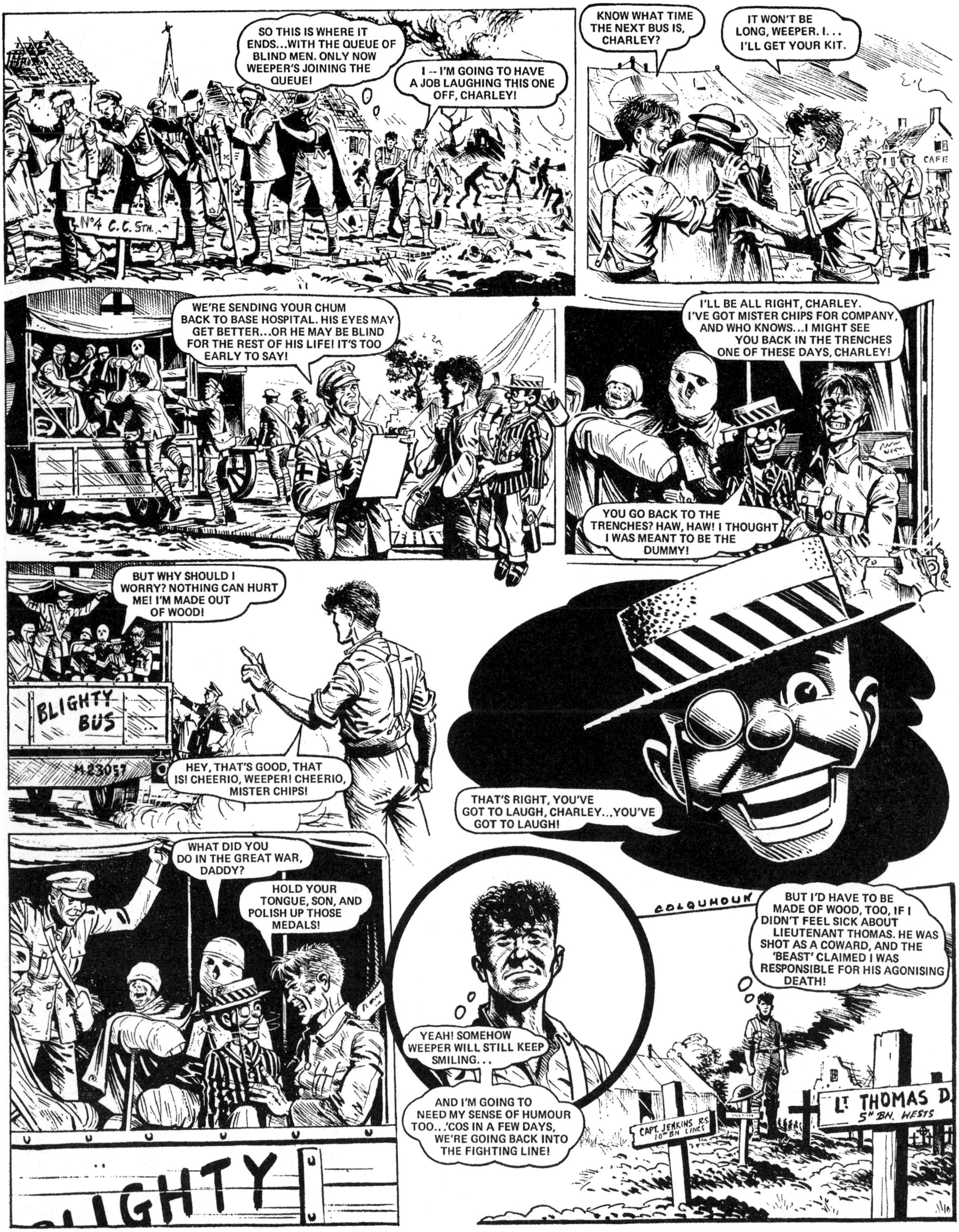

SO THIS IS WHERE IT ENDS...WITH THE QUEUE OF BLIND MEN. ONLY NOW WEEPER'S JOINING THE QUEUE!
I -- I'M GOING TO HAVE A JOB LAUGHING THIS ONE OFF, CHARLEY!
N°4 C.C. STN.
KNOW WHAT TIME THE NEXT BUS IS, CHARLEY?
IT WON'T BE LONG, WEEPER. I... I'LL GET YOUR KIT.
CAFE
WE'RE SENDING YOUR CHUM BACK TO BASE HOSPITAL. HIS EYES MAY GET BETTER...OR HE MAY BE BLIND FOR THE REST OF HIS LIFE! IT'S TOO EARLY TO SAY!
I'LL BE ALL RIGHT, CHARLEY. I'VE GOT MISTER CHIPS FOR COMPANY, AND WHO KNOWS...I MIGHT SEE YOU BACK IN THE TRENCHES ONE OF THESE DAYS, CHARLEY!
YOU GO BACK TO THE TRENCHES? HAW, HAW! I THOUGHT I WAS MEANT TO BE THE DUMMY!
BUT WHY SHOULD I WORRY? NOTHING CAN HURT ME! I'M MADE OUT OF WOOD!
BLIGHTY BUS
M.23057
HEY, THAT'S GOOD, THAT IS! CHEERIO, WEEPER! CHEERIO, MISTER CHIPS!
THAT'S RIGHT, YOU'VE GOT TO LAUGH, CHARLEY...YOU'VE GOT TO LAUGH!
WHAT DID YOU DO IN THE GREAT WAR, DADDY?
HOLD YOUR TONGUE, SON, AND POLISH UP THOSE MEDALS!
BLIGHTY
YEAH! SOMEHOW WEEPER WILL STILL KEEP SMILING...
AND I'M GOING TO NEED MY SENSE OF HUMOUR TOO...'COS IN A FEW DAYS, WE'RE GOING BACK INTO THE FIGHTING LINE!
COLQUHOUN
BUT I'D HAVE TO BE MADE OF WOOD, TOO, IF I DIDN'T FEEL SICK ABOUT LIEUTENANT THOMAS. HE WAS SHOT AS A COWARD, AND THE 'BEAST' CLAIMED I WAS RESPONSIBLE FOR HIS AGONISING DEATH!
CAPT. JENKINS R.S. 10TH BN LINCS
LT THOMAS D. 5TH BN. WESTS

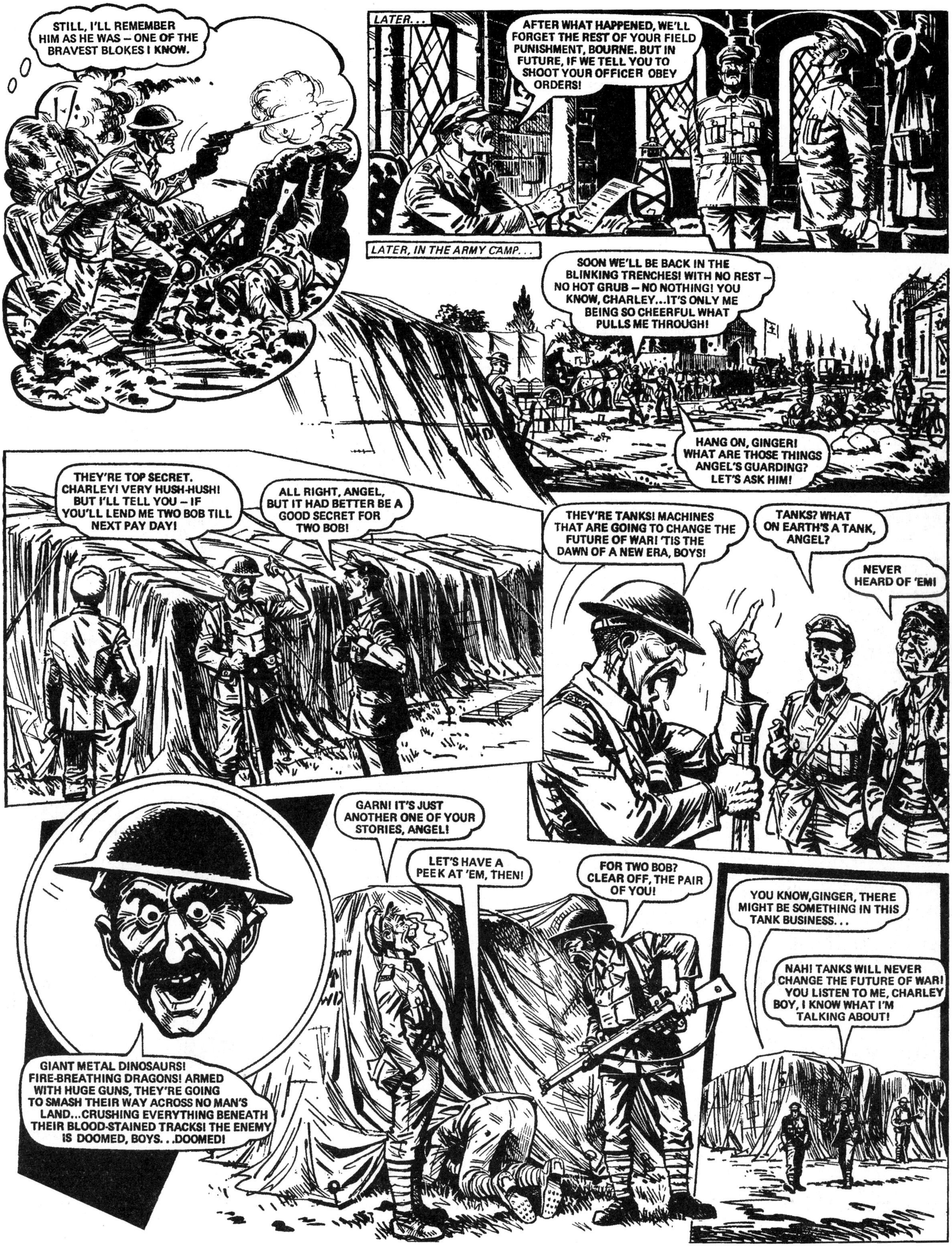
STILL, I'LL REMEMBER HIM AS HE WAS – ONE OF THE BRAVEST BLOKES I KNOW.
LATER...
AFTER WHAT HAPPENED, WE'LL FORGET THE REST OF YOUR FIELD PUNISHMENT, BOURNE. BUT IN FUTURE, IF WE TELL YOU TO SHOOT YOUR OFFICER OBEY ORDERS!
LATER, IN THE ARMY CAMP...
SOON WE'LL BE BACK IN THE BLINKING TRENCHES! WITH NO REST – NO HOT GRUB – NO NOTHING! YOU KNOW, CHARLEY...IT'S ONLY ME BEING SO CHEERFUL WHAT PULLS ME THROUGH!
HANG ON, GINGER! WHAT ARE THOSE THINGS ANGEL'S GUARDING? LET'S ASK HIM!
THEY'RE TOP SECRET, CHARLEY! VERY HUSH-HUSH! BUT I'LL TELL YOU – IF YOU'LL LEND ME TWO BOB TILL NEXT PAY DAY!
ALL RIGHT, ANGEL, BUT IT HAD BETTER BE A GOOD SECRET FOR TWO BOB!
THEY'RE TANKS! MACHINES THAT ARE GOING TO CHANGE THE FUTURE OF WAR! 'TIS THE DAWN OF A NEW ERA, BOYS!
TANKS? WHAT ON EARTH'S A TANK, ANGEL?
NEVER HEARD OF 'EM!
GIANT METAL DINOSAURS! FIRE-BREATHING DRAGONS! ARMED WITH HUGE GUNS, THEY'RE GOING TO SMASH THEIR WAY ACROSS NO MAN'S LAND...CRUSHING EVERYTHING BENEATH THEIR BLOOD-STAINED TRACKS! THE ENEMY IS DOOMED, BOYS...DOOMED!
GARN! IT'S JUST ANOTHER ONE OF YOUR STORIES, ANGEL!
LET'S HAVE A PEEK AT 'EM, THEN!
FOR TWO BOB? CLEAR OFF, THE PAIR OF YOU!
YOU KNOW, GINGER, THERE MIGHT BE SOMETHING IN THIS TANK BUSINESS...
NAH! TANKS WILL NEVER CHANGE THE FUTURE OF WAR! YOU LISTEN TO ME, CHARLEY BOY, I KNOW WHAT I'M TALKING ABOUT!

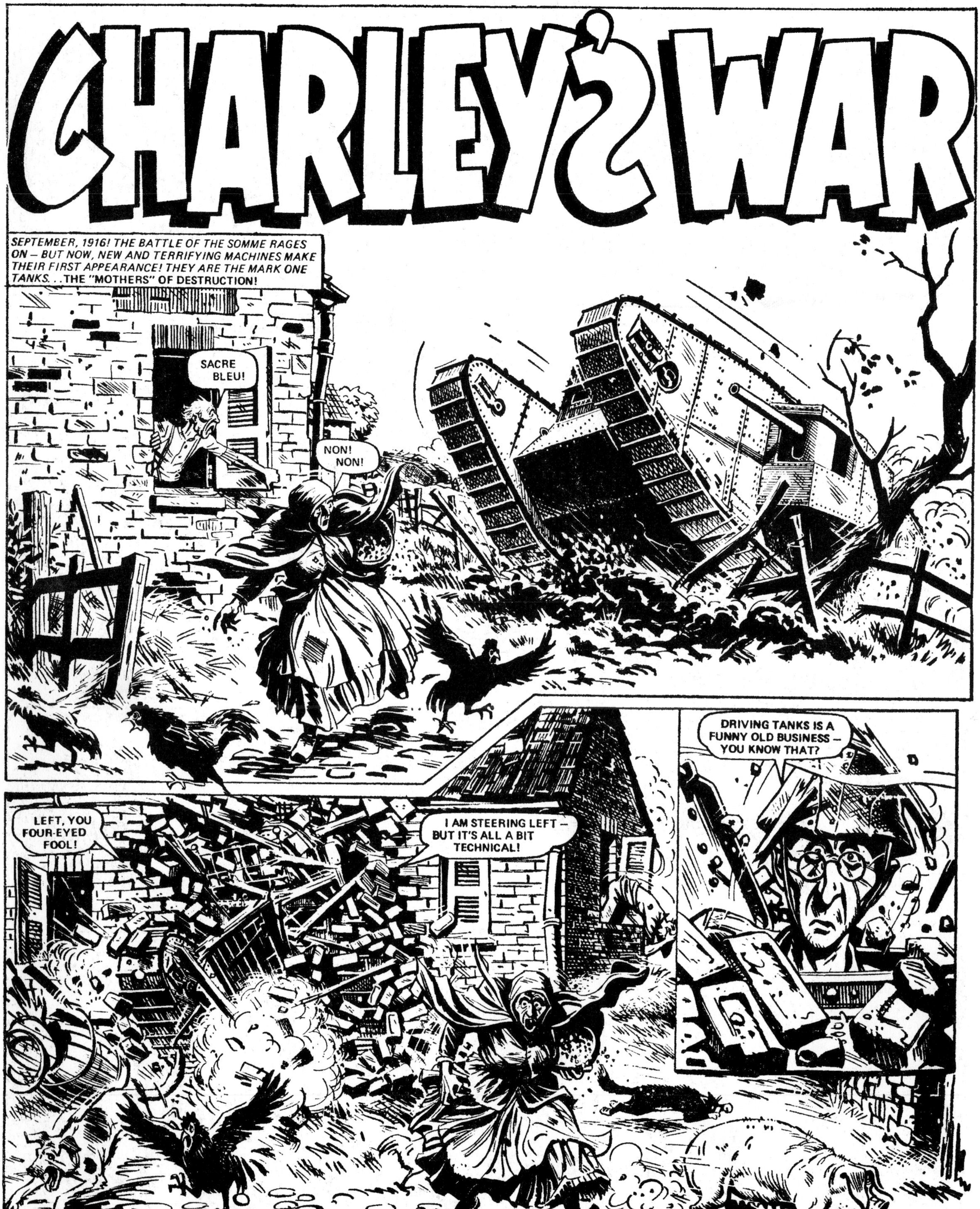
CHARLEY'S WAR
SEPTEMBER, 1916! THE BATTLE OF THE SOMME RAGES ON – BUT NOW, NEW AND TERRIFYING MACHINES MAKE THEIR FIRST APPEARANCE! THEY ARE THE MARK ONE TANKS. . . THE "MOTHERS" OF DESTRUCTION!
SACRE BLEU!
NON! NON!
LEFT, YOU FOUR-EYED FOOL!
I AM STEERING LEFT – BUT IT'S ALL A BIT TECHNICAL!
DRIVING TANKS IS A FUNNY OLD BUSINESS – YOU KNOW THAT?

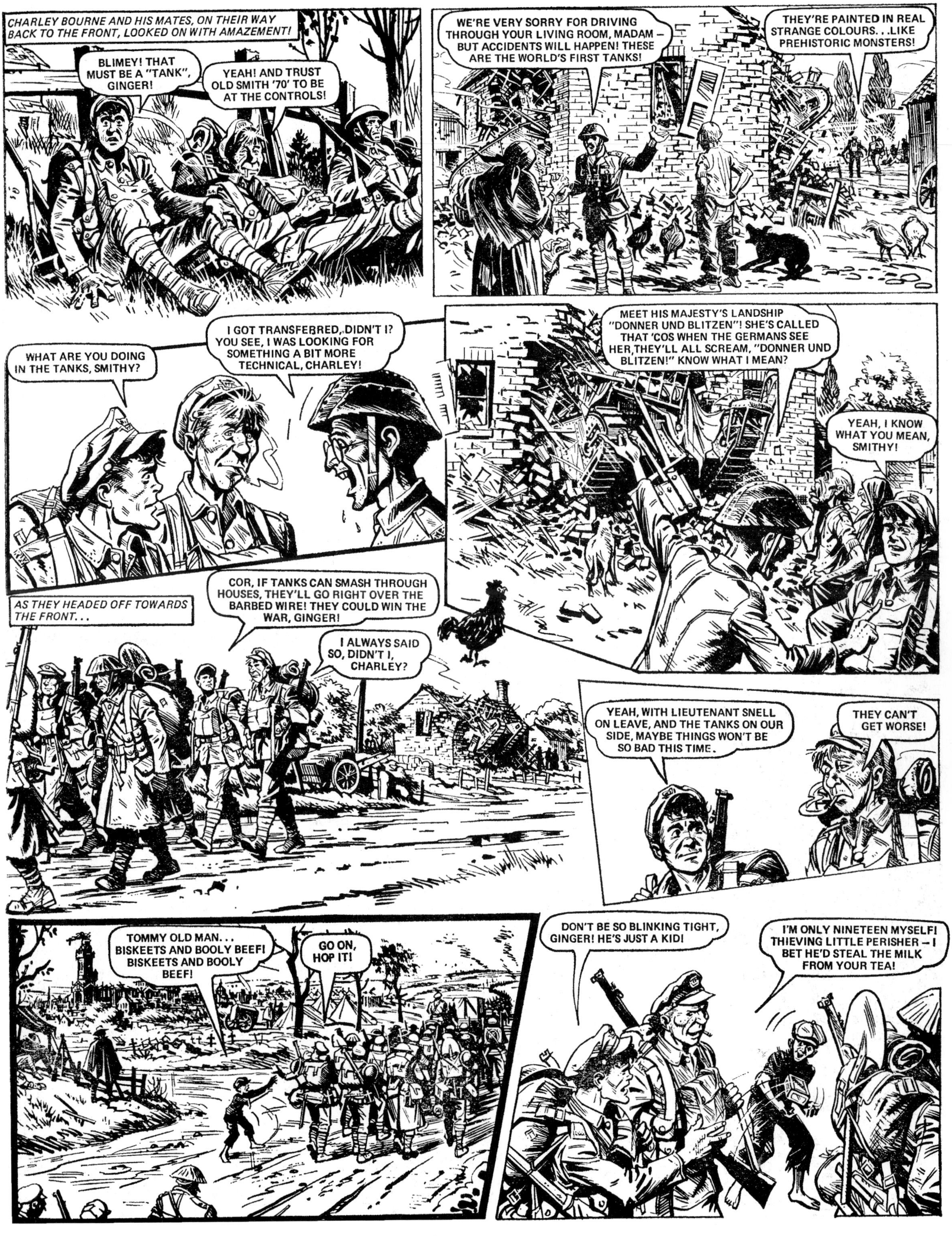
CHARLEY BOURNE AND HIS MATES, ON THEIR WAY BACK TO THE FRONT, LOOKED ON WITH AMAZEMENT!
BLIMEY! THAT MUST BE A "TANK", GINGER!
YEAH! AND TRUST OLD SMITH '70' TO BE AT THE CONTROLS!
WE'RE VERY SORRY FOR DRIVING THROUGH YOUR LIVING ROOM, MADAM – BUT ACCIDENTS WILL HAPPEN! THESE ARE THE WORLD'S FIRST TANKS!
THEY'RE PAINTED IN REAL STRANGE COLOURS. . .LIKE PREHISTORIC MONSTERS!
WHAT ARE YOU DOING IN THE TANKS, SMITHY?
I GOT TRANSFERRED, DIDN'T I? YOU SEE, I WAS LOOKING FOR SOMETHING A BIT MORE TECHNICAL, CHARLEY!
MEET HIS MAJESTY'S LANDSHIP "DONNER UND BLITZEN"! SHE'S CALLED THAT 'COS WHEN THE GERMANS SEE HER,THEY'LL ALL SCREAM, "DONNER UND BLITZEN!" KNOW WHAT I MEAN?
YEAH, I KNOW WHAT YOU MEAN, SMITHY!
AS THEY HEADED OFF TOWARDS THE FRONT. . .
COR, IF TANKS CAN SMASH THROUGH HOUSES, THEY'LL GO RIGHT OVER THE BARBED WIRE! THEY COULD WIN THE WAR, GINGER!
I ALWAYS SAID SO, DIDN'T I, CHARLEY?
YEAH, WITH LIEUTENANT SNELL ON LEAVE, AND THE TANKS ON OUR SIDE, MAYBE THINGS WON'T BE SO BAD THIS TIME.
THEY CAN'T GET WORSE!
TOMMY OLD MAN. . . BISKEETS AND BOOLY BEEF! BISKEETS AND BOOLY BEEF!
GO ON, HOP IT!
DON'T BE SO BLINKING TIGHT, GINGER! HE'S JUST A KID!
I'M ONLY NINETEEN MYSELF! THIEVING LITTLE PERISHER – I BET HE'D STEAL THE MILK FROM YOUR TEA!

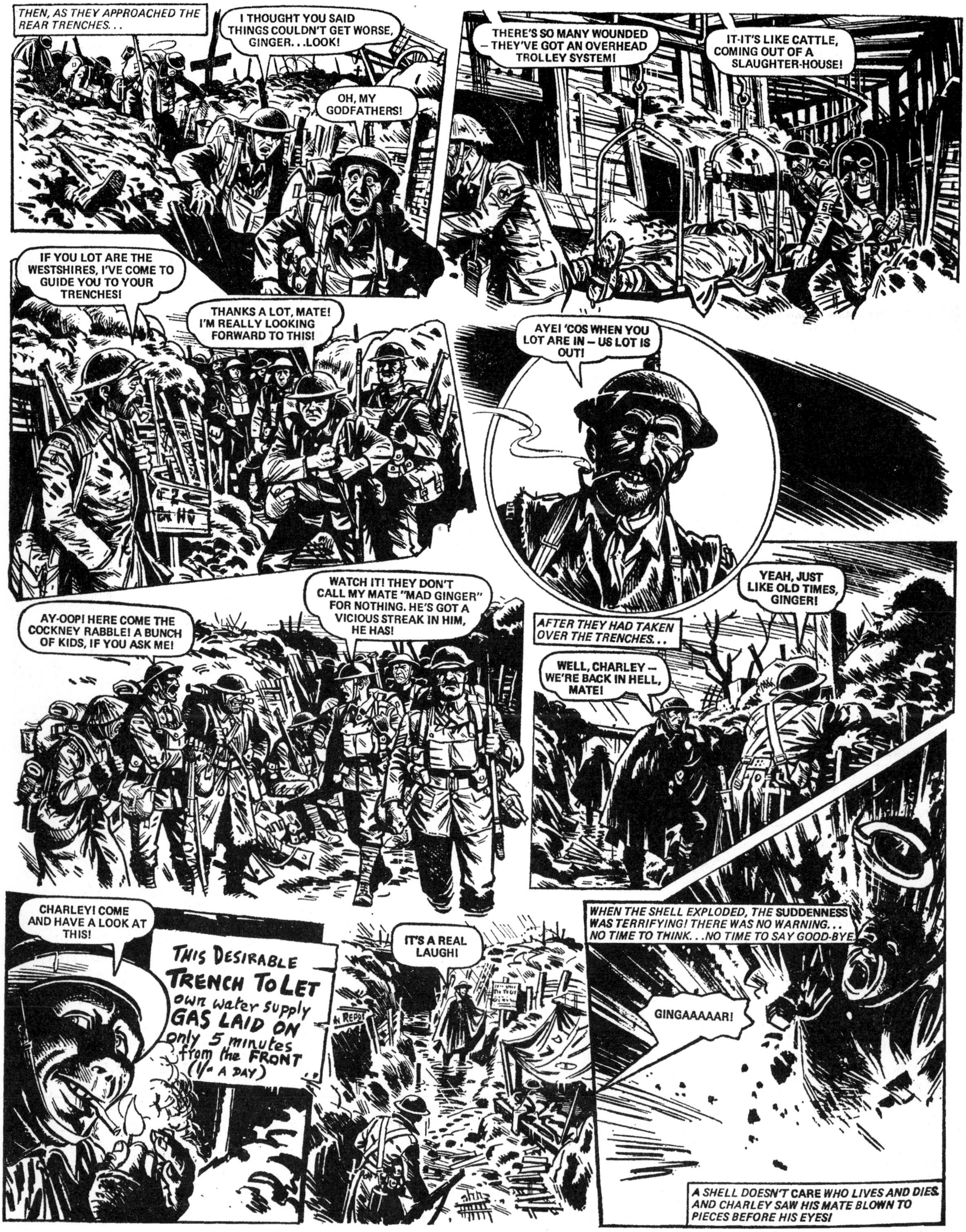
THEN, AS THEY APPROACHED THE REAR TRENCHES...
I THOUGHT YOU SAID THINGS COULDN'T GET WORSE, GINGER...LOOK!
OH, MY GODFATHERS!
THERE'S SO MANY WOUNDED – THEY'VE GOT AN OVERHEAD TROLLEY SYSTEM!
IT-IT'S LIKE CATTLE, COMING OUT OF A SLAUGHTER-HOUSE!
IF YOU LOT ARE THE WESTSHIRES, I'VE COME TO GUIDE YOU TO YOUR TRENCHES!
THANKS A LOT, MATE! I'M REALLY LOOKING FORWARD TO THIS!
AYE! 'COS WHEN YOU LOT ARE IN – US LOT IS OUT!
AY-OOP! HERE COME THE COCKNEY RABBLE! A BUNCH OF KIDS, IF YOU ASK ME!
WATCH IT! THEY DON'T CALL MY MATE "MAD GINGER" FOR NOTHING. HE'S GOT A VICIOUS STREAK IN HIM, HE HAS!
AFTER THEY HAD TAKEN OVER THE TRENCHES...
WELL, CHARLEY – WE'RE BACK IN HELL, MATE!
YEAH, JUST LIKE OLD TIMES, GINGER!
CHARLEY! COME AND HAVE A LOOK AT THIS!
THIS DESIRABLE TRENCH TO LET own water supply GAS LAID ON only 5 minutes from the FRONT (1/- A DAY)
IT'S A REAL LAUGH!
WHEN THE SHELL EXPLODED, THE SUDDENNESS WAS TERRIFYING! THERE WAS NO WARNING... NO TIME TO THINK...NO TIME TO SAY GOOD-BYE.
GINGAAAAAR!
A SHELL DOESN'T CARE WHO LIVES AND DIES. AND CHARLEY SAW HIS MATE BLOWN TO PIECES BEFORE HIS EYES!

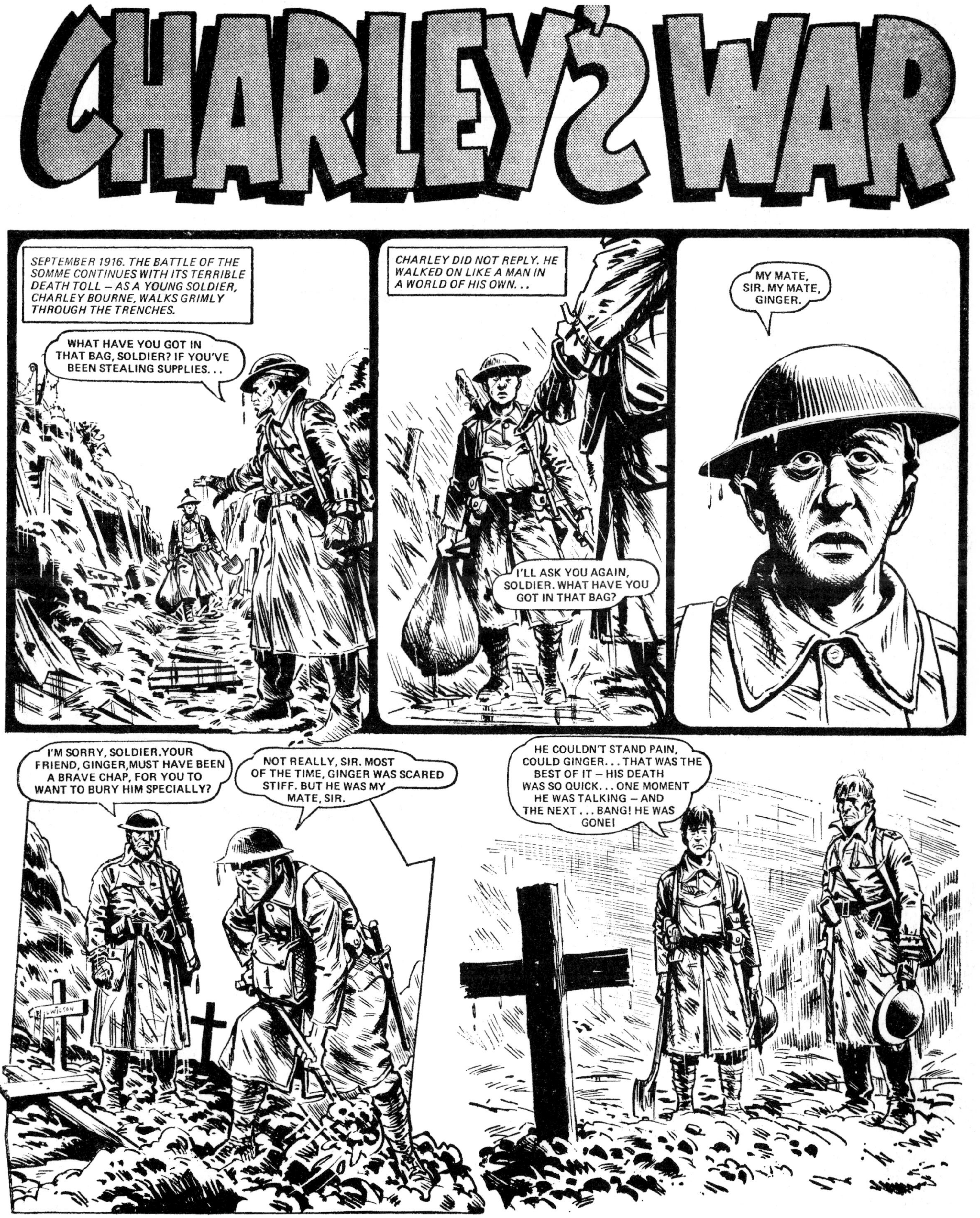
CHARLEY'S WAR
SEPTEMBER 1916. THE BATTLE OF THE SOMME CONTINUES WITH ITS TERRIBLE DEATH TOLL – AS A YOUNG SOLDIER, CHARLEY BOURNE, WALKS GRIMLY THROUGH THE TRENCHES.
WHAT HAVE YOU GOT IN THAT BAG, SOLDIER? IF YOU'VE BEEN STEALING SUPPLIES. . .
CHARLEY DID NOT REPLY. HE WALKED ON LIKE A MAN IN A WORLD OF HIS OWN. . .
I'LL ASK YOU AGAIN, SOLDIER. WHAT HAVE YOU GOT IN THAT BAG?
MY MATE, SIR. MY MATE, GINGER.
I'M SORRY, SOLDIER. YOUR FRIEND, GINGER, MUST HAVE BEEN A BRAVE CHAP, FOR YOU TO WANT TO BURY HIM SPECIALLY?
NOT REALLY, SIR. MOST OF THE TIME, GINGER WAS SCARED STIFF. BUT HE WAS MY MATE, SIR.
HE COULDN'T STAND PAIN, COULD GINGER. . . THAT WAS THE BEST OF IT – HIS DEATH WAS SO QUICK. . . ONE MOMENT HE WAS TALKING – AND THE NEXT . . . BANG! HE WAS GONE!

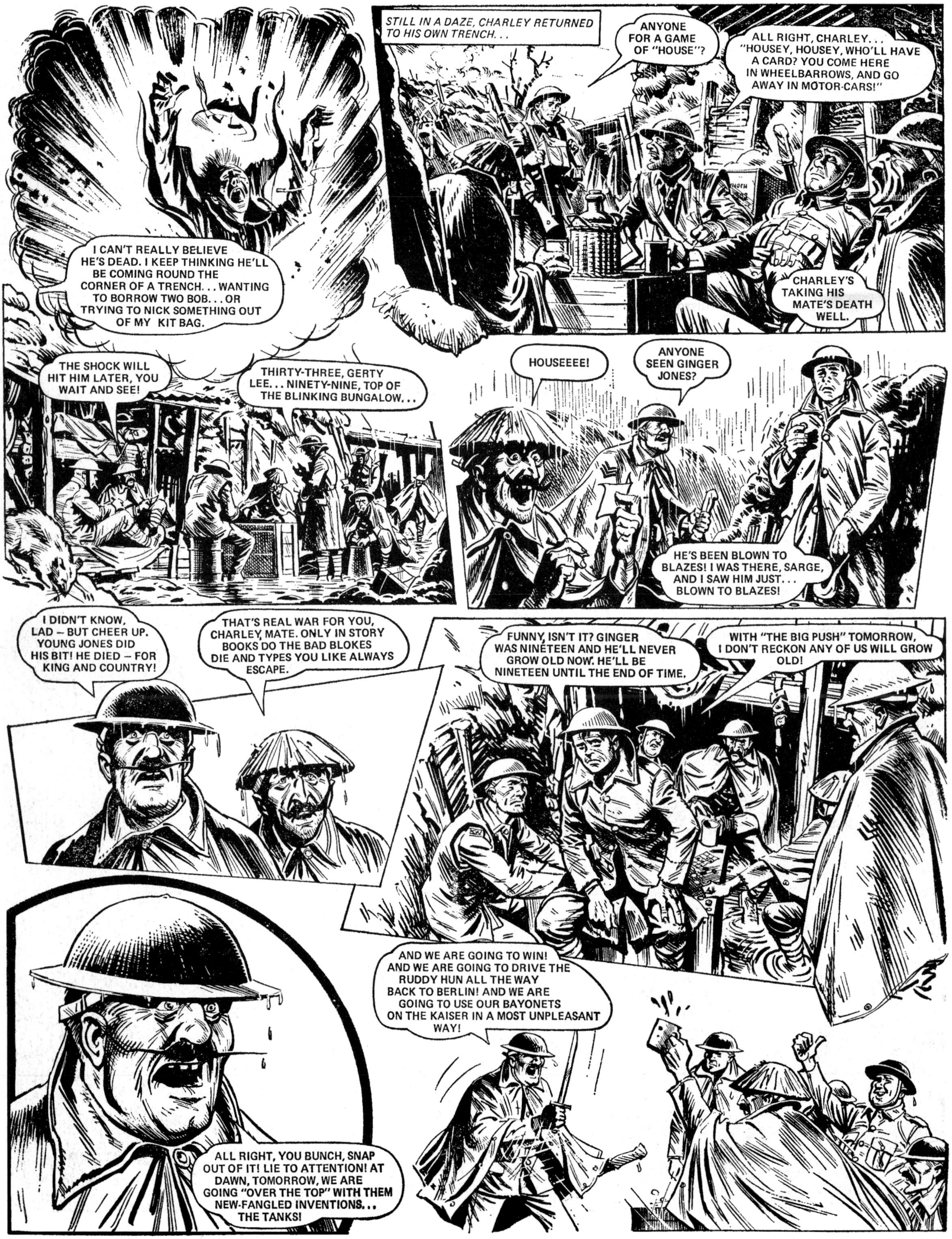

I CAN'T REALLY BELIEVE HE'S DEAD. I KEEP THINKING HE'LL BE COMING ROUND THE CORNER OF A TRENCH. . . WANTING TO BORROW TWO BOB. . . OR TRYING TO NICK SOMETHING OUT OF MY KIT BAG.
STILL IN A DAZE, CHARLEY RETURNED TO HIS OWN TRENCH. . .
ANYONE FOR A GAME OF "HOUSE"?
ALL RIGHT, CHARLEY. . . "HOUSEY, HOUSEY, WHO'LL HAVE A CARD? YOU COME HERE IN WHEELBARROWS, AND GO AWAY IN MOTOR-CARS!"
CHARLEY'S TAKING HIS MATE'S DEATH WELL.
THE SHOCK WILL HIT HIM LATER, YOU WAIT AND SEE!
THIRTY-THREE, GERTY LEE. . . NINETY-NINE, TOP OF THE BLINKING BUNGALOW. . .
HOUSEEEE!
ANYONE SEEN GINGER JONES?
HE'S BEEN BLOWN TO BLAZES! I WAS THERE, SARGE, AND I SAW HIM JUST. . . BLOWN TO BLAZES!
I DIDN'T KNOW, LAD – BUT CHEER UP. YOUNG JONES DID HIS BIT! HE DIED – FOR KING AND COUNTRY!
THAT'S REAL WAR FOR YOU, CHARLEY, MATE. ONLY IN STORY BOOKS DO THE BAD BLOKES DIE AND TYPES YOU LIKE ALWAYS ESCAPE.
FUNNY, ISN'T IT? GINGER WAS NINETEEN AND HE'LL NEVER GROW OLD NOW. HE'LL BE NINETEEN UNTIL THE END OF TIME.
WITH "THE BIG PUSH" TOMORROW, I DON'T RECKON ANY OF US WILL GROW OLD!
ALL RIGHT, YOU BUNCH, SNAP OUT OF IT! LIE TO ATTENTION! AT DAWN, TOMORROW, WE ARE GOING "OVER THE TOP" WITH THEM NEW-FANGLED INVENTIONS. . . THE TANKS!
AND WE ARE GOING TO WIN! AND WE ARE GOING TO DRIVE THE RUDDY HUN ALL THE WAY BACK TO BERLIN! AND WE ARE GOING TO USE OUR BAYONETS ON THE KAISER IN A MOST UNPLEASANT WAY!

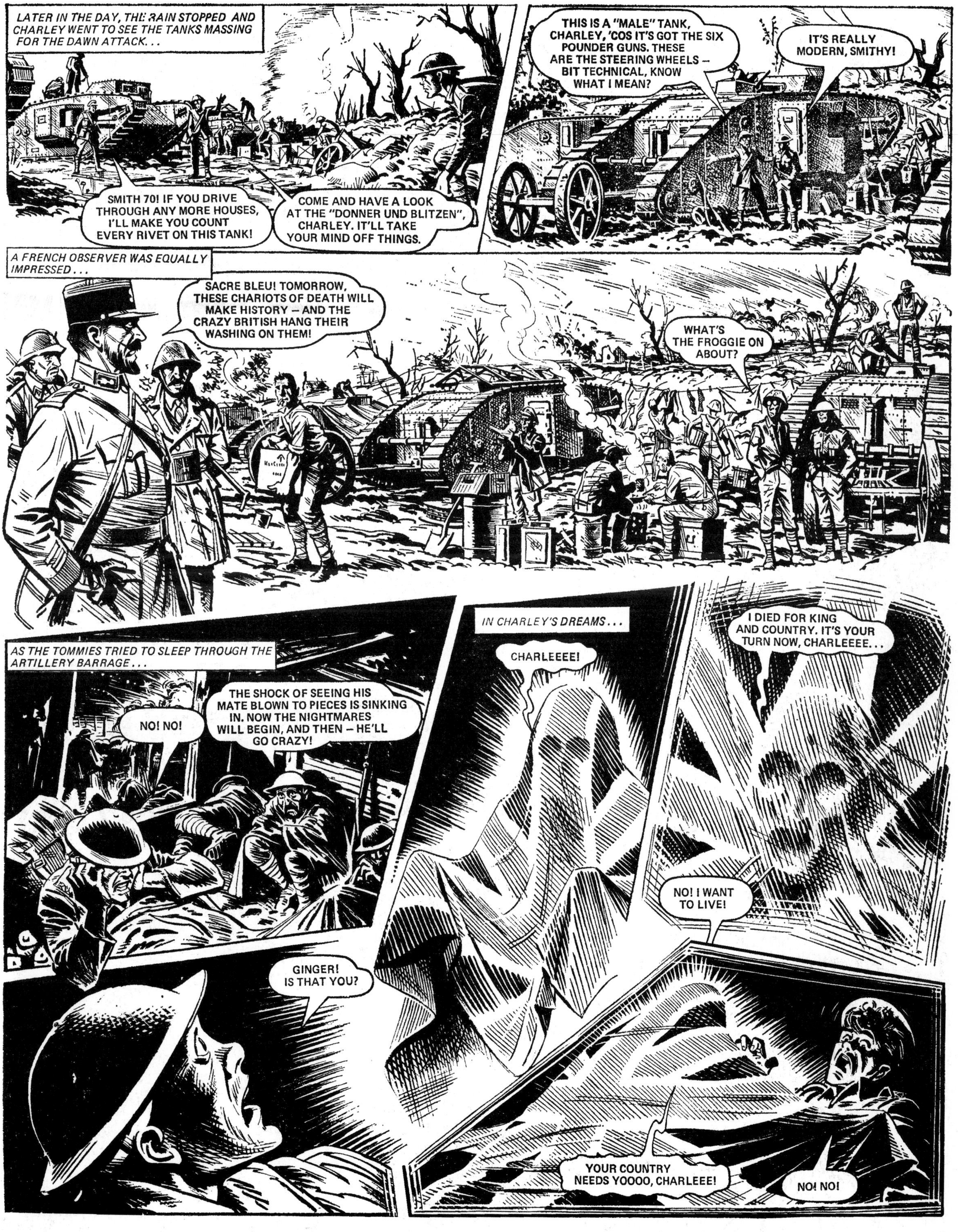
LATER IN THE DAY, THE RAIN STOPPED AND CHARLEY WENT TO SEE THE TANKS MASSING FOR THE DAWN ATTACK...
SMITH 70! IF YOU DRIVE THROUGH ANY MORE HOUSES, I'LL MAKE YOU COUNT EVERY RIVET ON THIS TANK!
COME AND HAVE A LOOK AT THE "DONNER UND BLITZEN", CHARLEY. IT'LL TAKE YOUR MIND OFF THINGS.
THIS IS A "MALE" TANK, CHARLEY, 'COS IT'S GOT THE SIX POUNDER GUNS. THESE ARE THE STEERING WHEELS — BIT TECHNICAL, KNOW WHAT I MEAN?
IT'S REALLY MODERN, SMITHY!
A FRENCH OBSERVER WAS EQUALLY IMPRESSED...
SACRE BLEU! TOMORROW, THESE CHARIOTS OF DEATH WILL MAKE HISTORY — AND THE CRAZY BRITISH HANG THEIR WASHING ON THEM!
WHAT'S THE FROGGIE ON ABOUT?
AS THE TOMMIES TRIED TO SLEEP THROUGH THE ARTILLERY BARRAGE...
NO! NO!
THE SHOCK OF SEEING HIS MATE BLOWN TO PIECES IS SINKING IN. NOW THE NIGHTMARES WILL BEGIN, AND THEN — HE'LL GO CRAZY!
IN CHARLEY'S DREAMS...
CHARLEEEE!
I DIED FOR KING AND COUNTRY. IT'S YOUR TURN NOW, CHARLEEEE...
NO! I WANT TO LIVE!
GINGER! IS THAT YOU?
YOUR COUNTRY NEEDS YOOOO, CHARLEEE!
NO! NO!

CHARLEY'S WAR

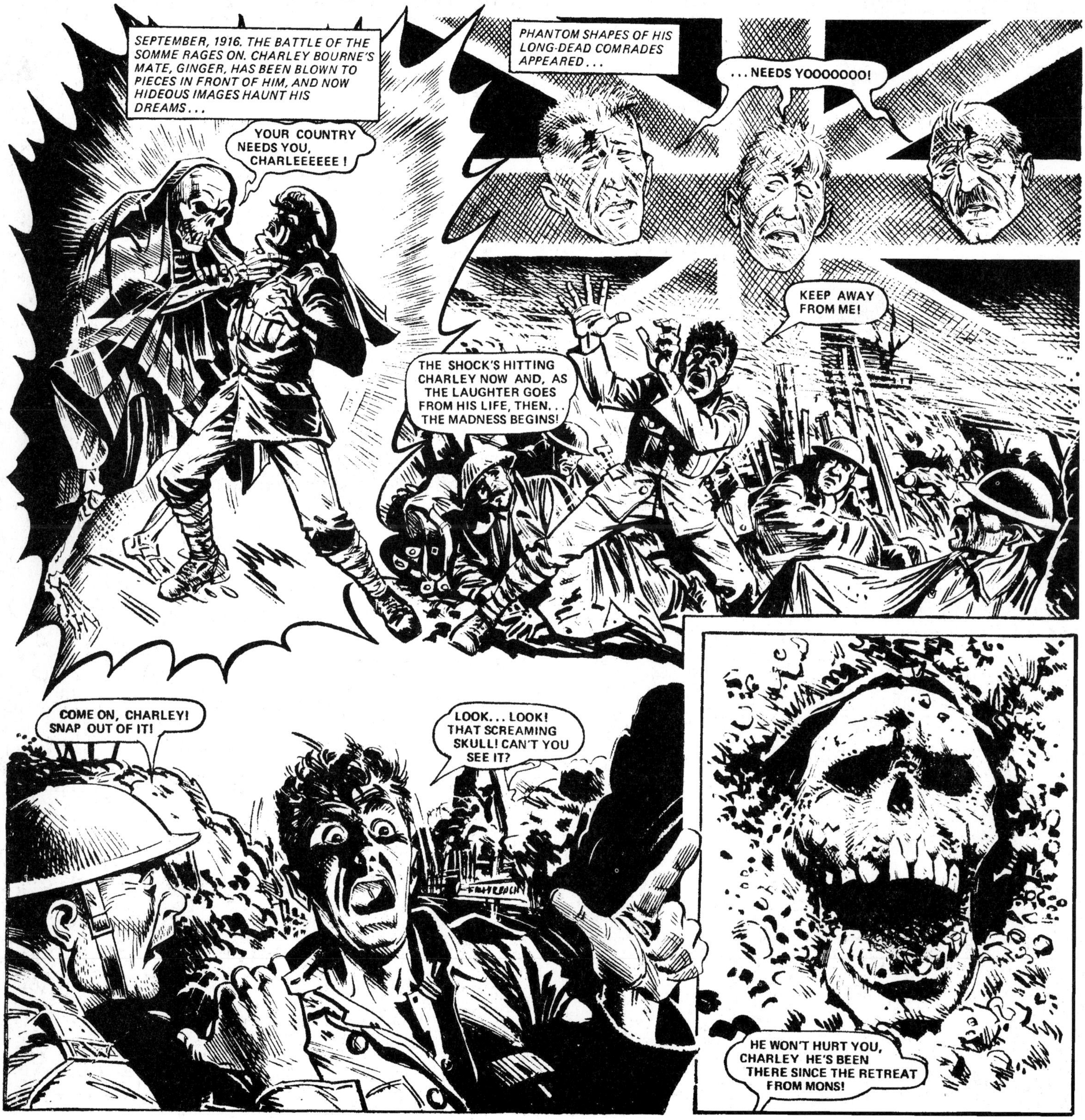

SEPTEMBER, 1916. THE BATTLE OF THE SOMME RAGES ON. CHARLEY BOURNE'S MATE, GINGER, HAS BEEN BLOWN TO PIECES IN FRONT OF HIM, AND NOW HIDEOUS IMAGES HAUNT HIS DREAMS...
YOUR COUNTRY NEEDS YOU, CHARLEEEEEE !
PHANTOM SHAPES OF HIS LONG-DEAD COMRADES APPEARED...
...NEEDS YOOOOOOO!
KEEP AWAY FROM ME!
THE SHOCK'S HITTING CHARLEY NOW AND, AS THE LAUGHTER GOES FROM HIS LIFE, THEN... THE MADNESS BEGINS!
COME ON, CHARLEY! SNAP OUT OF IT!
LOOK... LOOK! THAT SCREAMING SKULL! CAN'T YOU SEE IT?
HE WON'T HURT YOU, CHARLEY HE'S BEEN THERE SINCE THE RETREAT FROM MONS!

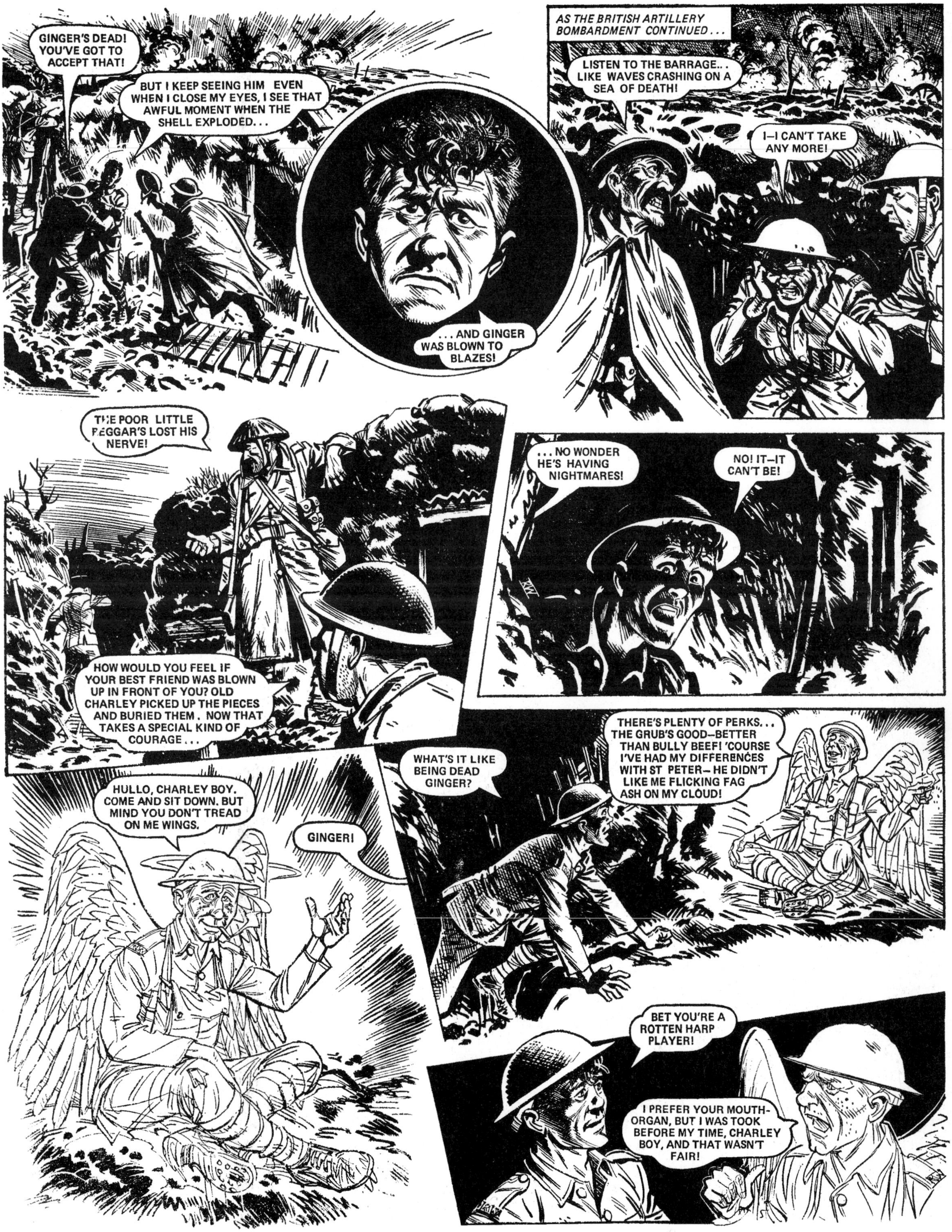
GINGER'S DEAD! YOU'VE GOT TO ACCEPT THAT!
BUT I KEEP SEEING HIM EVEN WHEN I CLOSE MY EYES, I SEE THAT AWFUL MOMENT WHEN THE SHELL EXPLODED...
...AND GINGER WAS BLOWN TO BLAZES!
AS THE BRITISH ARTILLERY BOMBARDMENT CONTINUED...
LISTEN TO THE BARRAGE.. LIKE WAVES CRASHING ON A SEA OF DEATH!
I–I CAN'T TAKE ANY MORE!
THE POOR LITTLE BEGGAR'S LOST HIS NERVE!
HOW WOULD YOU FEEL IF YOUR BEST FRIEND WAS BLOWN UP IN FRONT OF YOU? OLD CHARLEY PICKED UP THE PIECES AND BURIED THEM. NOW THAT TAKES A SPECIAL KIND OF COURAGE...
...NO WONDER HE'S HAVING NIGHTMARES!
NO! IT–IT CAN'T BE!
HULLO, CHARLEY BOY. COME AND SIT DOWN. BUT MIND YOU DON'T TREAD ON ME WINGS.
GINGER!
WHAT'S IT LIKE BEING DEAD GINGER?
THERE'S PLENTY OF PERKS... THE GRUB'S GOOD–BETTER THAN BULLY BEEF! 'COURSE I'VE HAD MY DIFFERENCES WITH ST PETER– HE DIDN'T LIKE ME FLICKING FAG ASH ON MY CLOUD!
BET YOU'RE A ROTTEN HARP PLAYER!
I PREFER YOUR MOUTH-ORGAN, BUT I WAS TOOK BEFORE MY TIME, CHARLEY BOY, AND THAT WASN'T FAIR!

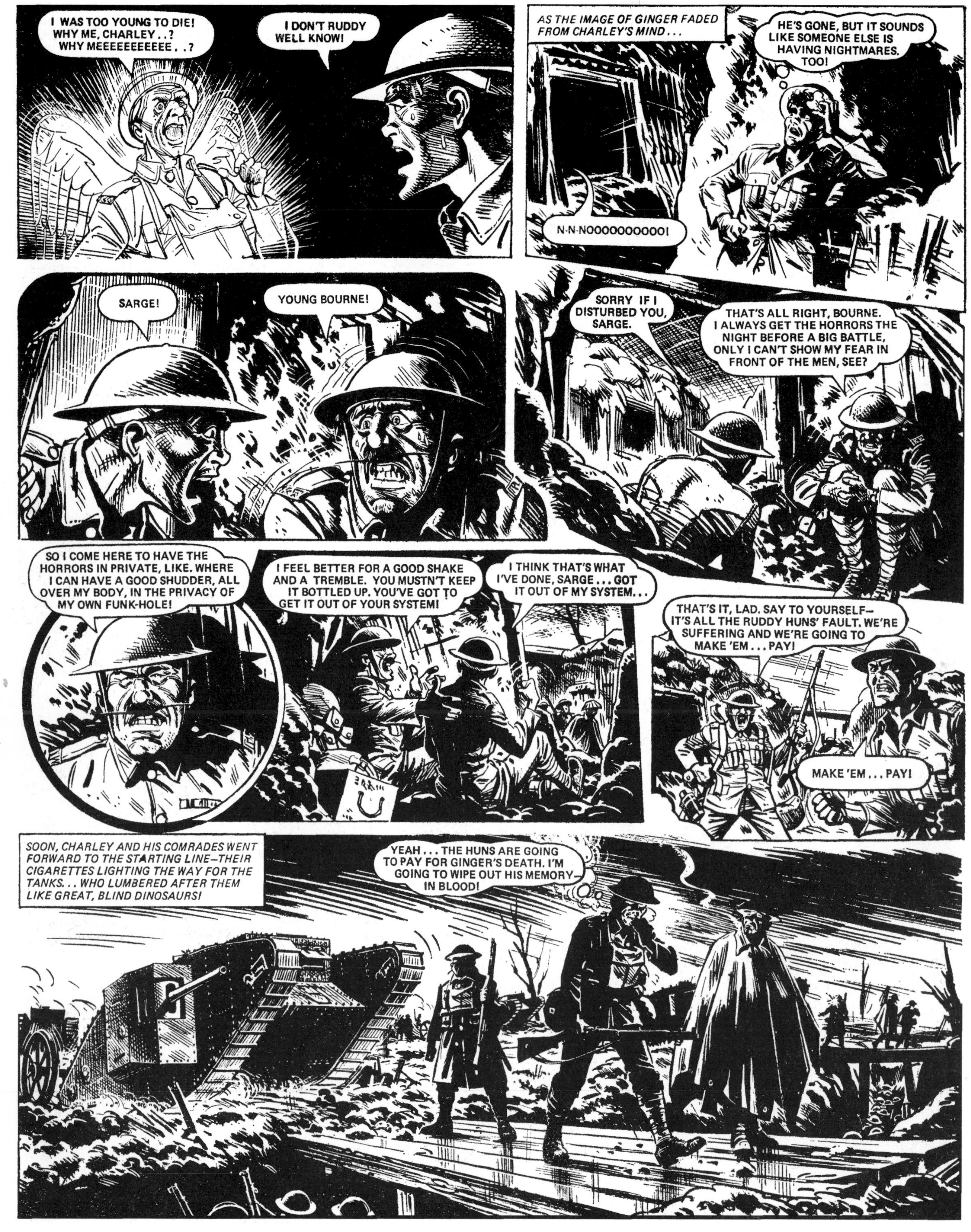
I WAS TOO YOUNG TO DIE! WHY ME, CHARLEY . . ? WHY MEEEEEEEEEEE . . ?
I DON'T RUDDY WELL KNOW!
AS THE IMAGE OF GINGER FADED FROM CHARLEY'S MIND . . .
HE'S GONE, BUT IT SOUNDS LIKE SOMEONE ELSE IS HAVING NIGHTMARES, TOO!
N-N-NOOOOOOOOOOO!
SARGE!
YOUNG BOURNE!
SORRY IF I DISTURBED YOU, SARGE.
THAT'S ALL RIGHT, BOURNE. I ALWAYS GET THE HORRORS THE NIGHT BEFORE A BIG BATTLE, ONLY I CAN'T SHOW MY FEAR IN FRONT OF THE MEN, SEE?
SO I COME HERE TO HAVE THE HORRORS IN PRIVATE, LIKE. WHERE I CAN HAVE A GOOD SHUDDER, ALL OVER MY BODY, IN THE PRIVACY OF MY OWN FUNK-HOLE!
I FEEL BETTER FOR A GOOD SHAKE AND A TREMBLE. YOU MUSTN'T KEEP IT BOTTLED UP. YOU'VE GOT TO GET IT OUT OF YOUR SYSTEM!
I THINK THAT'S WHAT I'VE DONE, SARGE . . . GOT IT OUT OF MY SYSTEM . . .
THAT'S IT, LAD. SAY TO YOURSELF— IT'S ALL THE RUDDY HUNS' FAULT. WE'RE SUFFERING AND WE'RE GOING TO MAKE 'EM . . . PAY!
MAKE 'EM . . . PAY!
SOON, CHARLEY AND HIS COMRADES WENT FORWARD TO THE STARTING LINE—THEIR CIGARETTES LIGHTING THE WAY FOR THE TANKS. . . WHO LUMBERED AFTER THEM LIKE GREAT, BLIND DINOSAURS!
YEAH . . . THE HUNS ARE GOING TO PAY FOR GINGER'S DEATH. I'M GOING TO WIPE OUT HIS MEMORY— IN BLOOD!

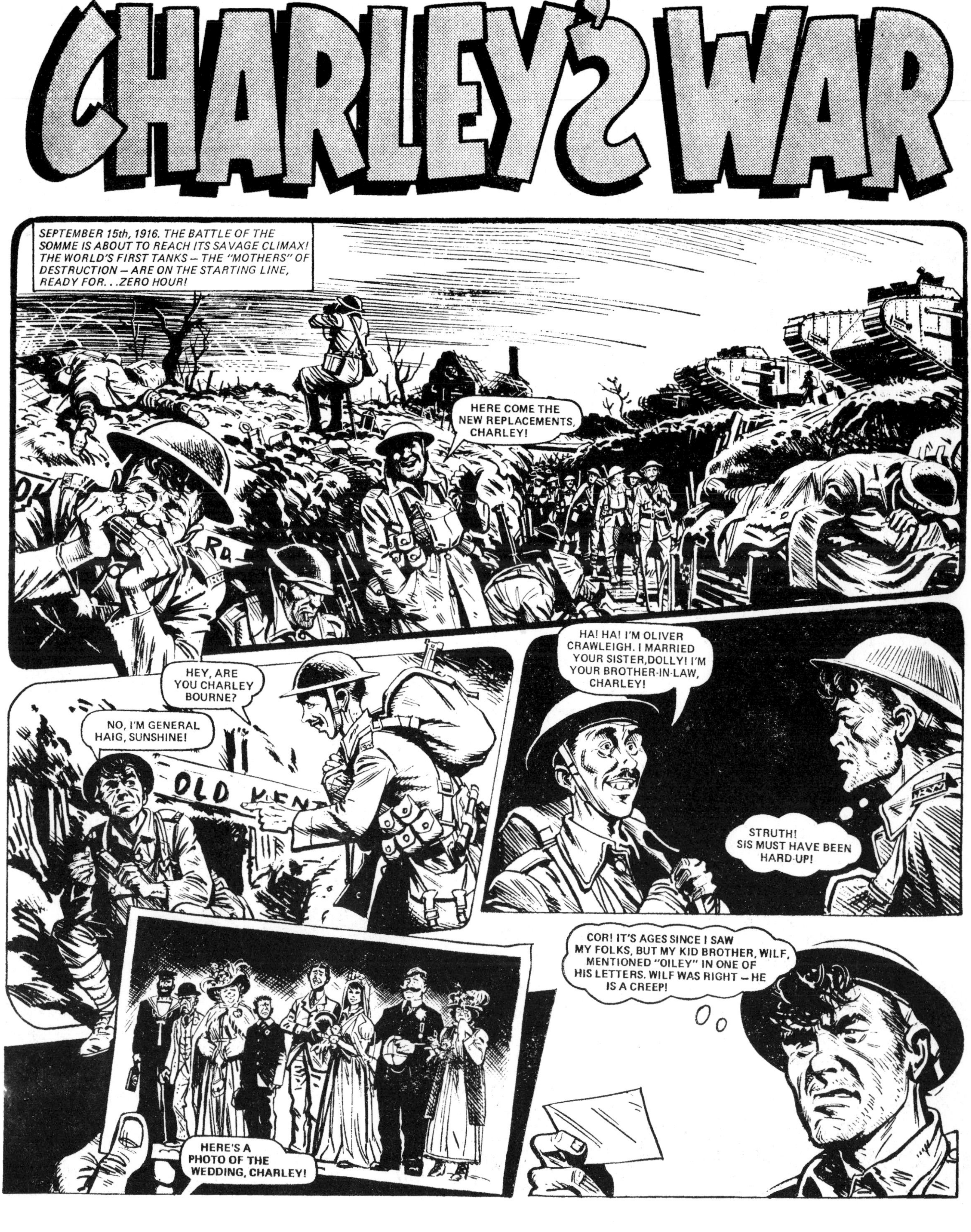
CHARLEY'S WAR
SEPTEMBER 15th, 1916. THE BATTLE OF THE SOMME IS ABOUT TO REACH ITS SAVAGE CLIMAX! THE WORLD'S FIRST TANKS – THE "MOTHERS" OF DESTRUCTION – ARE ON THE STARTING LINE, READY FOR. . .ZERO HOUR!
HERE COME THE NEW REPLACEMENTS, CHARLEY!
HEY, ARE YOU CHARLEY BOURNE?
NO, I'M GENERAL HAIG, SUNSHINE!
OLD KENT
HA! HA! I'M OLIVER CRAWLEIGH. I MARRIED YOUR SISTER, DOLLY! I'M YOUR BROTHER-IN-LAW, CHARLEY!
STRUTH! SIS MUST HAVE BEEN HARD-UP!
HERE'S A PHOTO OF THE WEDDING, CHARLEY!
COR! IT'S AGES SINCE I SAW MY FOLKS, BUT MY KID BROTHER, WILF, MENTIONED "OILEY" IN ONE OF HIS LETTERS. WILF WAS RIGHT – HE IS A CREEP!

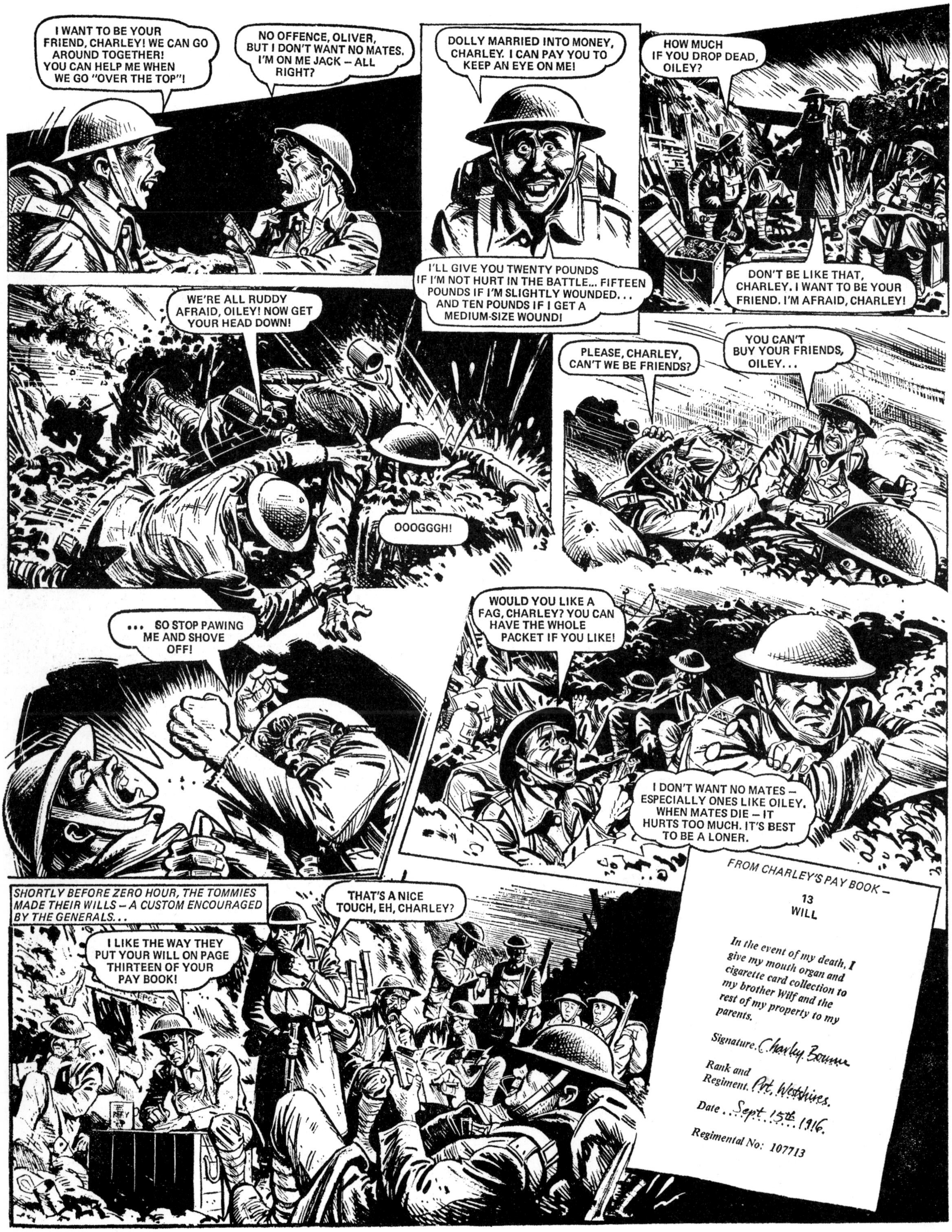

I WANT TO BE YOUR FRIEND, CHARLEY! WE CAN GO AROUND TOGETHER! YOU CAN HELP ME WHEN WE GO "OVER THE TOP"!
NO OFFENCE, OLIVER, BUT I DON'T WANT NO MATES. I'M ON ME JACK — ALL RIGHT?
DOLLY MARRIED INTO MONEY, CHARLEY. I CAN PAY YOU TO KEEP AN EYE ON ME!
I'LL GIVE YOU TWENTY POUNDS IF I'M NOT HURT IN THE BATTLE... FIFTEEN POUNDS IF I'M SLIGHTLY WOUNDED... AND TEN POUNDS IF I GET A MEDIUM-SIZE WOUND!
HOW MUCH IF YOU DROP DEAD, OILEY?
DON'T BE LIKE THAT, CHARLEY. I WANT TO BE YOUR FRIEND. I'M AFRAID, CHARLEY!
WE'RE ALL RUDDY AFRAID, OILEY! NOW GET YOUR HEAD DOWN!
OOOGGGH!
PLEASE, CHARLEY, CAN'T WE BE FRIENDS?
YOU CAN'T BUY YOUR FRIENDS, OILEY...
... SO STOP PAWING ME AND SHOVE OFF!
WOULD YOU LIKE A FAG, CHARLEY? YOU CAN HAVE THE WHOLE PACKET IF YOU LIKE!
I DON'T WANT NO MATES — ESPECIALLY ONES LIKE OILEY. WHEN MATES DIE — IT HURTS TOO MUCH. IT'S BEST TO BE A LONER.
SHORTLY BEFORE ZERO HOUR, THE TOMMIES MADE THEIR WILLS — A CUSTOM ENCOURAGED BY THE GENERALS...
I LIKE THE WAY THEY PUT YOUR WILL ON PAGE THIRTEEN OF YOUR PAY BOOK!
THAT'S A NICE TOUCH, EH, CHARLEY?
FROM CHARLEY'S PAY BOOK —
13
WILL
In the event of my death, I give my mouth organ and cigarette card collection to my brother Wilf and the rest of my property to my parents.
Signature. Charley Bourne
Rank and Regiment. Pvt. Westshires.
Date .. Sept. 15th. 1916.
Regimental No: 107713

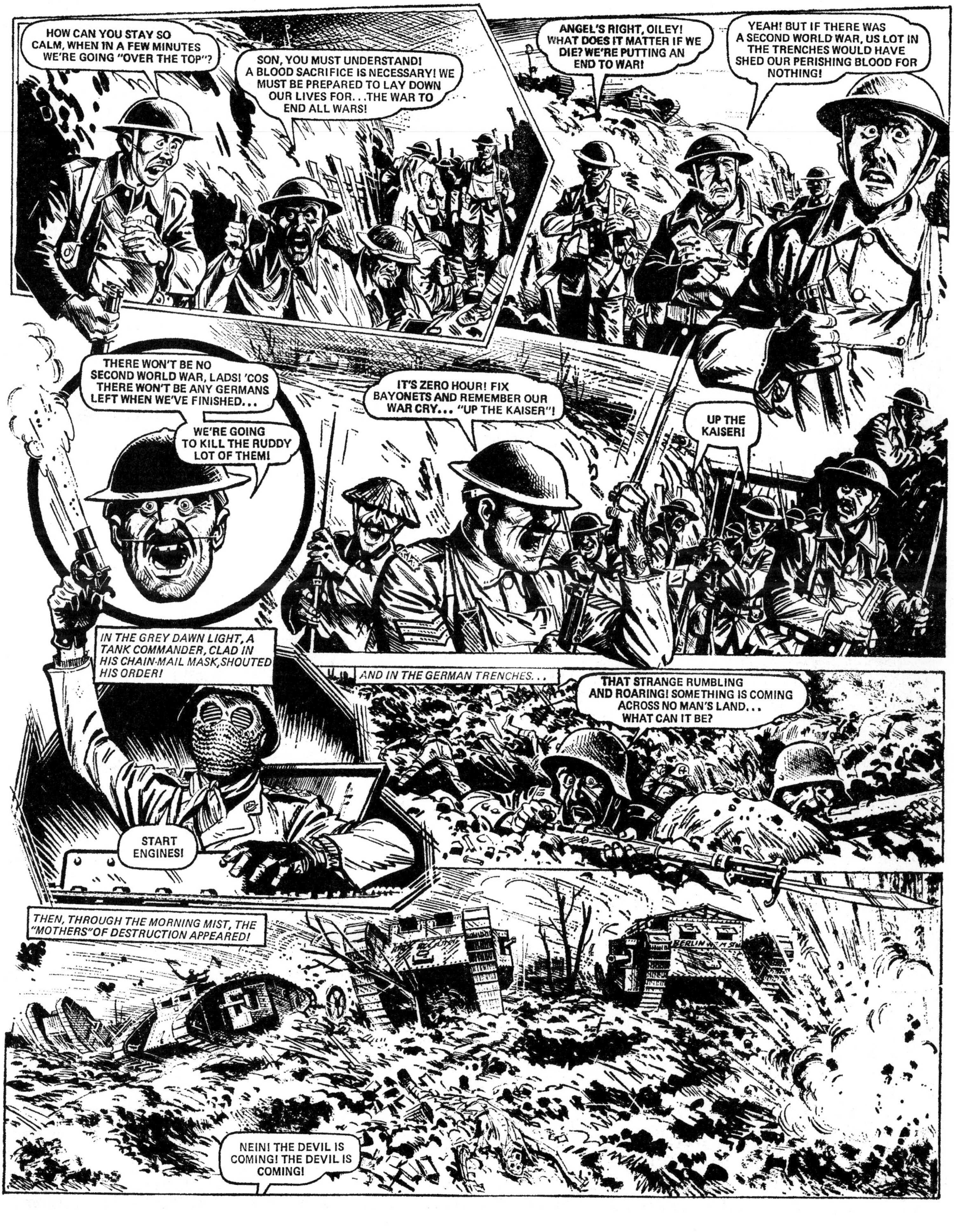
HOW CAN YOU STAY SO CALM, WHEN IN A FEW MINUTES WE'RE GOING "OVER THE TOP"?
SON, YOU MUST UNDERSTAND! A BLOOD SACRIFICE IS NECESSARY! WE MUST BE PREPARED TO LAY DOWN OUR LIVES FOR. . .THE WAR TO END ALL WARS!
ANGEL'S RIGHT, OILEY! WHAT DOES IT MATTER IF WE DIE? WE'RE PUTTING AN END TO WAR!
YEAH! BUT IF THERE WAS A SECOND WORLD WAR, US LOT IN THE TRENCHES WOULD HAVE SHED OUR PERISHING BLOOD FOR NOTHING!
THERE WON'T BE NO SECOND WORLD WAR, LADS! 'COS THERE WON'T BE ANY GERMANS LEFT WHEN WE'VE FINISHED...
WE'RE GOING TO KILL THE RUDDY LOT OF THEM!
IT'S ZERO HOUR! FIX BAYONETS AND REMEMBER OUR WAR CRY... "UP THE KAISER"!
UP THE KAISER!
IN THE GREY DAWN LIGHT, A TANK COMMANDER, CLAD IN HIS CHAIN-MAIL MASK, SHOUTED HIS ORDER!
START ENGINES!
AND IN THE GERMAN TRENCHES...
THAT STRANGE RUMBLING AND ROARING! SOMETHING IS COMING ACROSS NO MAN'S LAND... WHAT CAN IT BE?
THEN, THROUGH THE MORNING MIST, THE "MOTHERS" OF DESTRUCTION APPEARED!
NEIN! THE DEVIL IS COMING! THE DEVIL IS COMING!

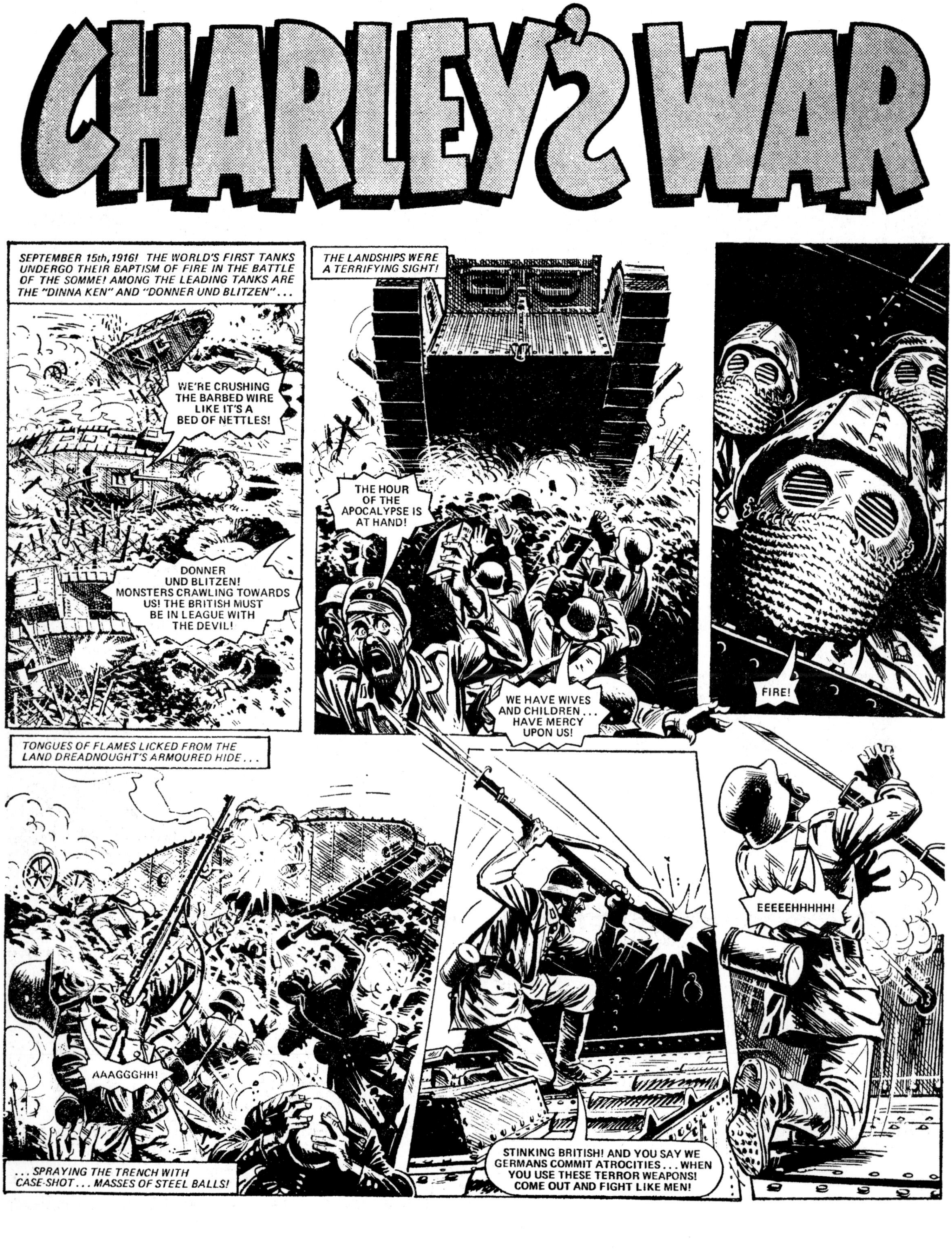
CHARLEY'S WAR
SEPTEMBER 15th, 1916! THE WORLD'S FIRST TANKS UNDERGO THEIR BAPTISM OF FIRE IN THE BATTLE OF THE SOMME! AMONG THE LEADING TANKS ARE THE "DINNA KEN" AND "DONNER UND BLITZEN"...
WE'RE CRUSHING THE BARBED WIRE LIKE IT'S A BED OF NETTLES!
DONNER UND BLITZEN! MONSTERS CRAWLING TOWARDS US! THE BRITISH MUST BE IN LEAGUE WITH THE DEVIL!
THE LANDSHIPS WERE A TERRIFYING SIGHT!
THE HOUR OF THE APOCALYPSE IS AT HAND!
WE HAVE WIVES AND CHILDREN... HAVE MERCY UPON US!
FIRE!
TONGUES OF FLAMES LICKED FROM THE LAND DREADNOUGHT'S ARMOURED HIDE...
AAAGGGHH!
... SPRAYING THE TRENCH WITH CASE-SHOT... MASSES OF STEEL BALLS!
STINKING BRITISH! AND YOU SAY WE GERMANS COMMIT ATROCITIES... WHEN YOU USE THESE TERROR WEAPONS! COME OUT AND FIGHT LIKE MEN!
EEEEEHHHHH!

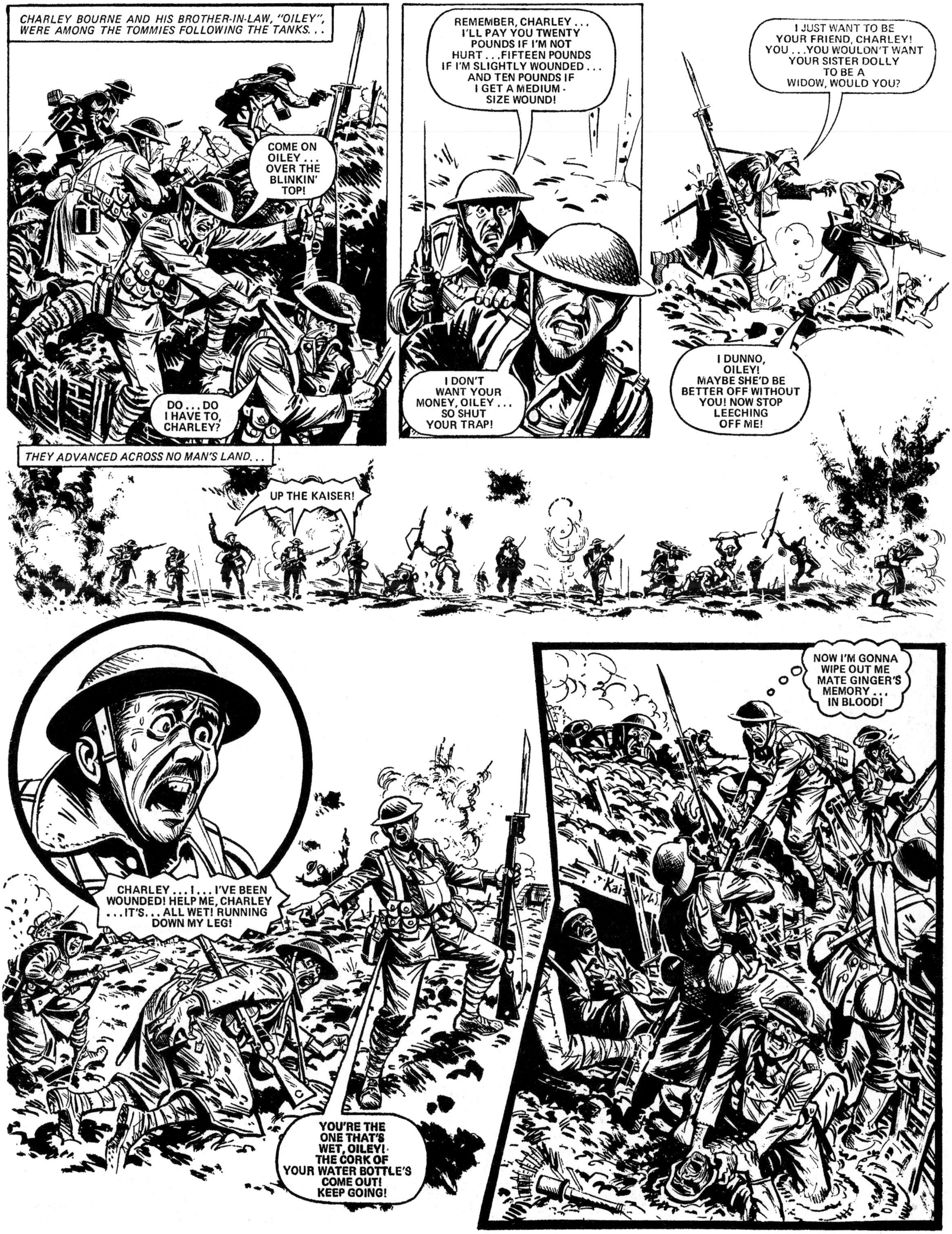
CHARLEY BOURNE AND HIS BROTHER-IN-LAW, "OILEY", WERE AMONG THE TOMMIES FOLLOWING THE TANKS. . .
COME ON OILEY . . . OVER THE BLINKIN' TOP!
DO . . . DO I HAVE TO, CHARLEY?
REMEMBER, CHARLEY . . . I'LL PAY YOU TWENTY POUNDS IF I'M NOT HURT . . . FIFTEEN POUNDS IF I'M SLIGHTLY WOUNDED . . . AND TEN POUNDS IF I GET A MEDIUM - SIZE WOUND!
I DON'T WANT YOUR MONEY, OILEY . . . SO SHUT YOUR TRAP!
I JUST WANT TO BE YOUR FRIEND, CHARLEY! YOU . . . YOU WOULDN'T WANT YOUR SISTER DOLLY TO BE A WIDOW, WOULD YOU?
I DUNNO, OILEY! MAYBE SHE'D BE BETTER OFF WITHOUT YOU! NOW STOP LEECHING OFF ME!
THEY ADVANCED ACROSS NO MAN'S LAND. . .
UP THE KAISER!
CHARLEY . . . I . . . I'VE BEEN WOUNDED! HELP ME, CHARLEY . . . IT'S . . . ALL WET! RUNNING DOWN MY LEG!
YOU'RE THE ONE THAT'S WET, OILEY! THE CORK OF YOUR WATER BOTTLE'S COME OUT! KEEP GOING!
NOW I'M GONNA WIPE OUT ME MATE GINGER'S MEMORY . . . IN BLOOD!

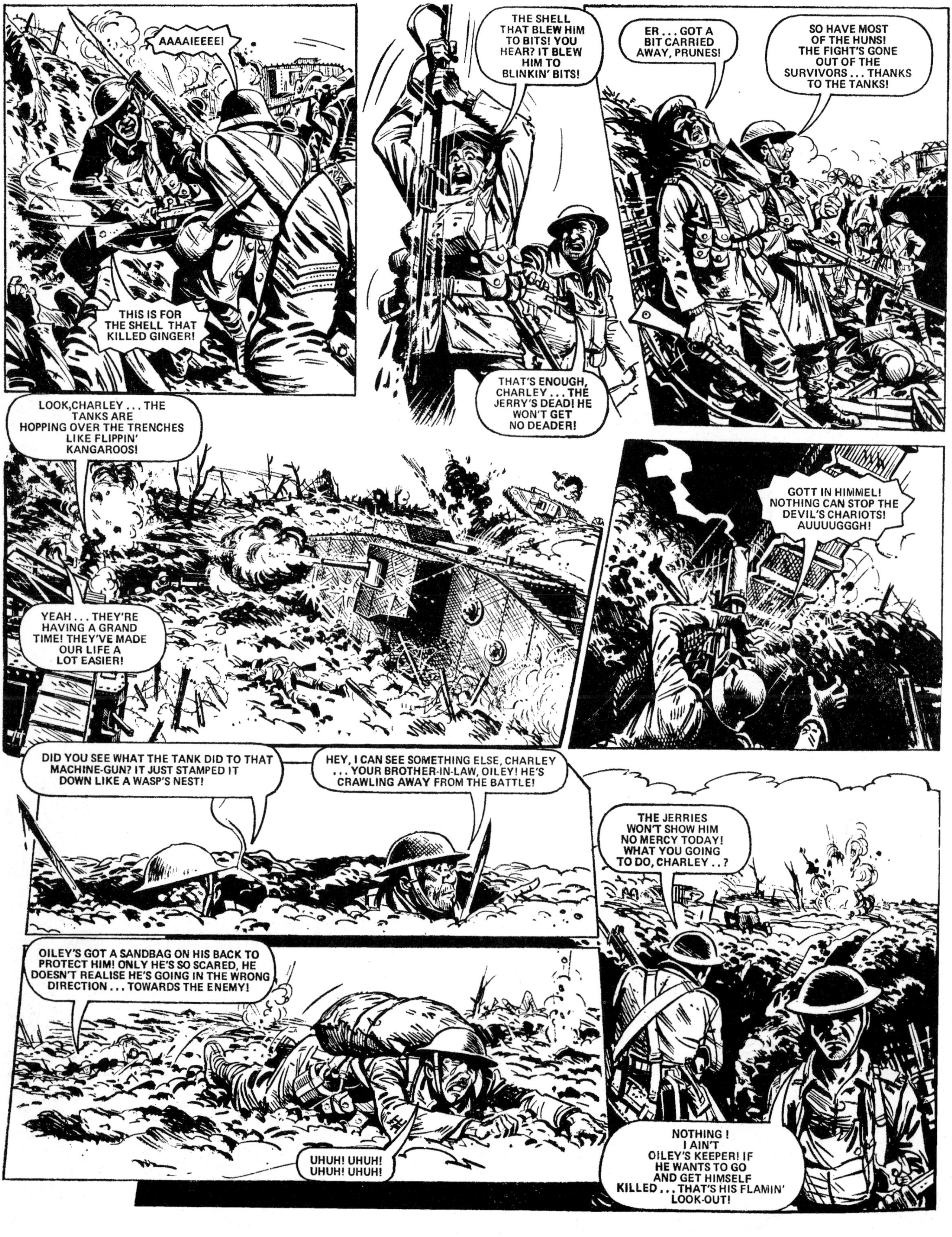

AAAAIEEEE!
THIS IS FOR THE SHELL THAT KILLED GINGER!
THE SHELL THAT BLEW HIM TO BITS! YOU HEAR? IT BLEW HIM TO BLINKIN' BITS!
THAT'S ENOUGH, CHARLEY . . . THE JERRY'S DEAD! HE WON'T GET NO DEADER!
ER . . . GOT A BIT CARRIED AWAY, PRUNES!
SO HAVE MOST OF THE HUNS! THE FIGHT'S GONE OUT OF THE SURVIVORS . . . THANKS TO THE TANKS!
LOOK,CHARLEY . . . THE TANKS ARE HOPPING OVER THE TRENCHES LIKE FLIPPIN' KANGAROOS!
YEAH . . . THEY'RE HAVING A GRAND TIME! THEY'VE MADE OUR LIFE A LOT EASIER!
GOTT IN HIMMEL! NOTHING CAN STOP THE DEVIL'S CHARIOTS! AUUUUGGGH!
DID YOU SEE WHAT THE TANK DID TO THAT MACHINE-GUN? IT JUST STAMPED IT DOWN LIKE A WASP'S NEST!
HEY, I CAN SEE SOMETHING ELSE, CHARLEY . . . YOUR BROTHER-IN-LAW, OILEY! HE'S CRAWLING AWAY FROM THE BATTLE!
OILEY'S GOT A SANDBAG ON HIS BACK TO PROTECT HIM! ONLY HE'S SO SCARED, HE DOESN'T REALISE HE'S GOING IN THE WRONG DIRECTION . . . TOWARDS THE ENEMY!
UHUH! UHUH! UHUH! UHUH!
THE JERRIES WON'T SHOW HIM NO MERCY TODAY! WHAT YOU GOING TO DO, CHARLEY . . ?
NOTHING ! I AIN'T OILEY'S KEEPER! IF HE WANTS TO GO AND GET HIMSELF KILLED . . . THAT'S HIS FLAMIN' LOOK-OUT!

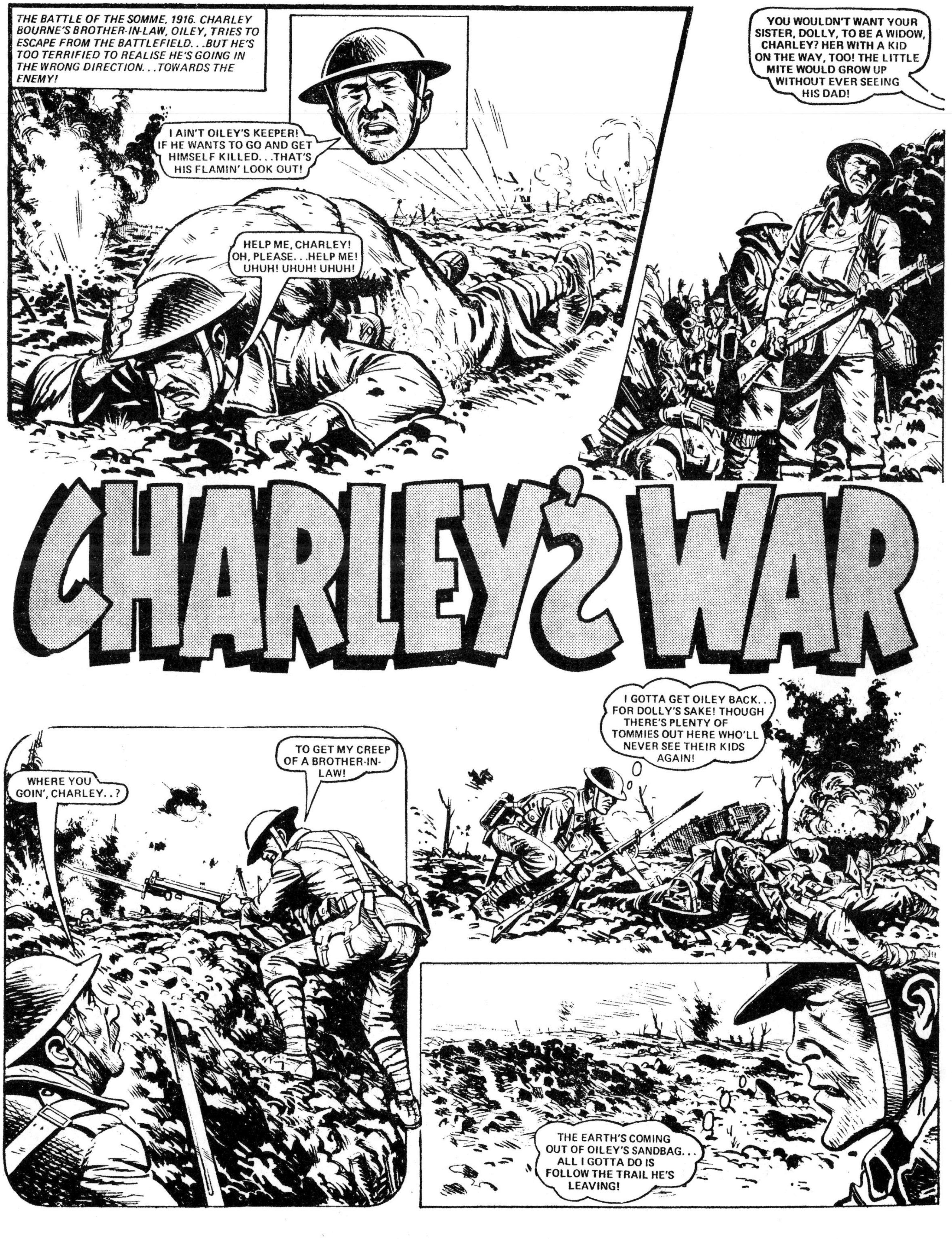
THE BATTLE OF THE SOMME, 1916. CHARLEY BOURNE'S BROTHER-IN-LAW, OILEY, TRIES TO ESCAPE FROM THE BATTLEFIELD. . .BUT HE'S TOO TERRIFIED TO REALISE HE'S GOING IN THE WRONG DIRECTION. . .TOWARDS THE ENEMY!
I AIN'T OILEY'S KEEPER! IF HE WANTS TO GO AND GET HIMSELF KILLED. . .THAT'S HIS FLAMIN' LOOK OUT!
HELP ME, CHARLEY! OH, PLEASE. . .HELP ME! UHUH! UHUH! UHUH!
YOU WOULDN'T WANT YOUR SISTER, DOLLY, TO BE A WIDOW, CHARLEY? HER WITH A KID ON THE WAY, TOO! THE LITTLE MITE WOULD GROW UP WITHOUT EVER SEEING HIS DAD!
CHARLEY'S WAR
WHERE YOU GOIN', CHARLEY. . ?
TO GET MY CREEP OF A BROTHER-IN-LAW!
I GOTTA GET OILEY BACK. . . FOR DOLLY'S SAKE! THOUGH THERE'S PLENTY OF TOMMIES OUT HERE WHO'LL NEVER SEE THEIR KIDS AGAIN!
THE EARTH'S COMING OUT OF OILEY'S SANDBAG. . . ALL I GOTTA DO IS FOLLOW THE TRAIL HE'S LEAVING!

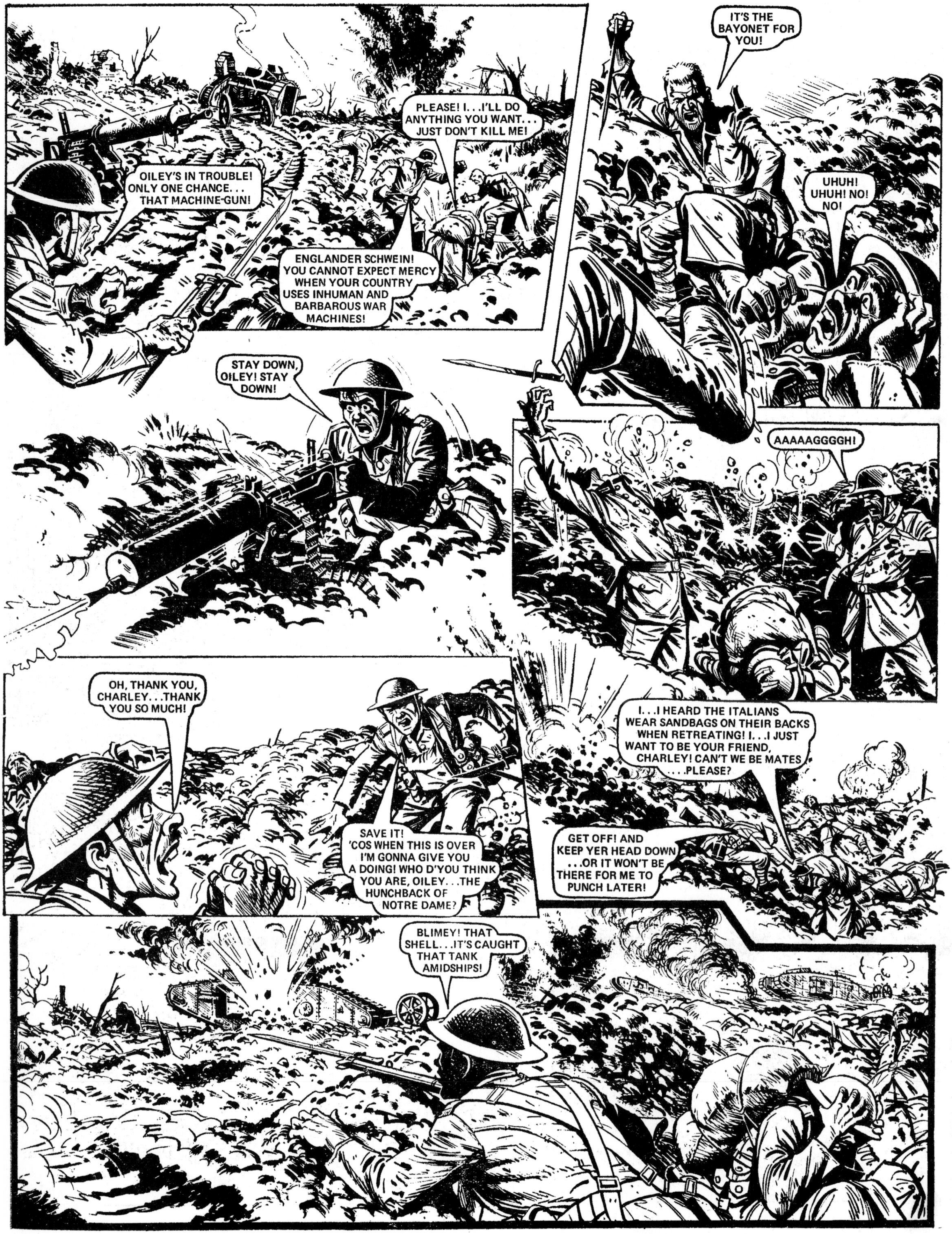
OILEY'S IN TROUBLE! ONLY ONE CHANCE. . . THAT MACHINE-GUN!
PLEASE! I. . .I'LL DO ANYTHING YOU WANT. . . JUST DON'T KILL ME!
ENGLANDER SCHWEIN! YOU CANNOT EXPECT MERCY WHEN YOUR COUNTRY USES INHUMAN AND BARBAROUS WAR MACHINES!
IT'S THE BAYONET FOR YOU!
UHUH! UHUH! NO! NO!
STAY DOWN, OILEY! STAY DOWN!
AAAAAGGGGH!
OH, THANK YOU, CHARLEY. . .THANK YOU SO MUCH!
SAVE IT! 'COS WHEN THIS IS OVER I'M GONNA GIVE YOU A DOING! WHO D'YOU THINK YOU ARE, OILEY. . .THE HUNCHBACK OF NOTRE DAME?
I. . .I HEARD THE ITALIANS WEAR SANDBAGS ON THEIR BACKS WHEN RETREATING! I. . .I JUST WANT TO BE YOUR FRIEND, CHARLEY! CAN'T WE BE MATES . . .PLEASE?
GET OFF! AND KEEP YER HEAD DOWN . . .OR IT WON'T BE THERE FOR ME TO PUNCH LATER!
BLIMEY! THAT SHELL. . .IT'S CAUGHT THAT TANK AMIDSHIPS!

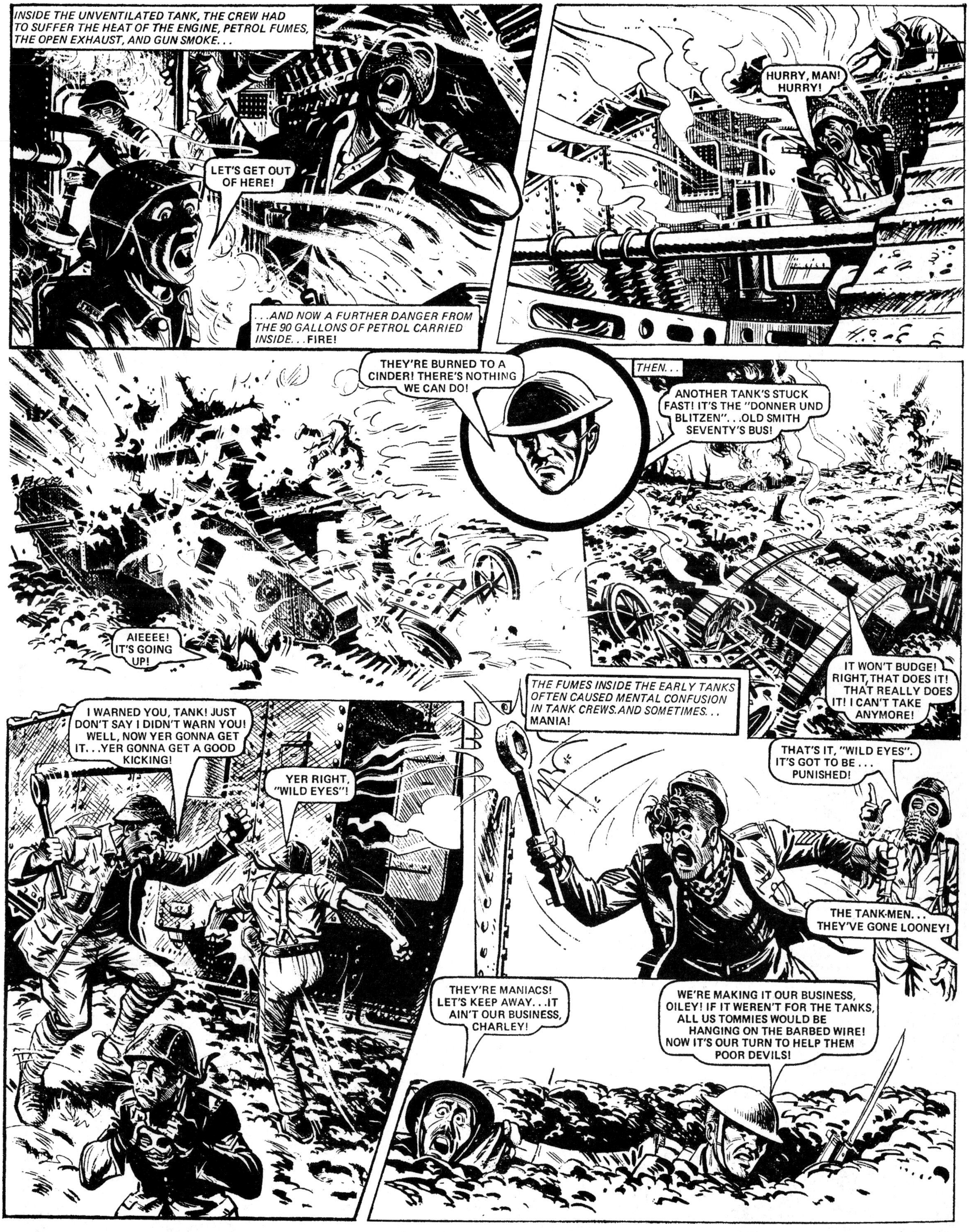
INSIDE THE UNVENTILATED TANK, THE CREW HAD TO SUFFER THE HEAT OF THE ENGINE, PETROL FUMES, THE OPEN EXHAUST, AND GUN SMOKE...
LET'S GET OUT OF HERE!
...AND NOW A FURTHER DANGER FROM THE 90 GALLONS OF PETROL CARRIED INSIDE...FIRE!
HURRY, MAN! HURRY!
AIEEEE! IT'S GOING UP!
THEY'RE BURNED TO A CINDER! THERE'S NOTHING WE CAN DO!
THEN...
ANOTHER TANK'S STUCK FAST! IT'S THE "DONNER UND BLITZEN"...OLD SMITH SEVENTY'S BUS!
IT WON'T BUDGE! RIGHT, THAT DOES IT! THAT REALLY DOES IT! I CAN'T TAKE ANYMORE!
I WARNED YOU, TANK! JUST DON'T SAY I DIDN'T WARN YOU! WELL, NOW YER GONNA GET IT...YER GONNA GET A GOOD KICKING!
YER RIGHT, "WILD EYES"!
THE FUMES INSIDE THE EARLY TANKS OFTEN CAUSED MENTAL CONFUSION IN TANK CREWS.AND SOMETIMES... MANIA!
THAT'S IT, "WILD EYES". IT'S GOT TO BE ... PUNISHED!
THE TANK-MEN... THEY'VE GONE LOONEY!
THEY'RE MANIACS! LET'S KEEP AWAY...IT AIN'T OUR BUSINESS, CHARLEY!
WE'RE MAKING IT OUR BUSINESS, OILEY! IF IT WEREN'T FOR THE TANKS, ALL US TOMMIES WOULD BE HANGING ON THE BARBED WIRE! NOW IT'S OUR TURN TO HELP THEM POOR DEVILS!

CHARLEY'S WAR

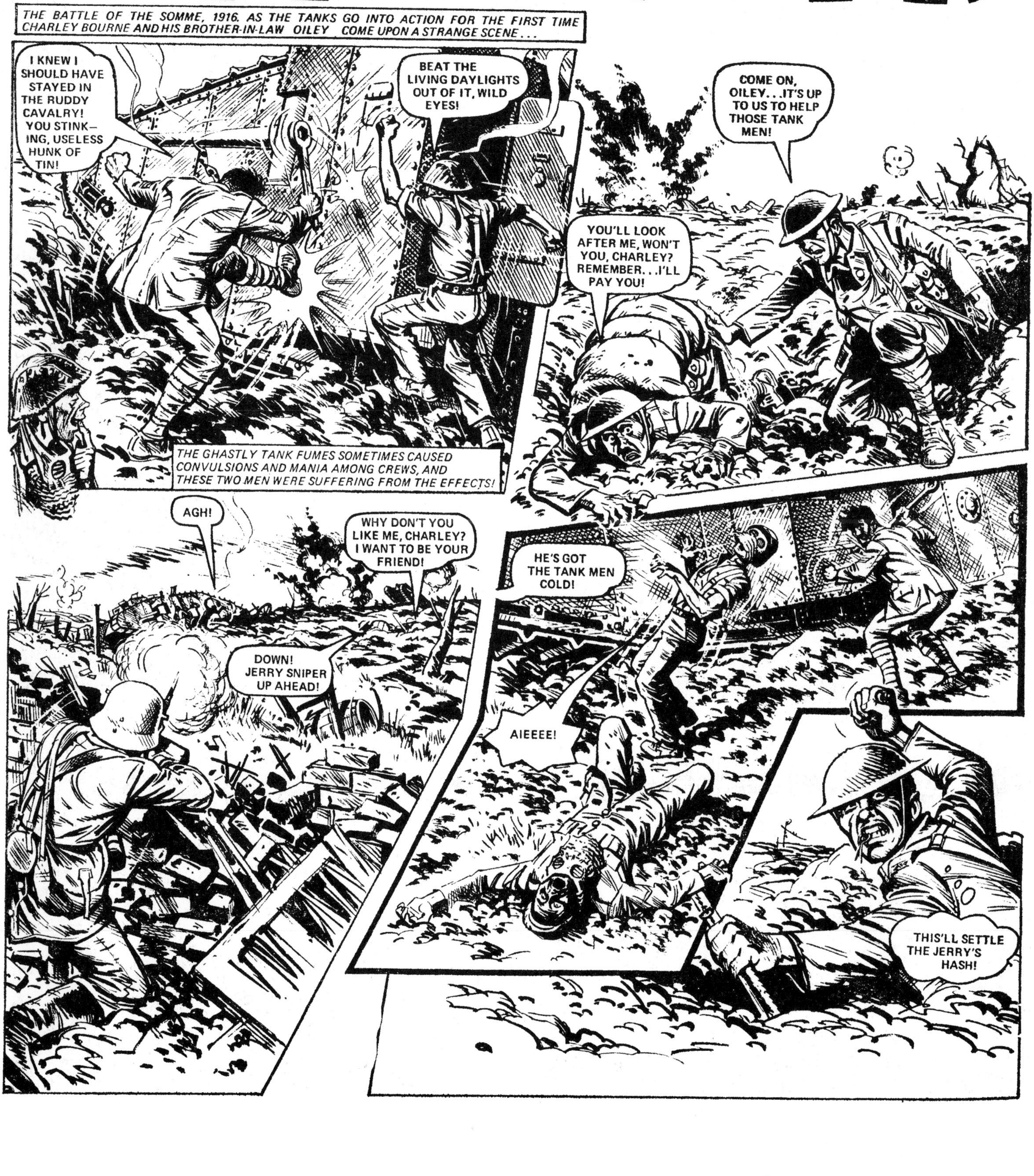

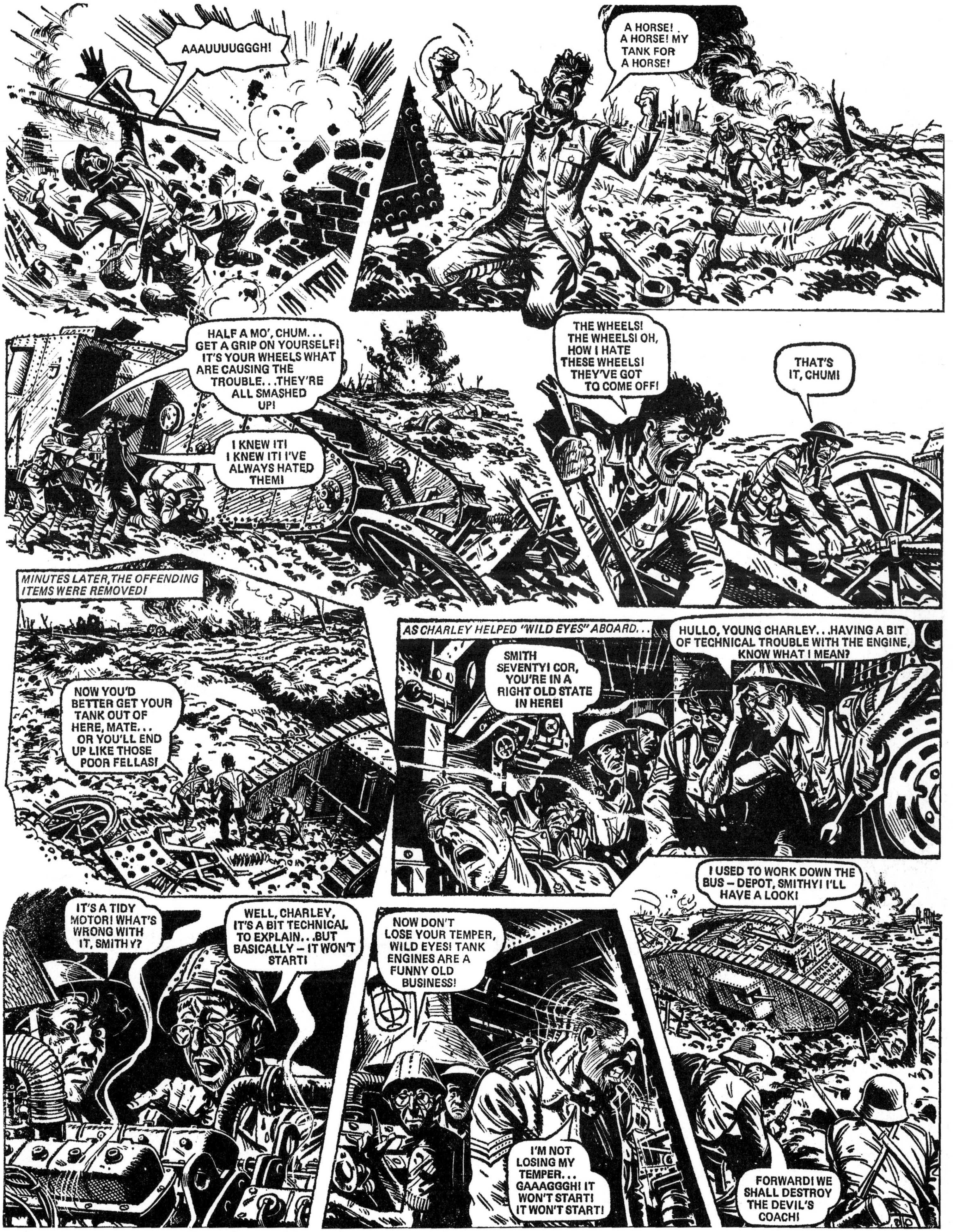
AAAUUUUGGGH!
A HORSE! A HORSE! MY TANK FOR A HORSE!
HALF A MO', CHUM... GET A GRIP ON YOURSELF! IT'S YOUR WHEELS WHAT ARE CAUSING THE TROUBLE...THEY'RE ALL SMASHED UP!
I KNEW IT! I KNEW IT! I'VE ALWAYS HATED THEM!
THE WHEELS! THE WHEELS! OH, HOW I HATE THESE WHEELS! THEY'VE GOT TO COME OFF!
THAT'S IT, CHUM!
MINUTES LATER, THE OFFENDING ITEMS WERE REMOVED!
NOW YOU'D BETTER GET YOUR TANK OUT OF HERE, MATE... OR YOU'LL END UP LIKE THOSE POOR FELLAS!
AS CHARLEY HELPED "WILD EYES" ABOARD...
SMITH SEVENTY! COR, YOU'RE IN A RIGHT OLD STATE IN HERE!
HULLO, YOUNG CHARLEY...HAVING A BIT OF TECHNICAL TROUBLE WITH THE ENGINE, KNOW WHAT I MEAN?
IT'S A TIDY MOTOR! WHAT'S WRONG WITH IT, SMITHY?
WELL, CHARLEY, IT'S A BIT TECHNICAL TO EXPLAIN...BUT BASICALLY – IT WON'T START!
NOW DON'T LOSE YOUR TEMPER, WILD EYES! TANK ENGINES ARE A FUNNY OLD BUSINESS!
I'M NOT LOSING MY TEMPER... GAAAGGGH! IT WON'T START! IT WON'T START!
I USED TO WORK DOWN THE BUS – DEPOT, SMITHY! I'LL HAVE A LOOK!
FORWARD! WE SHALL DESTROY THE DEVIL'S COACH!

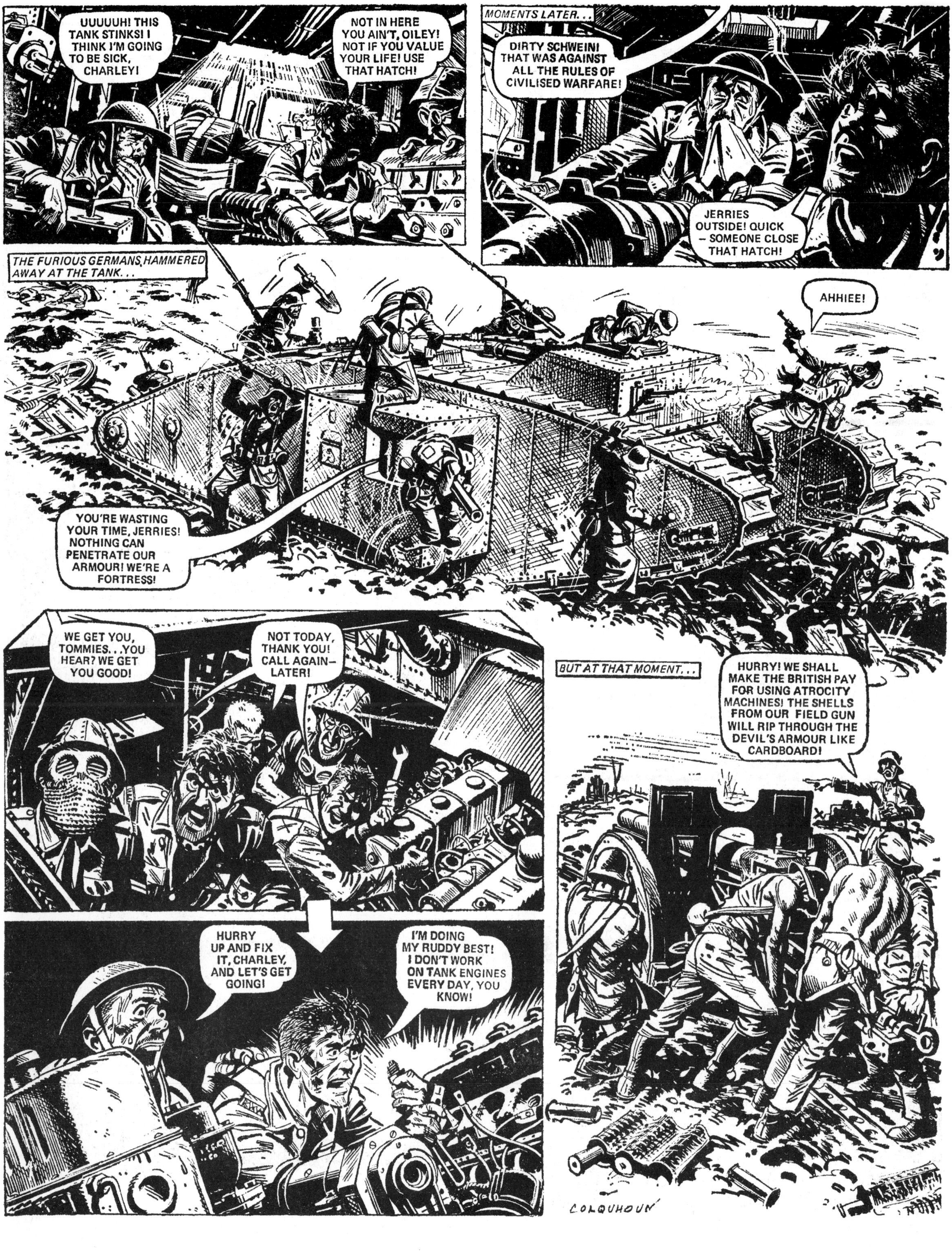
UUUUUH! THIS TANK STINKS! I THINK I'M GOING TO BE SICK, CHARLEY!
NOT IN HERE YOU AIN'T, OILEY! NOT IF YOU VALUE YOUR LIFE! USE THAT HATCH!
MOMENTS LATER...
DIRTY SCHWEIN! THAT WAS AGAINST ALL THE RULES OF CIVILISED WARFARE!
JERRIES OUTSIDE! QUICK – SOMEONE CLOSE THAT HATCH!
THE FURIOUS GERMANS HAMMERED AWAY AT THE TANK...
AHHIEE!
YOU'RE WASTING YOUR TIME, JERRIES! NOTHING CAN PENETRATE OUR ARMOUR! WE'RE A FORTRESS!
WE GET YOU, TOMMIES...YOU HEAR? WE GET YOU GOOD!
NOT TODAY, THANK YOU! CALL AGAIN–LATER!
HURRY UP AND FIX IT, CHARLEY, AND LET'S GET GOING!
I'M DOING MY RUDDY BEST! I DON'T WORK ON TANK ENGINES EVERY DAY, YOU KNOW!
BUT AT THAT MOMENT...
HURRY! WE SHALL MAKE THE BRITISH PAY FOR USING ATROCITY MACHINES! THE SHELLS FROM OUR FIELD GUN WILL RIP THROUGH THE DEVIL'S ARMOUR LIKE CARDBOARD!
COLQUHOUN

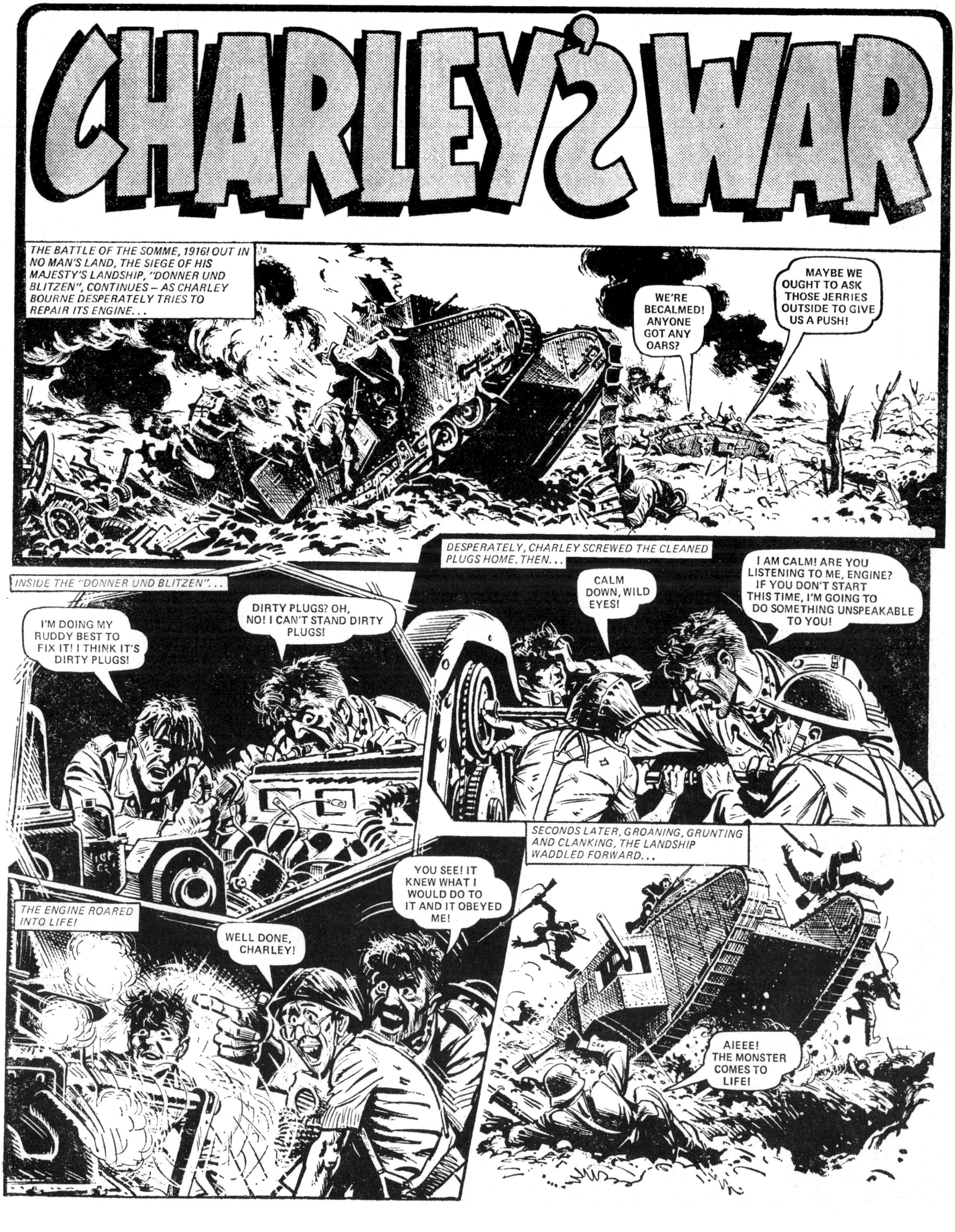
CHARLEY'S WAR
THE BATTLE OF THE SOMME, 1916! OUT IN NO MAN'S LAND, THE SIEGE OF HIS MAJESTY'S LANDSHIP, "DONNER UND BLITZEN", CONTINUES – AS CHARLEY BOURNE DESPERATELY TRIES TO REPAIR ITS ENGINE...
WE'RE BECALMED! ANYONE GOT ANY OARS?
MAYBE WE OUGHT TO ASK THOSE JERRIES OUTSIDE TO GIVE US A PUSH!
INSIDE THE "DONNER UND BLITZEN"...
I'M DOING MY RUDDY BEST TO FIX IT! I THINK IT'S DIRTY PLUGS!
DIRTY PLUGS? OH, NO! I CAN'T STAND DIRTY PLUGS!
DESPERATELY, CHARLEY SCREWED THE CLEANED PLUGS HOME. THEN...
CALM DOWN, WILD EYES!
I AM CALM! ARE YOU LISTENING TO ME, ENGINE? IF YOU DON'T START THIS TIME, I'M GOING TO DO SOMETHING UNSPEAKABLE TO YOU!
THE ENGINE ROARED INTO LIFE!
WELL DONE, CHARLEY!
YOU SEE! IT KNEW WHAT I WOULD DO TO IT AND IT OBEYED ME!
SECONDS LATER, GROANING, GRUNTING AND CLANKING, THE LANDSHIP WADDLED FORWARD...
AIEEE! THE MONSTER COMES TO LIFE!

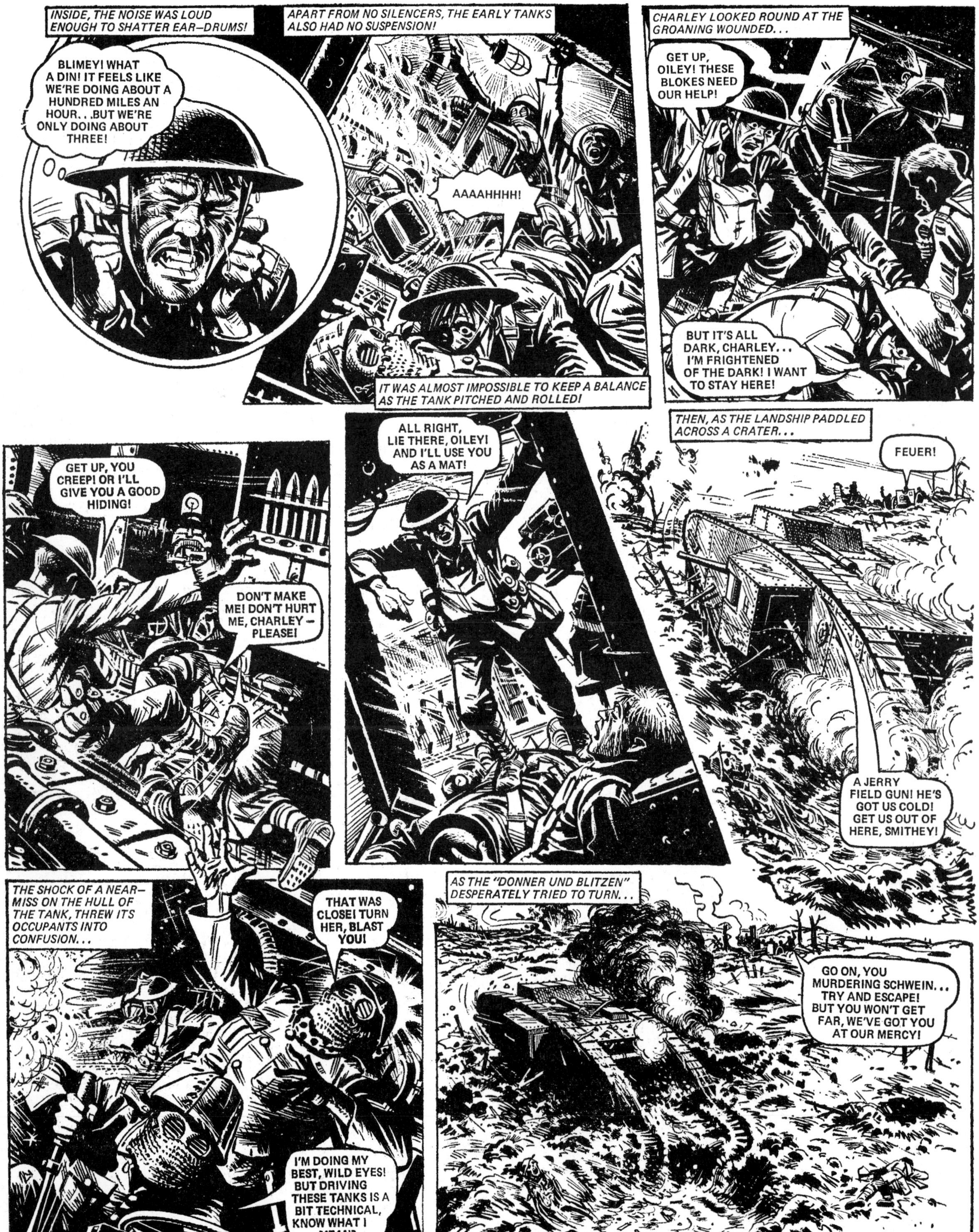
INSIDE, THE NOISE WAS LOUD ENOUGH TO SHATTER EAR-DRUMS!
BLIMEY! WHAT A DIN! IT FEELS LIKE WE'RE DOING ABOUT A HUNDRED MILES AN HOUR.. .BUT WE'RE ONLY DOING ABOUT THREE!
APART FROM NO SILENCERS, THE EARLY TANKS ALSO HAD NO SUSPENSION!
AAAAHHHH!
IT WAS ALMOST IMPOSSIBLE TO KEEP A BALANCE AS THE TANK PITCHED AND ROLLED!
CHARLEY LOOKED ROUND AT THE GROANING WOUNDED...
GET UP, OILEY! THESE BLOKES NEED OUR HELP!
BUT IT'S ALL DARK, CHARLEY... I'M FRIGHTENED OF THE DARK! I WANT TO STAY HERE!
GET UP, YOU CREEP! OR I'LL GIVE YOU A GOOD HIDING!
DON'T MAKE ME! DON'T HURT ME, CHARLEY – PLEASE!
ALL RIGHT, LIE THERE, OILEY! AND I'LL USE YOU AS A MAT!
THEN, AS THE LANDSHIP PADDLED ACROSS A CRATER...
FEUER!
A JERRY FIELD GUN! HE'S GOT US COLD! GET US OUT OF HERE, SMITHEY!
THE SHOCK OF A NEAR-MISS ON THE HULL OF THE TANK, THREW ITS OCCUPANTS INTO CONFUSION...
THAT WAS CLOSE! TURN HER, BLAST YOU!
I'M DOING MY BEST, WILD EYES! BUT DRIVING THESE TANKS IS A BIT TECHNICAL, KNOW WHAT I MEAN?
AS THE "DONNER UND BLITZEN" DESPERATELY TRIED TO TURN...
GO ON, YOU MURDERING SCHWEIN... TRY AND ESCAPE! BUT YOU WON'T GET FAR, WE'VE GOT YOU AT OUR MERCY!

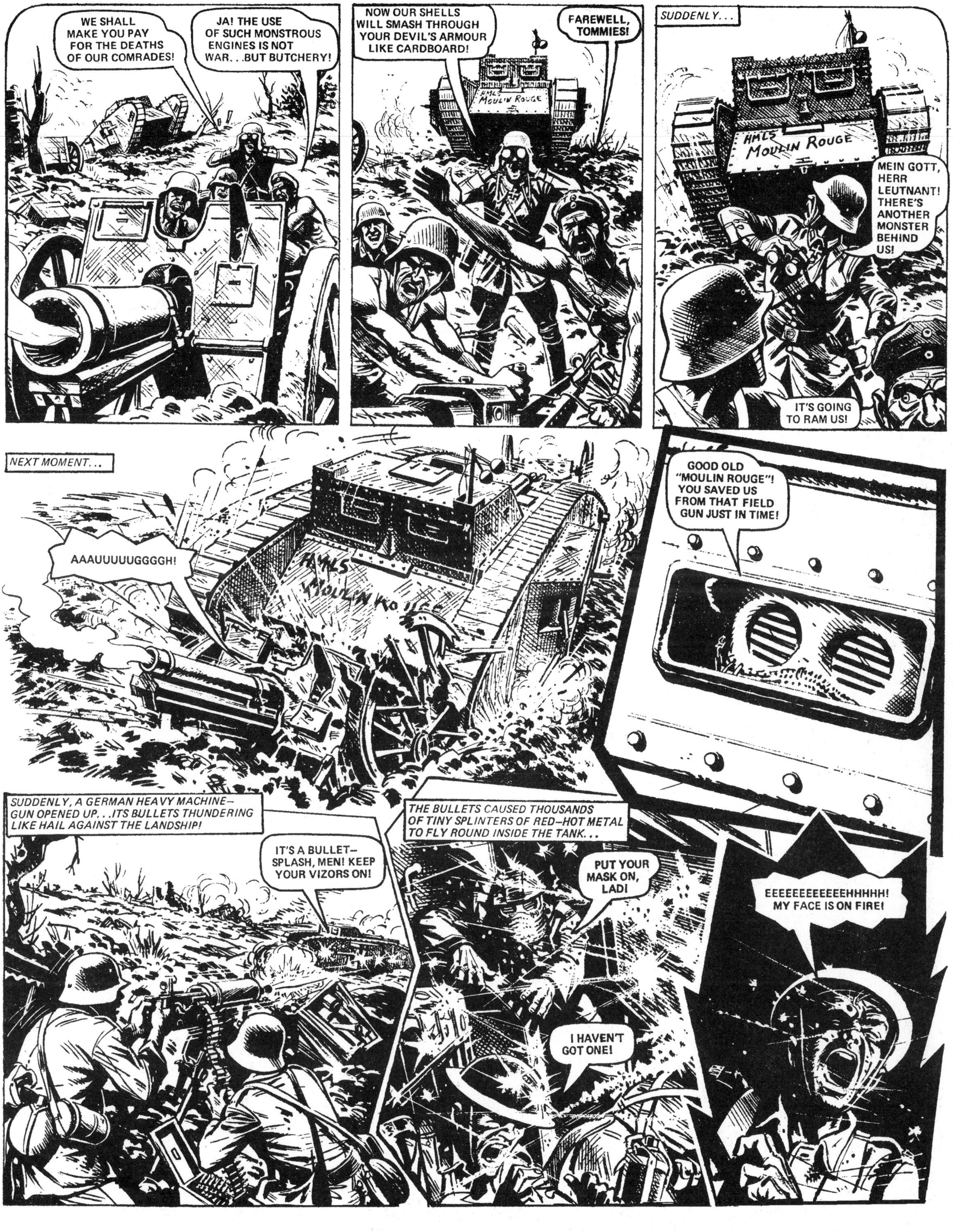
WE SHALL MAKE YOU PAY FOR THE DEATHS OF OUR COMRADES!
JA! THE USE OF SUCH MONSTROUS ENGINES IS NOT WAR. . .BUT BUTCHERY!
NOW OUR SHELLS WILL SMASH THROUGH YOUR DEVIL'S ARMOUR LIKE CARDBOARD!
FAREWELL, TOMMIES!
HMLS MOULIN ROUGE
SUDDENLY. . .
HMLS MOULIN ROUGE
MEIN GOTT, HERR LEUTNANT! THERE'S ANOTHER MONSTER BEHIND US!
IT'S GOING TO RAM US!
NEXT MOMENT. . .
AAAUUUUUGGGGH!
GOOD OLD "MOULIN ROUGE"! YOU SAVED US FROM THAT FIELD GUN JUST IN TIME!
SUDDENLY, A GERMAN HEAVY MACHINE-GUN OPENED UP. . .ITS BULLETS THUNDERING LIKE HAIL AGAINST THE LANDSHIP!
IT'S A BULLET-SPLASH, MEN! KEEP YOUR VIZORS ON!
THE BULLETS CAUSED THOUSANDS OF TINY SPLINTERS OF RED-HOT METAL TO FLY ROUND INSIDE THE TANK. . .
PUT YOUR MASK ON, LAD!
I HAVEN'T GOT ONE!
EEEEEEEEEEEEHHHHH! MY FACE IS ON FIRE!

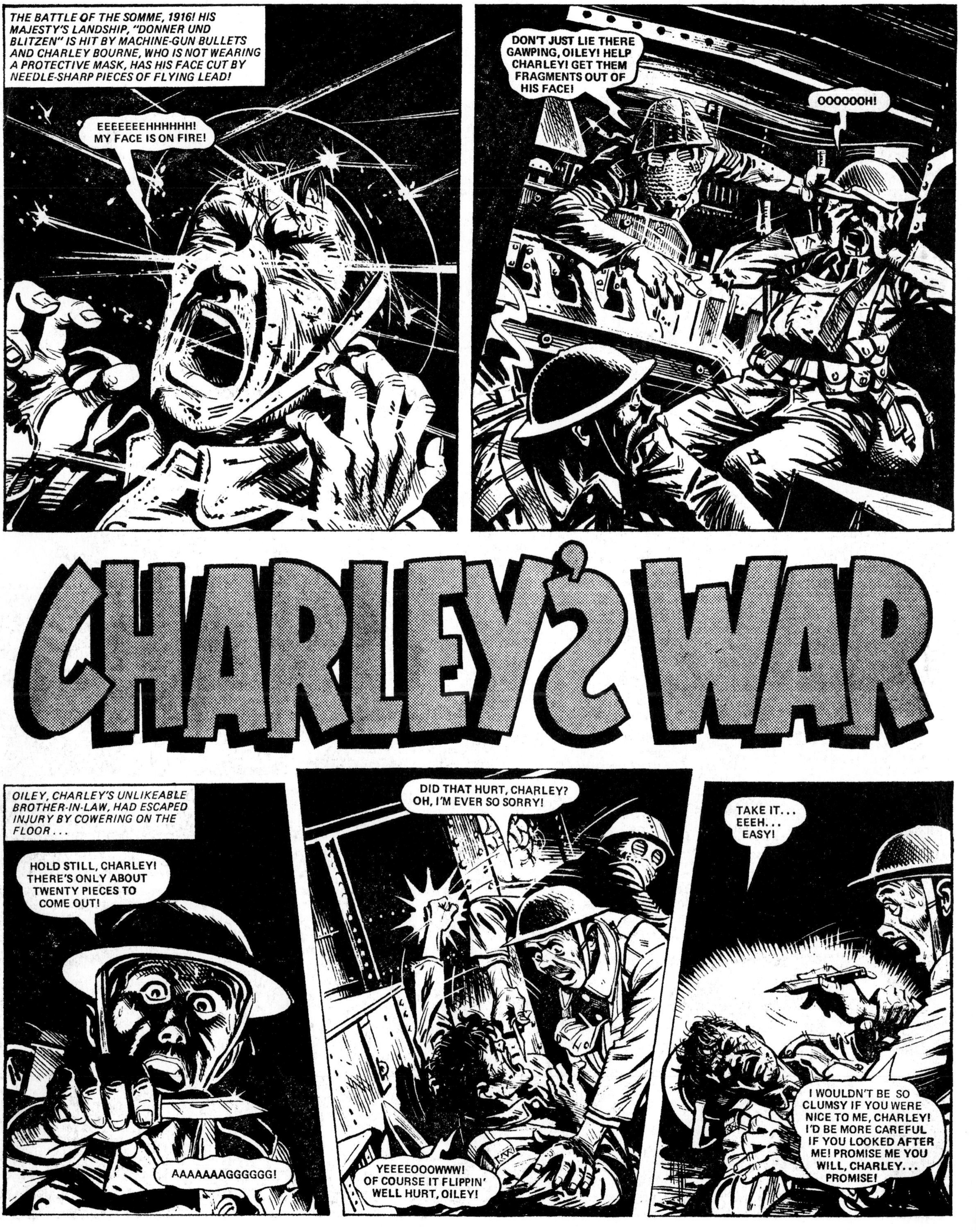
THE BATTLE OF THE SOMME, 1916! HIS MAJESTY'S LANDSHIP, "DONNER UND BLITZEN" IS HIT BY MACHINE-GUN BULLETS AND CHARLEY BOURNE, WHO IS NOT WEARING A PROTECTIVE MASK, HAS HIS FACE CUT BY NEEDLE-SHARP PIECES OF FLYING LEAD!
EEEEEEEHHHHHH! MY FACE IS ON FIRE!
DON'T JUST LIE THERE GAWPING, OILEY! HELP CHARLEY! GET THEM FRAGMENTS OUT OF HIS FACE!
OOOOOOH!
CHARLEY'S WAR
OILEY, CHARLEY'S UNLIKEABLE BROTHER-IN-LAW, HAD ESCAPED INJURY BY COWERING ON THE FLOOR...
HOLD STILL, CHARLEY! THERE'S ONLY ABOUT TWENTY PIECES TO COME OUT!
AAAAAAAGGGGGG!
DID THAT HURT, CHARLEY? OH, I'M EVER SO SORRY!
YEEEEOOOWWW! OF COURSE IT FLIPPIN' WELL HURT, OILEY!
TAKE IT... EEEH... EASY!
I WOULDN'T BE SO CLUMSY IF YOU WERE NICE TO ME, CHARLEY! I'D BE MORE CAREFUL IF YOU LOOKED AFTER ME! PROMISE ME YOU WILL, CHARLEY... PROMISE!

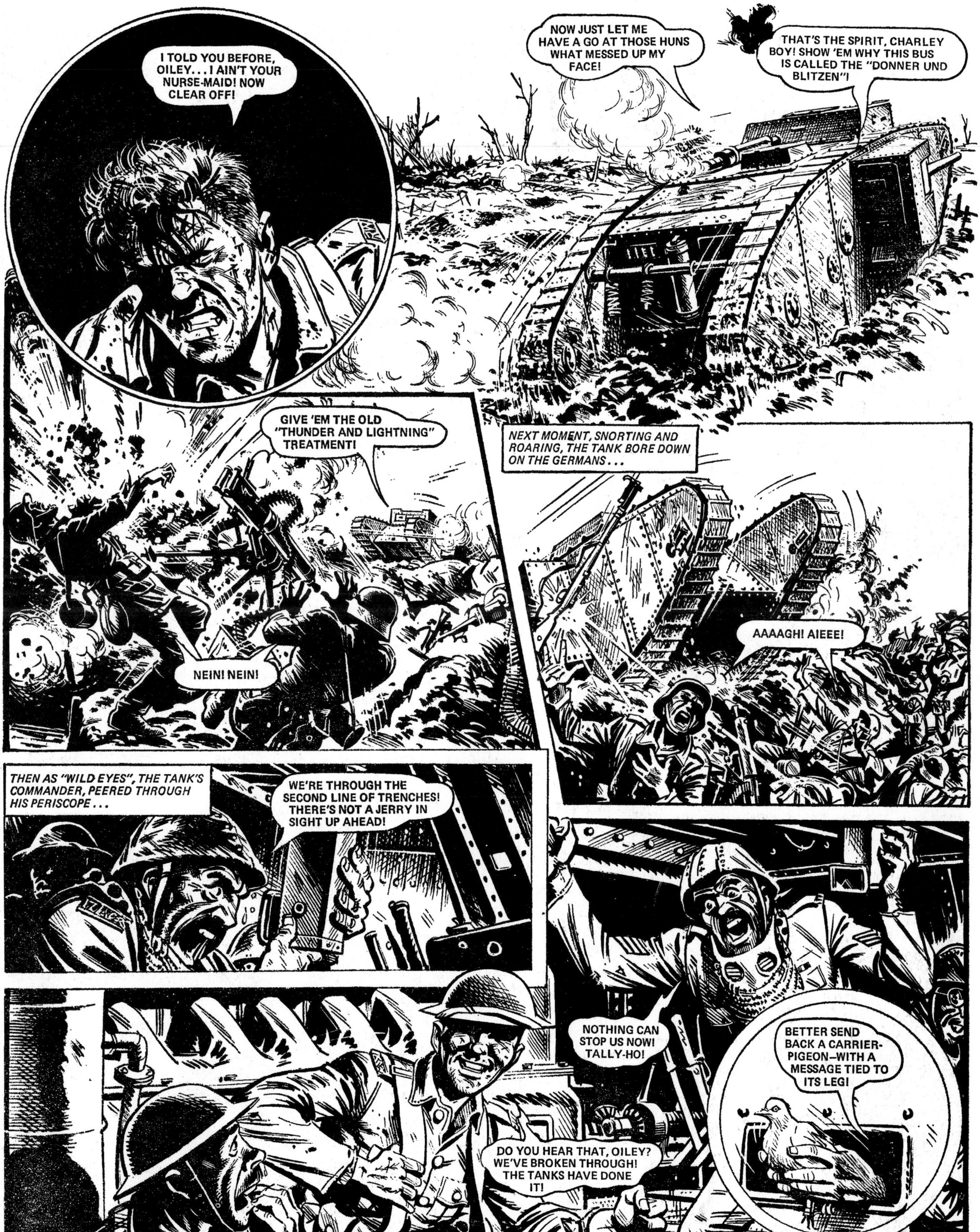
I TOLD YOU BEFORE, OILEY... I AIN'T YOUR NURSE-MAID! NOW CLEAR OFF!
NOW JUST LET ME HAVE A GO AT THOSE HUNS WHAT MESSED UP MY FACE!
THAT'S THE SPIRIT, CHARLEY BOY! SHOW 'EM WHY THIS BUS IS CALLED THE "DONNER UND BLITZEN"!
GIVE 'EM THE OLD "THUNDER AND LIGHTNING" TREATMENT!
NEIN! NEIN!
NEXT MOMENT, SNORTING AND ROARING, THE TANK BORE DOWN ON THE GERMANS...
AAAAGH! AIEEE!
THEN AS "WILD EYES", THE TANK'S COMMANDER, PEERED THROUGH HIS PERISCOPE...
WE'RE THROUGH THE SECOND LINE OF TRENCHES! THERE'S NOT A JERRY IN SIGHT UP AHEAD!
NOTHING CAN STOP US NOW! TALLY-HO!
DO YOU HEAR THAT, OILEY? WE'VE BROKEN THROUGH! THE TANKS HAVE DONE IT!
BETTER SEND BACK A CARRIER-PIGEON—WITH A MESSAGE TIED TO ITS LEG!

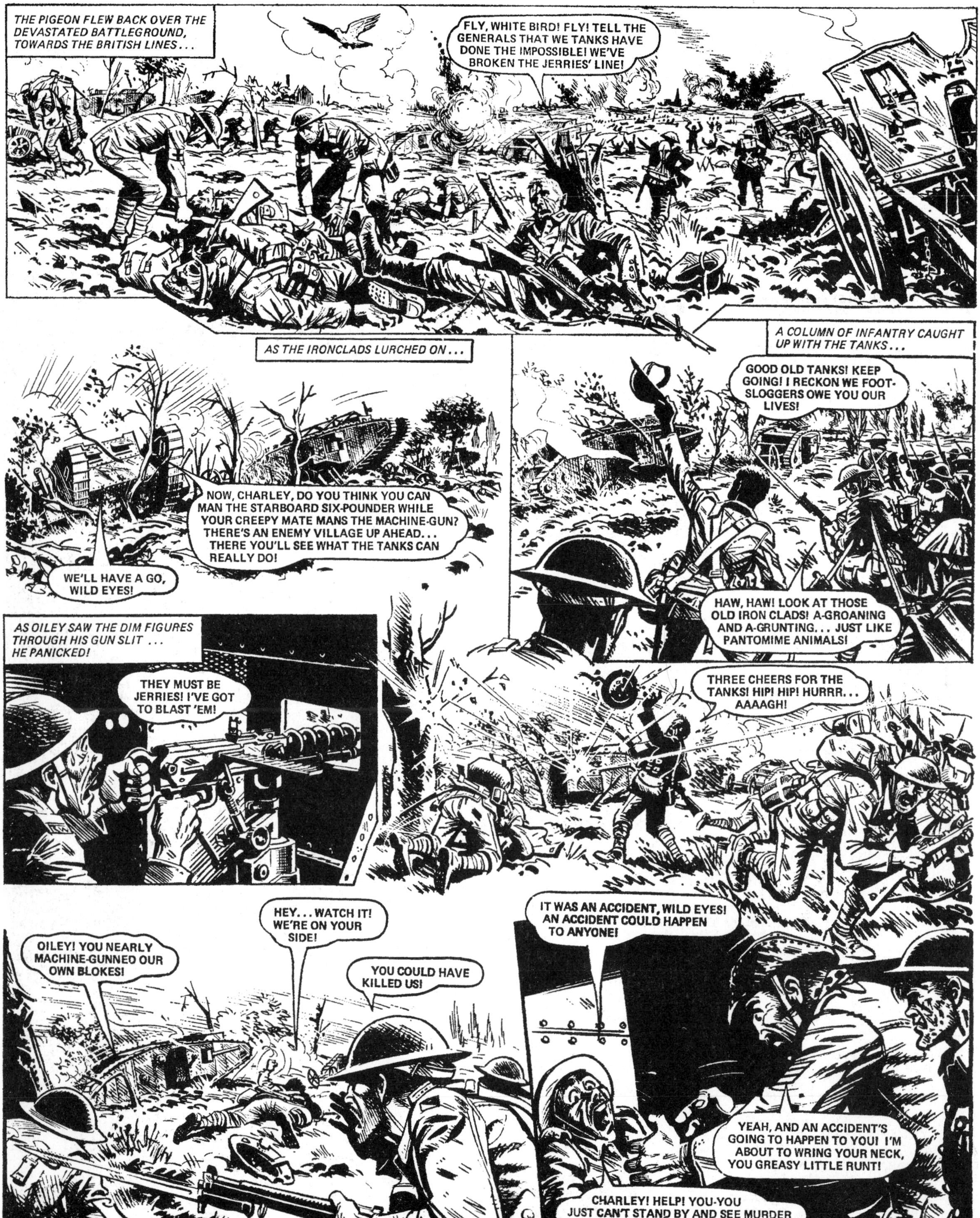

THE PIGEON FLEW BACK OVER THE DEVASTATED BATTLEGROUND, TOWARDS THE BRITISH LINES...
FLY, WHITE BIRD! FLY! TELL THE GENERALS THAT WE TANKS HAVE DONE THE IMPOSSIBLE! WE'VE BROKEN THE JERRIES' LINE!
AS THE IRONCLADS LURCHED ON...
NOW, CHARLEY, DO YOU THINK YOU CAN MAN THE STARBOARD SIX-POUNDER WHILE YOUR CREEPY MATE MANS THE MACHINE-GUN? THERE'S AN ENEMY VILLAGE UP AHEAD... THERE YOU'LL SEE WHAT THE TANKS CAN REALLY DO!
WE'LL HAVE A GO, WILD EYES!
A COLUMN OF INFANTRY CAUGHT UP WITH THE TANKS...
GOOD OLD TANKS! KEEP GOING! I RECKON WE FOOT-SLOGGERS OWE YOU OUR LIVES!
HAW, HAW! LOOK AT THOSE OLD IRON CLADS! A-GROANING AND A-GRUNTING... JUST LIKE PANTOMIME ANIMALS!
AS OILEY SAW THE DIM FIGURES THROUGH HIS GUN SLIT ... HE PANICKED!
THEY MUST BE JERRIES! I'VE GOT TO BLAST 'EM!
THREE CHEERS FOR THE TANKS! HIP! HIP! HURRR... AAAAGH!
OILEY! YOU NEARLY MACHINE-GUNNED OUR OWN BLOKES!
HEY... WATCH IT! WE'RE ON YOUR SIDE!
YOU COULD HAVE KILLED US!
IT WAS AN ACCIDENT, WILD EYES! AN ACCIDENT COULD HAPPEN TO ANYONE!
YEAH, AND AN ACCIDENT'S GOING TO HAPPEN TO YOU! I'M ABOUT TO WRING YOUR NECK, YOU GREASY LITTLE RUNT!
CHARLEY! HELP! YOU-YOU JUST CAN'T STAND BY AND SEE MURDER DONE! CAN YOU, CHARLEY — CAN YOU?

CHARLEY'S WAR

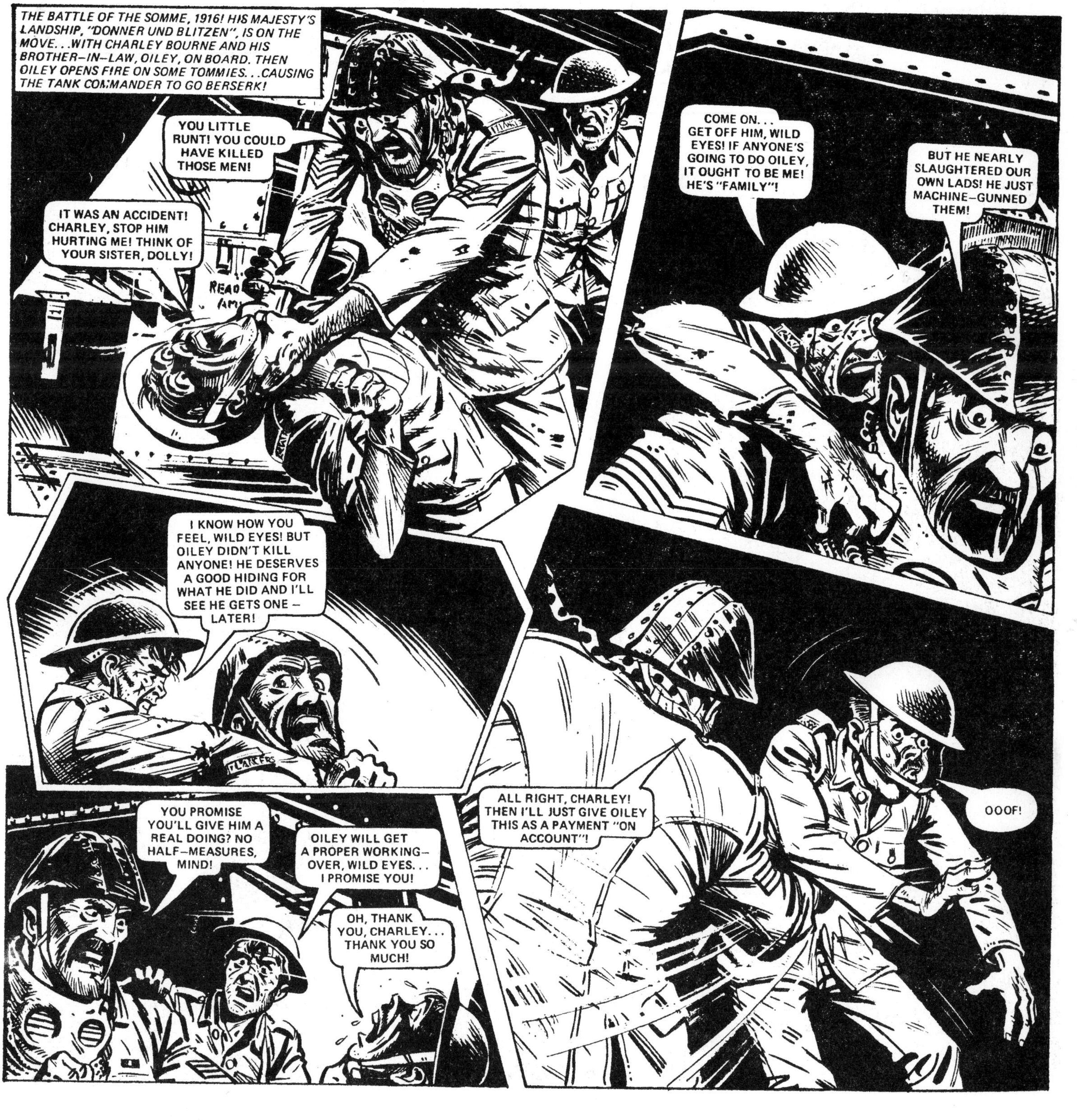

THE BATTLE OF THE SOMME, 1916! HIS MAJESTY'S LANDSHIP, "DONNER UND BLITZEN", IS ON THE MOVE. . . WITH CHARLEY BOURNE AND HIS BROTHER-IN-LAW, OILEY, ON BOARD. THEN OILEY OPENS FIRE ON SOME TOMMIES. . . CAUSING THE TANK COMMANDER TO GO BERSERK!
YOU LITTLE RUNT! YOU COULD HAVE KILLED THOSE MEN!
IT WAS AN ACCIDENT! CHARLEY, STOP HIM HURTING ME! THINK OF YOUR SISTER, DOLLY!
COME ON. . . GET OFF HIM, WILD EYES! IF ANYONE'S GOING TO DO OILEY, IT OUGHT TO BE ME! HE'S "FAMILY"!
BUT HE NEARLY SLAUGHTERED OUR OWN LADS! HE JUST MACHINE-GUNNED THEM!
I KNOW HOW YOU FEEL, WILD EYES! BUT OILEY DIDN'T KILL ANYONE! HE DESERVES A GOOD HIDING FOR WHAT HE DID AND I'LL SEE HE GETS ONE – LATER!
YOU PROMISE YOU'LL GIVE HIM A REAL DOING? NO HALF-MEASURES, MIND!
OILEY WILL GET A PROPER WORKING-OVER, WILD EYES. . . I PROMISE YOU!
OH, THANK YOU, CHARLEY. . . THANK YOU SO MUCH!
ALL RIGHT, CHARLEY! THEN I'LL JUST GIVE OILEY THIS AS A PAYMENT "ON ACCOUNT"!
OOOF!

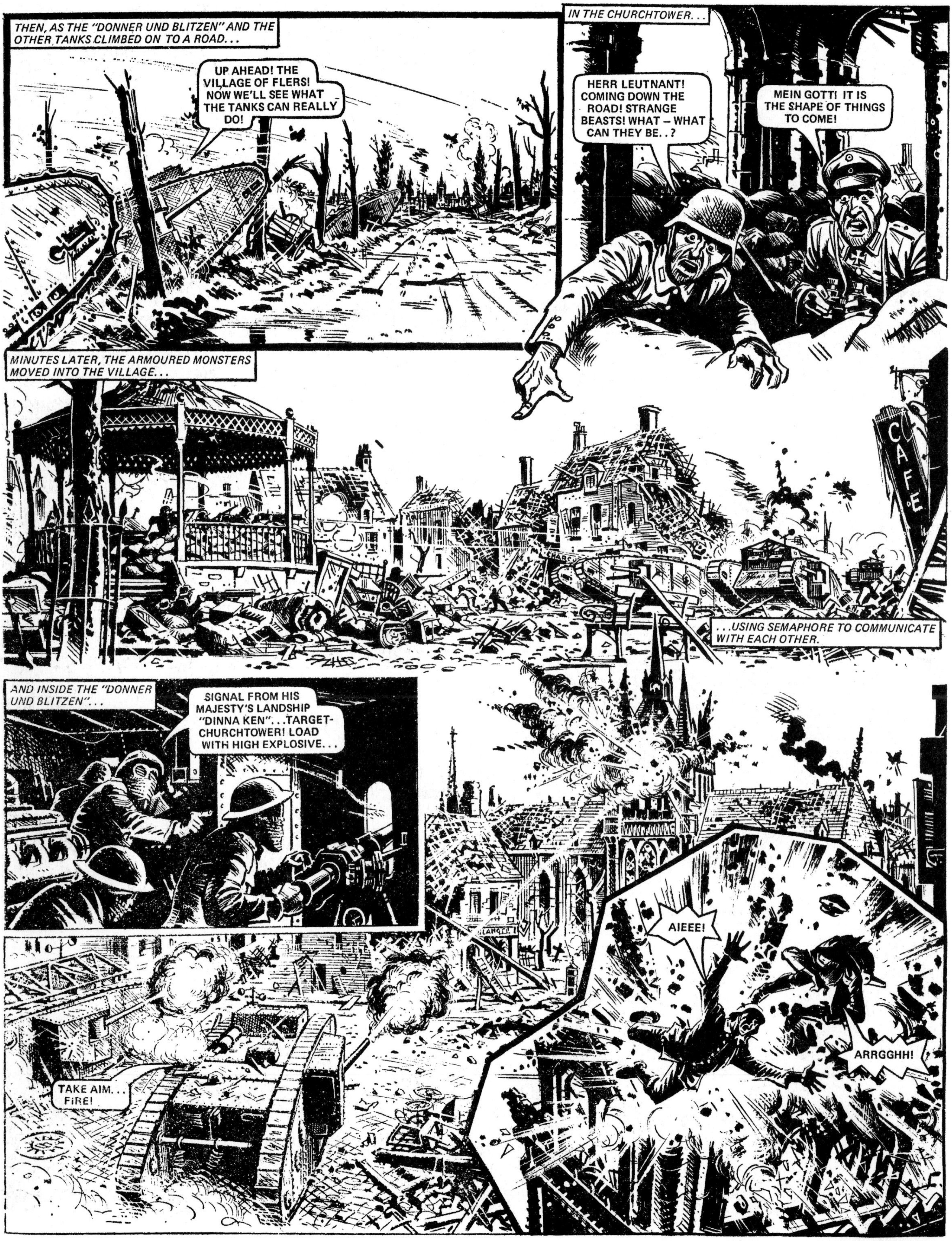
THEN, AS THE "DONNER UND BLITZEN" AND THE OTHER TANKS CLIMBED ON TO A ROAD...
UP AHEAD! THE VILLAGE OF FLERS! NOW WE'LL SEE WHAT THE TANKS CAN REALLY DO!
IN THE CHURCHTOWER...
HERR LEUTNANT! COMING DOWN THE ROAD! STRANGE BEASTS! WHAT – WHAT CAN THEY BE..?
MEIN GOTT! IT IS THE SHAPE OF THINGS TO COME!
MINUTES LATER, THE ARMOURED MONSTERS MOVED INTO THE VILLAGE...
CAFE
...USING SEMAPHORE TO COMMUNICATE WITH EACH OTHER.
AND INSIDE THE "DONNER UND BLITZEN"...
SIGNAL FROM HIS MAJESTY'S LANDSHIP "DINNA KEN"...TARGET-CHURCHTOWER! LOAD WITH HIGH EXPLOSIVE...
TAKE AIM... FIRE!
AIEEE!
ARRGGHH!

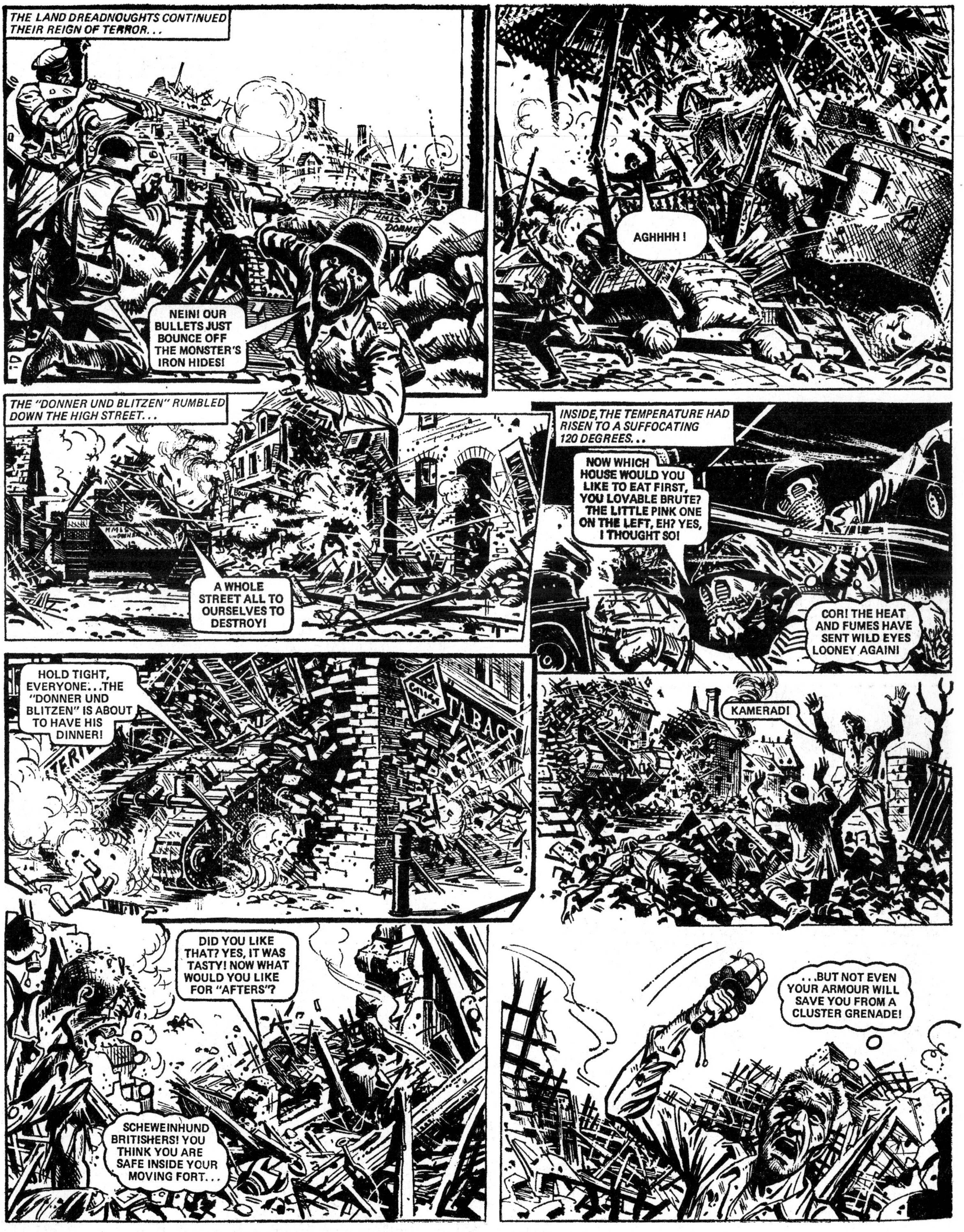
THE LAND DREADNOUGHTS CONTINUED THEIR REIGN OF TERROR...
NEIN! OUR BULLETS JUST BOUNCE OFF THE MONSTER'S IRON HIDES!
AGHHHH!
THE "DONNER UND BLITZEN" RUMBLED DOWN THE HIGH STREET...
A WHOLE STREET ALL TO OURSELVES TO DESTROY!
INSIDE, THE TEMPERATURE HAD RISEN TO A SUFFOCATING 120 DEGREES...
NOW WHICH HOUSE WOULD YOU LIKE TO EAT FIRST, YOU LOVABLE BRUTE? THE LITTLE PINK ONE ON THE LEFT, EH? YES, I THOUGHT SO!
COR! THE HEAT AND FUMES HAVE SENT WILD EYES LOONEY AGAIN!
HOLD TIGHT, EVERYONE...THE "DONNER UND BLITZEN" IS ABOUT TO HAVE HIS DINNER!
TABAC
KAMERAD!
DID YOU LIKE THAT? YES, IT WAS TASTY! NOW WHAT WOULD YOU LIKE FOR "AFTERS"?
SCHEWEINHUND BRITISHERS! YOU THINK YOU ARE SAFE INSIDE YOUR MOVING FORT...
...BUT NOT EVEN YOUR ARMOUR WILL SAVE YOU FROM A CLUSTER GRENADE!

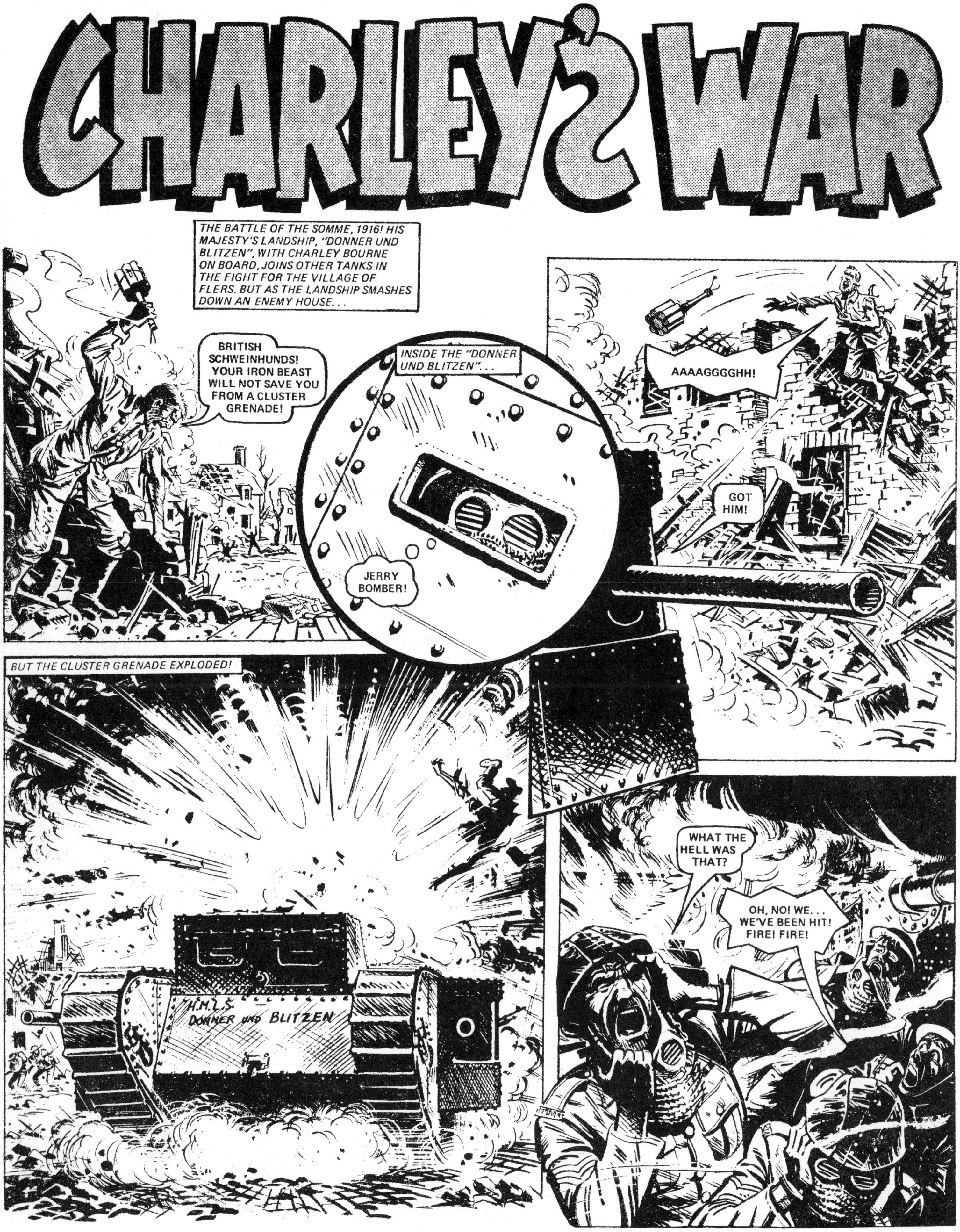
CHARLEY'S WAR
THE BATTLE OF THE SOMME, 1916! HIS MAJESTY'S LANDSHIP, "DONNER UND BLITZEN", WITH CHARLEY BOURNE ON BOARD, JOINS OTHER TANKS IN THE FIGHT FOR THE VILLAGE OF FLERS. BUT AS THE LANDSHIP SMASHES DOWN AN ENEMY HOUSE. . .
BRITISH SCHWEINHUNDS! YOUR IRON BEAST WILL NOT SAVE YOU FROM A CLUSTER GRENADE!
INSIDE THE "DONNER UND BLITZEN". . .
JERRY BOMBER!
AAAAGGGGHH!
GOT HIM!
BUT THE CLUSTER GRENADE EXPLODED!
H.M.L.S. DONNER UND BLITZEN
WHAT THE HELL WAS THAT?
OH, NO! WE. . . WE'VE BEEN HIT! FIRE! FIRE!

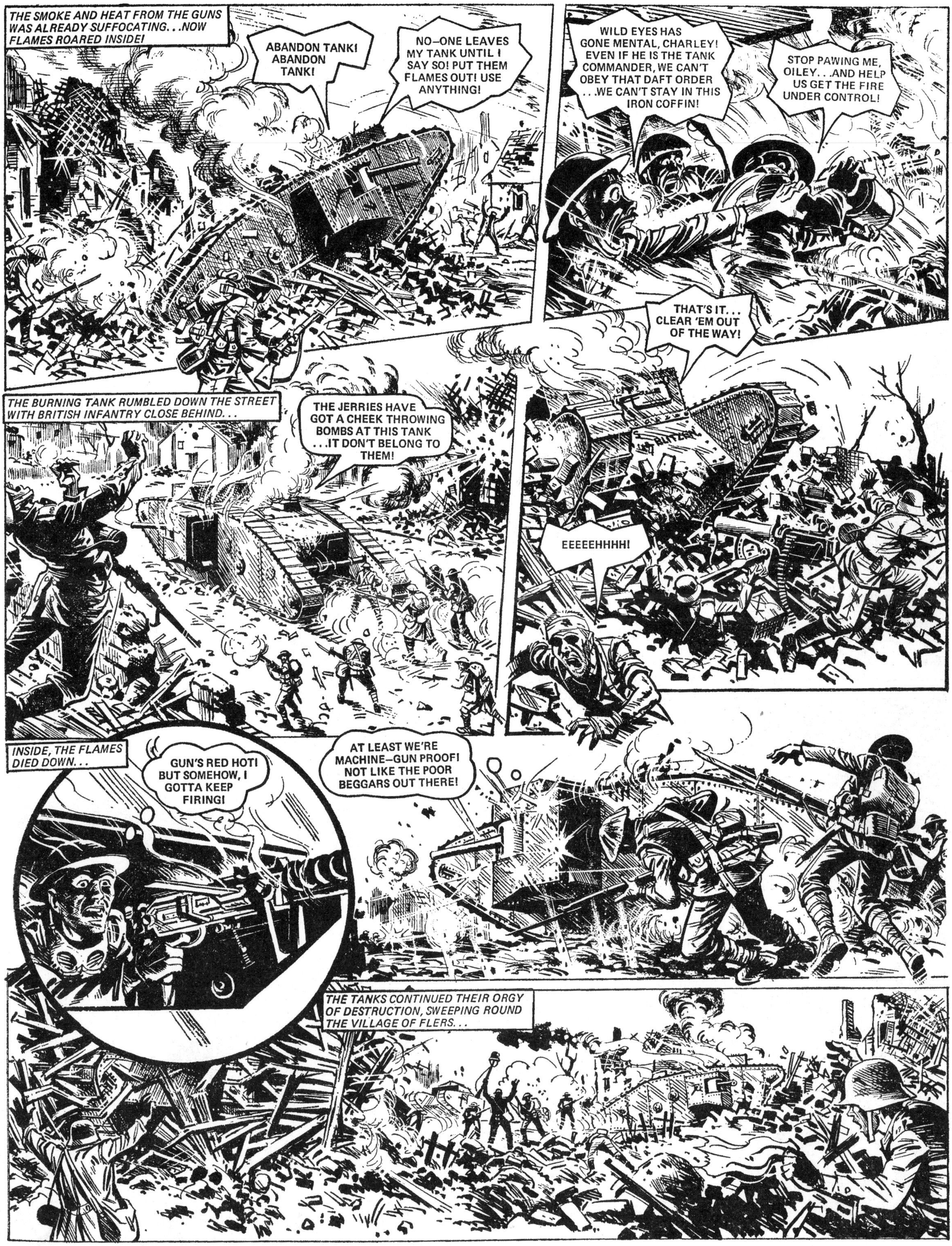

THE SMOKE AND HEAT FROM THE GUNS WAS ALREADY SUFFOCATING. . .NOW FLAMES ROARED INSIDE!
ABANDON TANK! ABANDON TANK!
NO–ONE LEAVES MY TANK UNTIL I SAY SO! PUT THEM FLAMES OUT! USE ANYTHING!
WILD EYES HAS GONE MENTAL, CHARLEY! EVEN IF HE IS THE TANK COMMANDER, WE CAN'T OBEY THAT DAFT ORDER . . .WE CAN'T STAY IN THIS IRON COFFIN!
STOP PAWING ME, OILEY. . .AND HELP US GET THE FIRE UNDER CONTROL!
THE BURNING TANK RUMBLED DOWN THE STREET WITH BRITISH INFANTRY CLOSE BEHIND. . .
THE JERRIES HAVE GOT A CHEEK THROWING BOMBS AT THIS TANK . . .IT DON'T BELONG TO THEM!
THAT'S IT. . . CLEAR 'EM OUT OF THE WAY!
EEEEEHHHH!
INSIDE, THE FLAMES DIED DOWN. . .
GUN'S RED HOT! BUT SOMEHOW, I GOTTA KEEP FIRING!
AT LEAST WE'RE MACHINE–GUN PROOF! NOT LIKE THE POOR BEGGARS OUT THERE!
THE TANKS CONTINUED THEIR ORGY OF DESTRUCTION, SWEEPING ROUND THE VILLAGE OF FLERS. . .

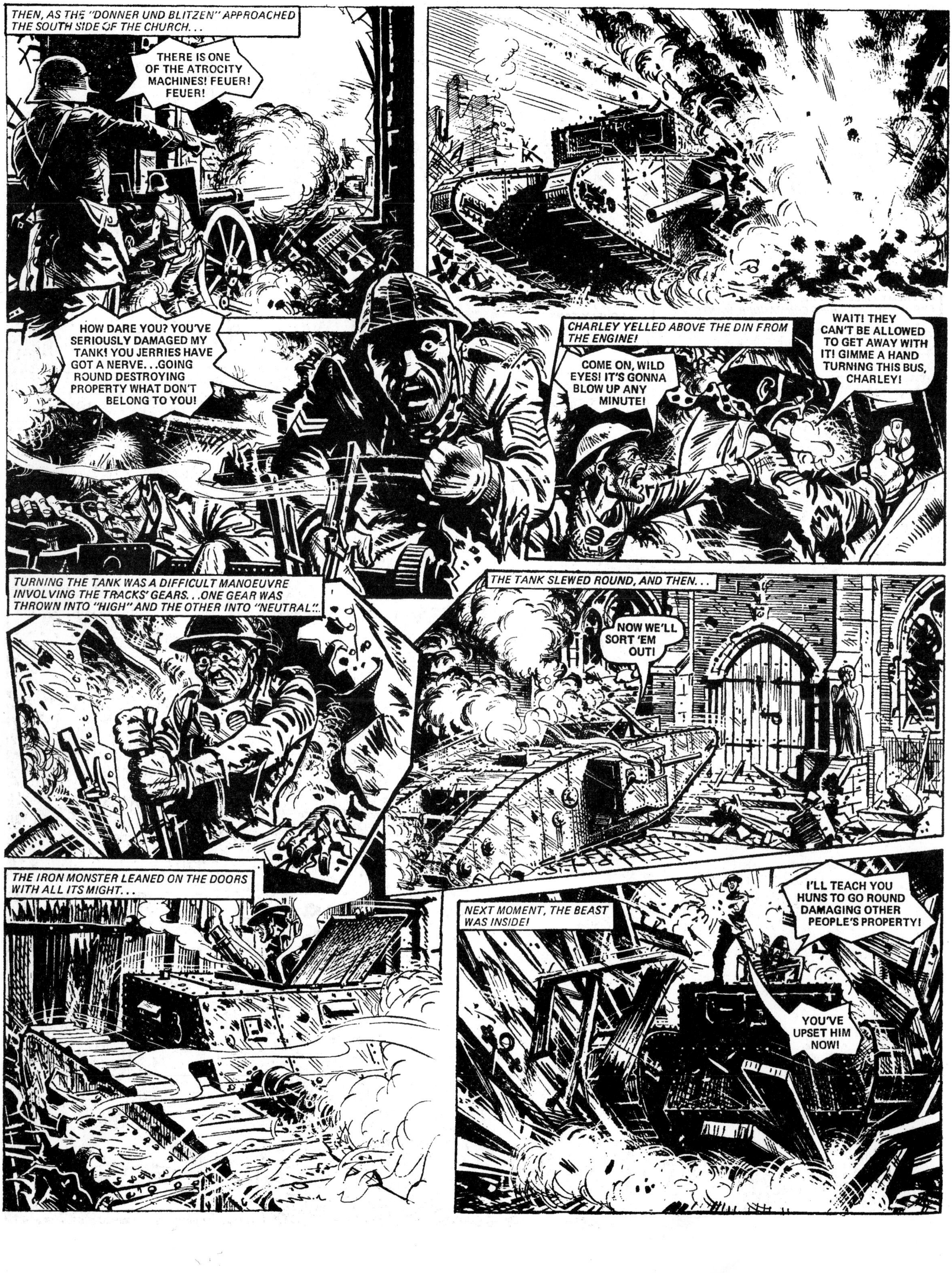
THEN, AS THE "DONNER UND BLITZEN" APPROACHED THE SOUTH SIDE OF THE CHURCH. . .
THERE IS ONE OF THE ATROCITY MACHINES! FEUER! FEUER!
HOW DARE YOU? YOU'VE SERIOUSLY DAMAGED MY TANK! YOU JERRIES HAVE GOT A NERVE. . .GOING ROUND DESTROYING PROPERTY WHAT DON'T BELONG TO YOU!
CHARLEY YELLED ABOVE THE DIN FROM THE ENGINE!
COME ON, WILD EYES! IT'S GONNA BLOW UP ANY MINUTE!
WAIT! THEY CAN'T BE ALLOWED TO GET AWAY WITH IT! GIMME A HAND TURNING THIS BUS, CHARLEY!
TURNING THE TANK WAS A DIFFICULT MANOEUVRE INVOLVING THE TRACKS' GEARS. . .ONE GEAR WAS THROWN INTO "HIGH" AND THE OTHER INTO "NEUTRAL".
THE TANK SLEWED ROUND, AND THEN. . .
NOW WE'LL SORT 'EM OUT!
THE IRON MONSTER LEANED ON THE DOORS WITH ALL ITS MIGHT. . .
NEXT MOMENT, THE BEAST WAS INSIDE!
I'LL TEACH YOU HUNS TO GO ROUND DAMAGING OTHER PEOPLE'S PROPERTY!
YOU'VE UPSET HIM NOW!

CHARLEY'S WAR

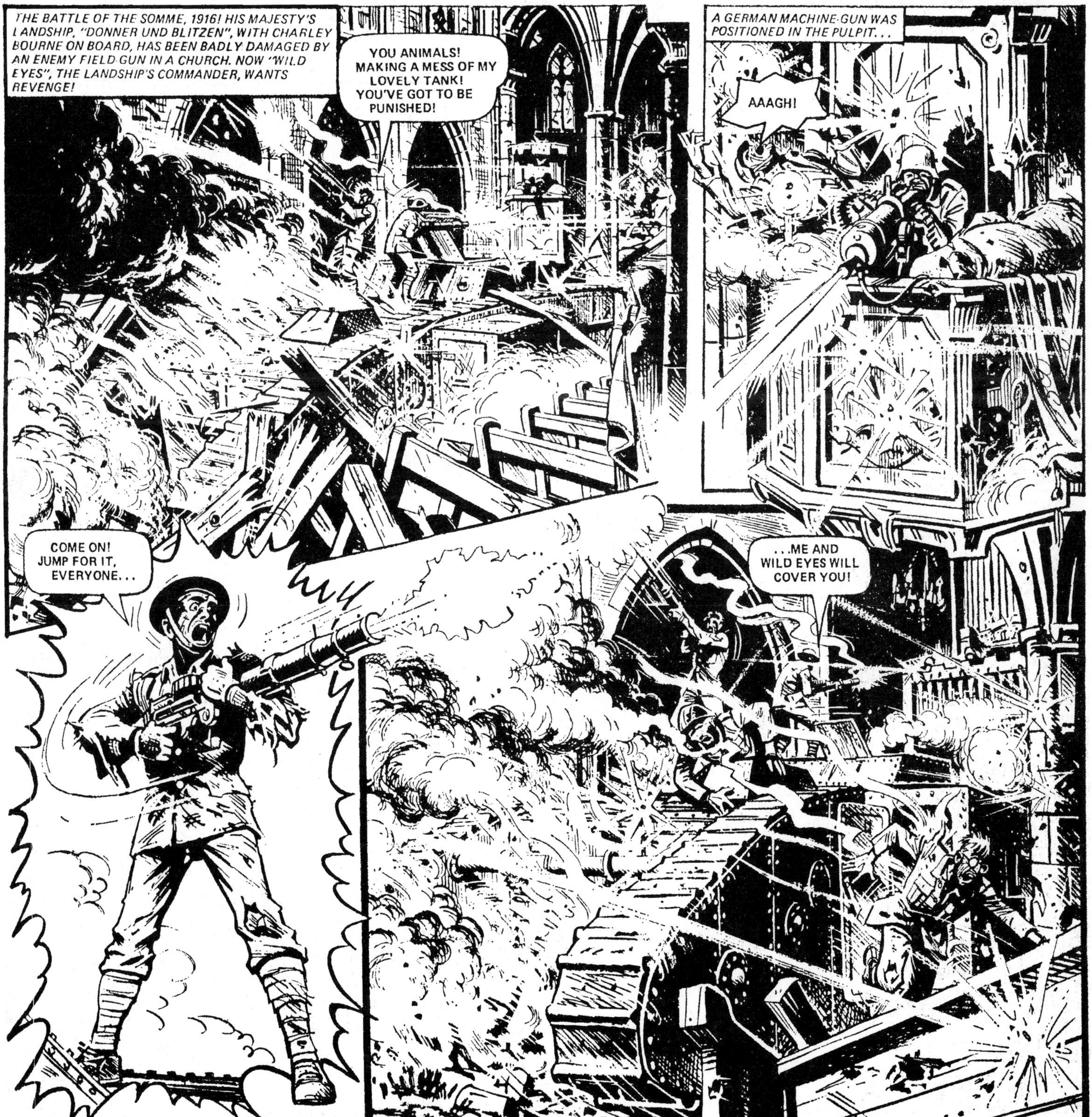

THE BATTLE OF THE SOMME, 1916! HIS MAJESTY'S LANDSHIP, "DONNER UND BLITZEN", WITH CHARLEY BOURNE ON BOARD, HAS BEEN BADLY DAMAGED BY AN ENEMY FIELD-GUN IN A CHURCH. NOW "WILD EYES", THE LANDSHIP'S COMMANDER, WANTS REVENGE!
YOU ANIMALS! MAKING A MESS OF MY LOVELY TANK! YOU'VE GOT TO BE PUNISHED!
A GERMAN MACHINE-GUN WAS POSITIONED IN THE PULPIT. . .
AAAGH!
COME ON! JUMP FOR IT, EVERYONE. . .
. . .ME AND WILD EYES WILL COVER YOU!

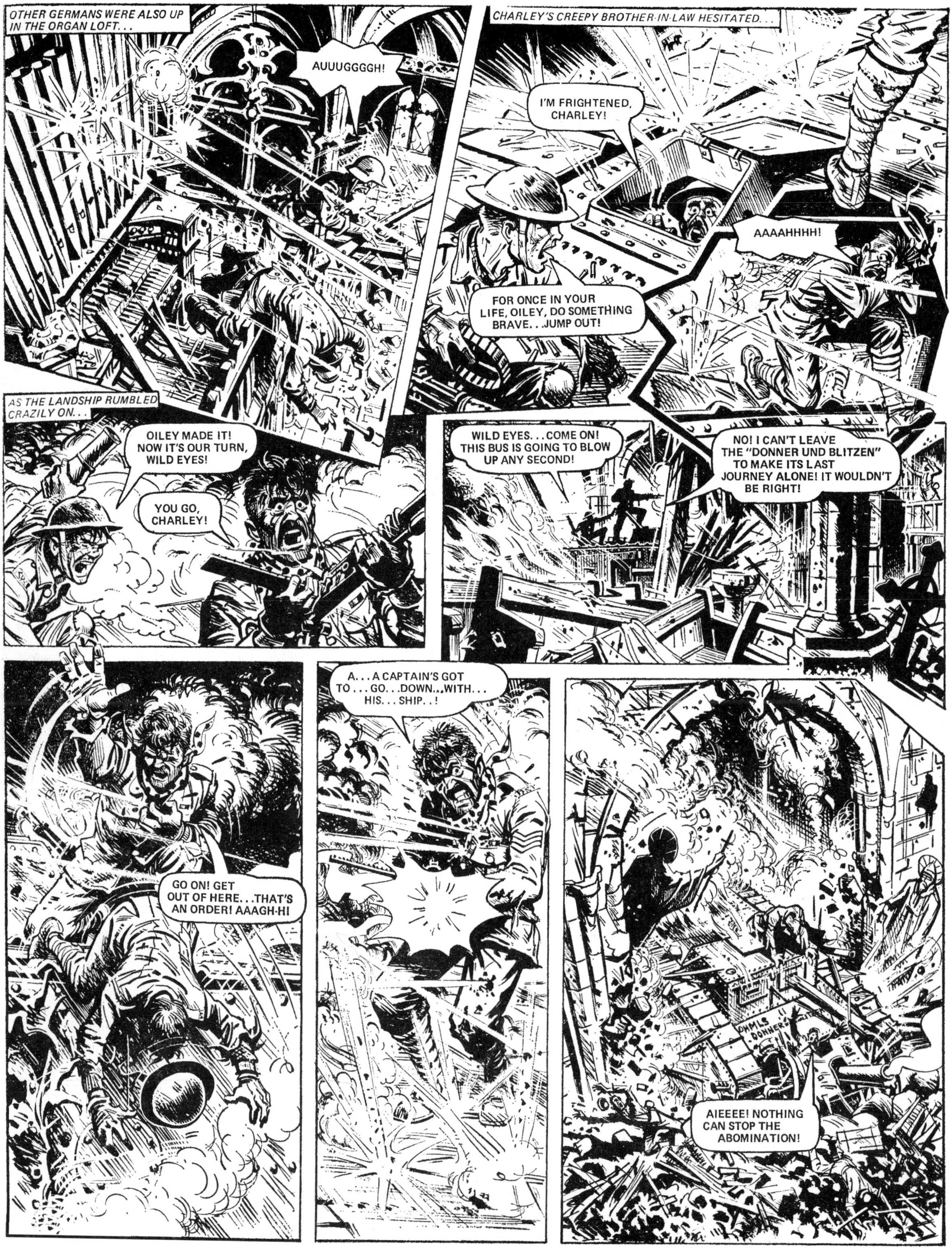
OTHER GERMANS WERE ALSO UP IN THE ORGAN LOFT...
AUUUGGGGH!
CHARLEY'S CREEPY BROTHER-IN-LAW HESITATED...
I'M FRIGHTENED, CHARLEY!
FOR ONCE IN YOUR LIFE, OILEY, DO SOMETHING BRAVE.. .JUMP OUT!
AAAAHHHH!
AS THE LANDSHIP RUMBLED CRAZILY ON...
OILEY MADE IT! NOW IT'S OUR TURN, WILD EYES!
YOU GO, CHARLEY!
WILD EYES...COME ON! THIS BUS IS GOING TO BLOW UP ANY SECOND!
NO! I CAN'T LEAVE THE "DONNER UND BLITZEN" TO MAKE ITS LAST JOURNEY ALONE! IT WOULDN'T BE RIGHT!
GO ON! GET OUT OF HERE...THAT'S AN ORDER! AAAGH-H!
A... A CAPTAIN'S GOT TO... GO...DOWN...WITH... HIS... SHIP..!
AIEEEE! NOTHING CAN STOP THE ABOMINATION!

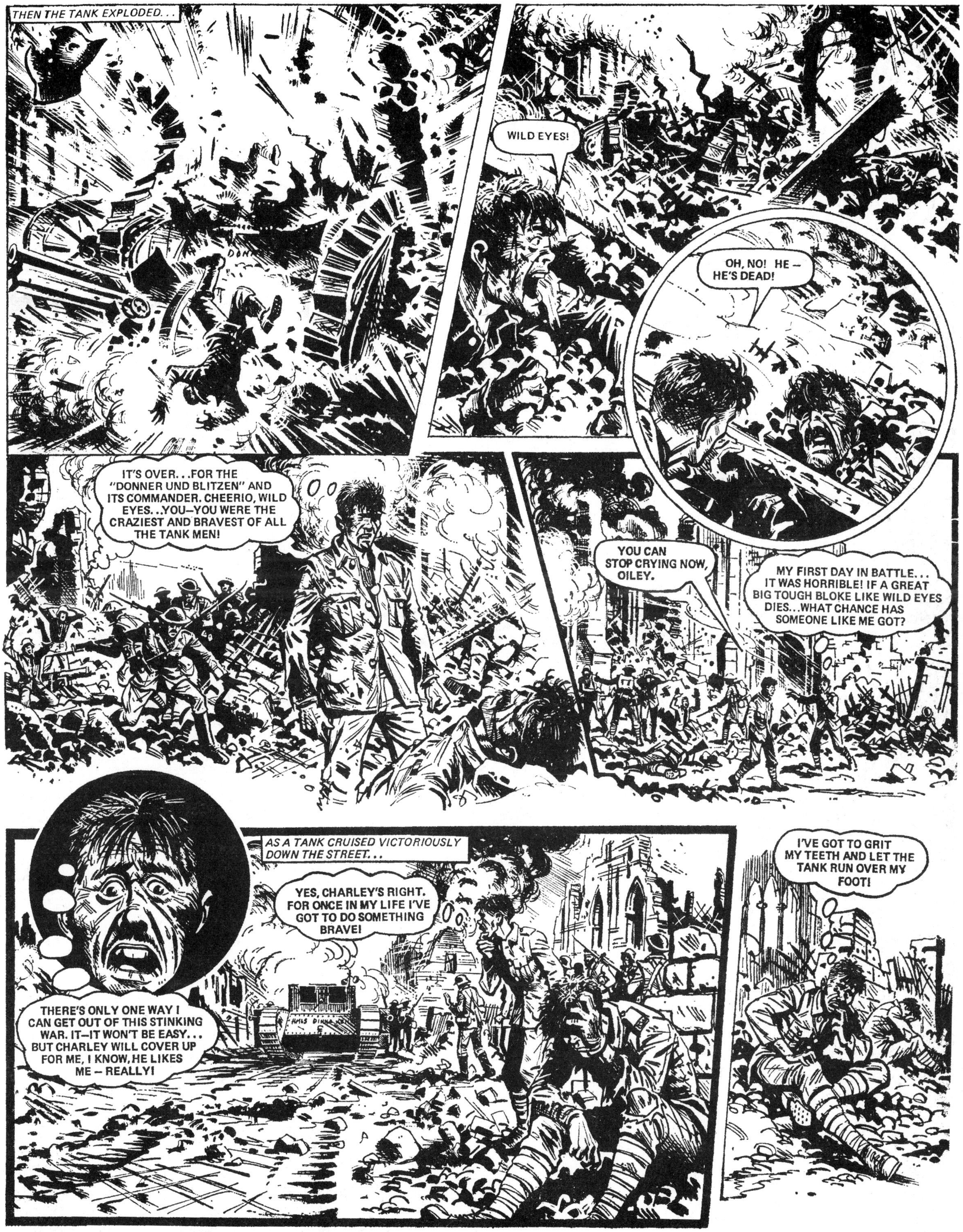
THEN THE TANK EXPLODED...
WILD EYES!
OH, NO! HE — HE'S DEAD!
IT'S OVER...FOR THE "DONNER UND BLITZEN" AND ITS COMMANDER. CHEERIO, WILD EYES...YOU—YOU WERE THE CRAZIEST AND BRAVEST OF ALL THE TANK MEN!
YOU CAN STOP CRYING NOW, OILEY.
MY FIRST DAY IN BATTLE... IT WAS HORRIBLE! IF A GREAT BIG TOUGH BLOKE LIKE WILD EYES DIES...WHAT CHANCE HAS SOMEONE LIKE ME GOT?
THERE'S ONLY ONE WAY I CAN GET OUT OF THIS STINKING WAR. IT—IT WON'T BE EASY... BUT CHARLEY WILL COVER UP FOR ME, I KNOW, HE LIKES ME — REALLY!
AS A TANK CRUISED VICTORIOUSLY DOWN THE STREET...
YES, CHARLEY'S RIGHT. FOR ONCE IN MY LIFE I'VE GOT TO DO SOMETHING BRAVE!
I'VE GOT TO GRIT MY TEETH AND LET THE TANK RUN OVER MY FOOT!

CHARLEY'S WAR

THE BATTLE OF THE SOMME, 1916! THE TANKS HAVE SCORED THEIR FIRST VICTORY BY CAPTURING THE VILLAGE OF FLERS. BUT CHARLEY BOURNE'S BROTHER-IN-LAW, OILEY, IS DETERMINED TO AVOID THE FIGHTING ANY WAY HE CAN...

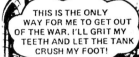

THIS IS THE ONLY WAY FOR ME TO GET OUT OF THE WAR. I'LL GRIT MY TEETH AND LET THE TANK CRUSH MY FOOT!

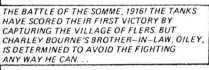

GREAT HUN DEFEAT SPECIAL

BUT AT THE LAST MOMENT, OILEY LOST HIS NERVE... SO THE TANK ONLY RAN OVER HIS TOES...

AAAAHHHHH!

AAAHHH!

WHAT THE DEVIL HAPPENED HERE?

IT...ER ...WAS AN ACCIDENT, SIR.

I MUST BE BONKERS COVERING UP FOR A CREEP LIKE OILEY. BUT IF THEY KNEW HE'D DONE IT DELIBERATELY...THEY'D SHOOT HIM!

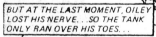

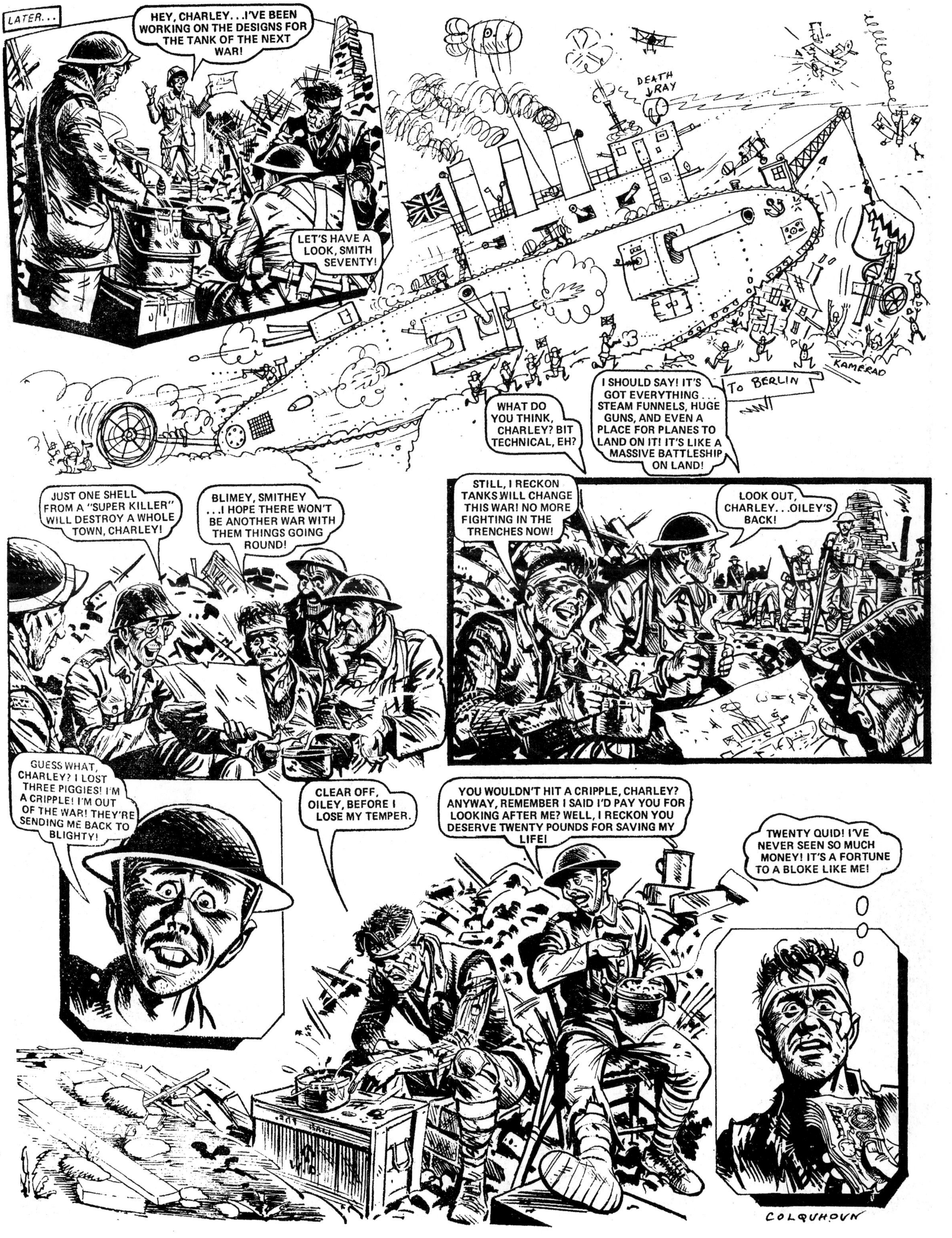
LATER...
HEY, CHARLEY...I'VE BEEN WORKING ON THE DESIGNS FOR THE TANK OF THE NEXT WAR!
LET'S HAVE A LOOK, SMITH SEVENTY!
DEATH RAY
TO BERLIN
KAMERAD
WHAT DO YOU THINK, CHARLEY? BIT TECHNICAL, EH?
I SHOULD SAY! IT'S GOT EVERYTHING . . . STEAM FUNNELS, HUGE GUNS, AND EVEN A PLACE FOR PLANES TO LAND ON IT! IT'S LIKE A MASSIVE BATTLESHIP ON LAND!
JUST ONE SHELL FROM A "SUPER KILLER" WILL DESTROY A WHOLE TOWN, CHARLEY!
BLIMEY, SMITHEY . . . I HOPE THERE WON'T BE ANOTHER WAR WITH THEM THINGS GOING ROUND!
STILL, I RECKON TANKS WILL CHANGE THIS WAR! NO MORE FIGHTING IN THE TRENCHES NOW!
LOOK OUT, CHARLEY. . . OILEY'S BACK!
GUESS WHAT, CHARLEY? I LOST THREE PIGGIES! I'M A CRIPPLE! I'M OUT OF THE WAR! THEY'RE SENDING ME BACK TO BLIGHTY!
CLEAR OFF, OILEY, BEFORE I LOSE MY TEMPER.
YOU WOULDN'T HIT A CRIPPLE, CHARLEY? ANYWAY, REMEMBER I SAID I'D PAY YOU FOR LOOKING AFTER ME? WELL, I RECKON YOU DESERVE TWENTY POUNDS FOR SAVING MY LIFE!
TWENTY QUID! I'VE NEVER SEEN SO MUCH MONEY! IT'S A FORTUNE TO A BLOKE LIKE ME!
COLQUHOUN

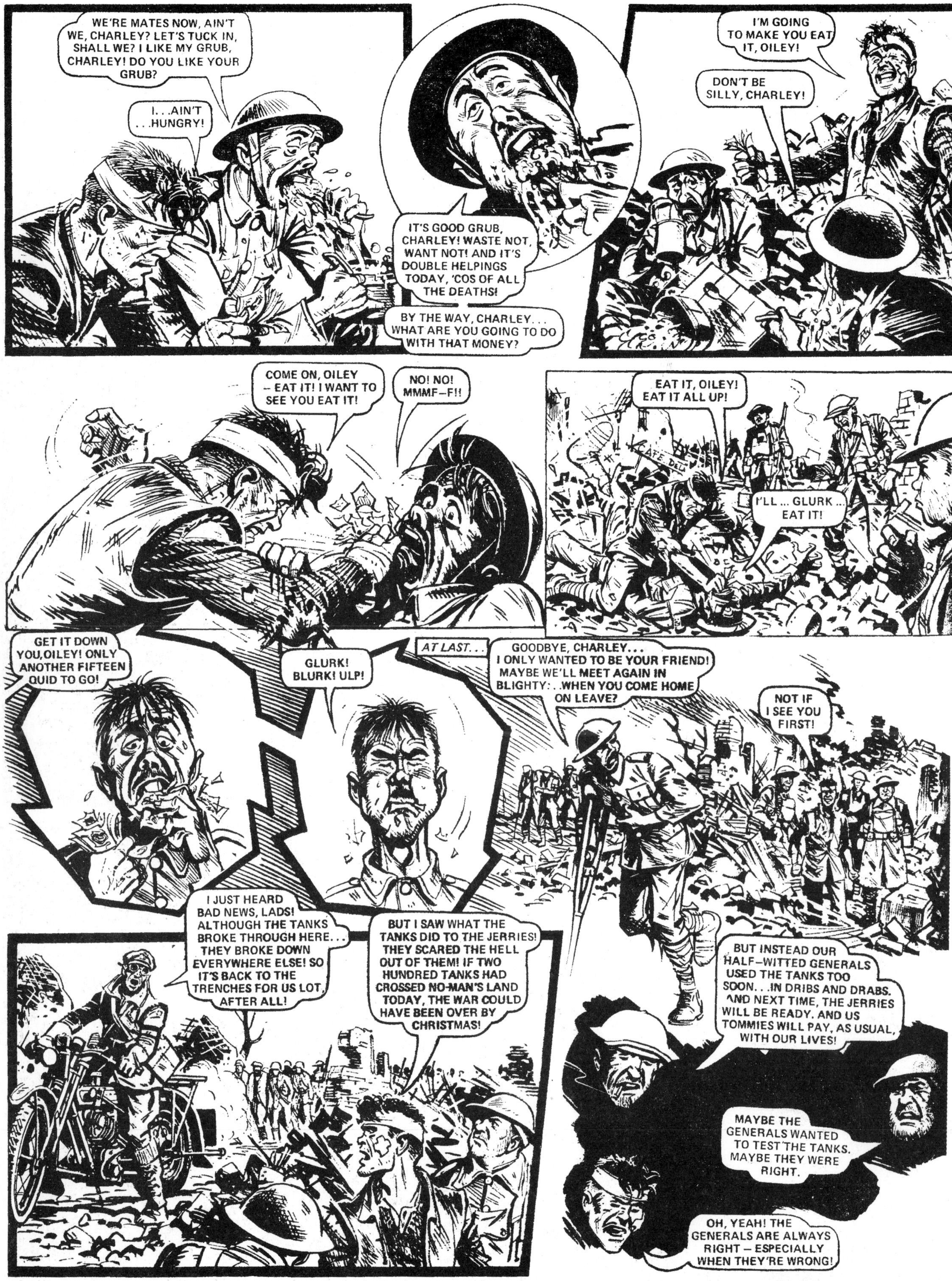
WE'RE MATES NOW, AIN'T WE, CHARLEY? LET'S TUCK IN, SHALL WE? I LIKE MY GRUB, CHARLEY! DO YOU LIKE YOUR GRUB?
I. . . AIN'T . . . HUNGRY!
IT'S GOOD GRUB, CHARLEY! WASTE NOT, WANT NOT! AND IT'S DOUBLE HELPINGS TODAY, 'COS OF ALL THE DEATHS!
BY THE WAY, CHARLEY. . . WHAT ARE YOU GOING TO DO WITH THAT MONEY?
I'M GOING TO MAKE YOU EAT IT, OILEY!
DON'T BE SILLY, CHARLEY!
COME ON, OILEY – EAT IT! I WANT TO SEE YOU EAT IT!
NO! NO! MMMF–F!!
EAT IT, OILEY! EAT IT ALL UP!
I'LL ... GLURK ... EAT IT!
GET IT DOWN YOU,OILEY! ONLY ANOTHER FIFTEEN QUID TO GO!
GLURK! BLURK! ULP!
AT LAST. . .
GOODBYE, CHARLEY. . . I ONLY WANTED TO BE YOUR FRIEND! MAYBE WE'LL MEET AGAIN IN BLIGHTY: . .WHEN YOU COME HOME ON LEAVE?
NOT IF I SEE YOU FIRST!
I JUST HEARD BAD NEWS, LADS! ALTHOUGH THE TANKS BROKE THROUGH HERE. . . THEY BROKE DOWN EVERYWHERE ELSE! SO IT'S BACK TO THE TRENCHES FOR US LOT, AFTER ALL!
BUT I SAW WHAT THE TANKS DID TO THE JERRIES! THEY SCARED THE HELL OUT OF THEM! IF TWO HUNDRED TANKS HAD CROSSED NO-MAN'S LAND TODAY, THE WAR COULD HAVE BEEN OVER BY CHRISTMAS!
BUT INSTEAD OUR HALF–WITTED GENERALS USED THE TANKS TOO SOON. . .IN DRIBS AND DRABS. AND NEXT TIME, THE JERRIES WILL BE READY. AND US TOMMIES WILL PAY, AS USUAL, WITH OUR LIVES!
MAYBE THE GENERALS WANTED TO TEST THE TANKS. MAYBE THEY WERE RIGHT.
OH, YEAH! THE GENERALS ARE ALWAYS RIGHT – ESPECIALLY WHEN THEY'RE WRONG!

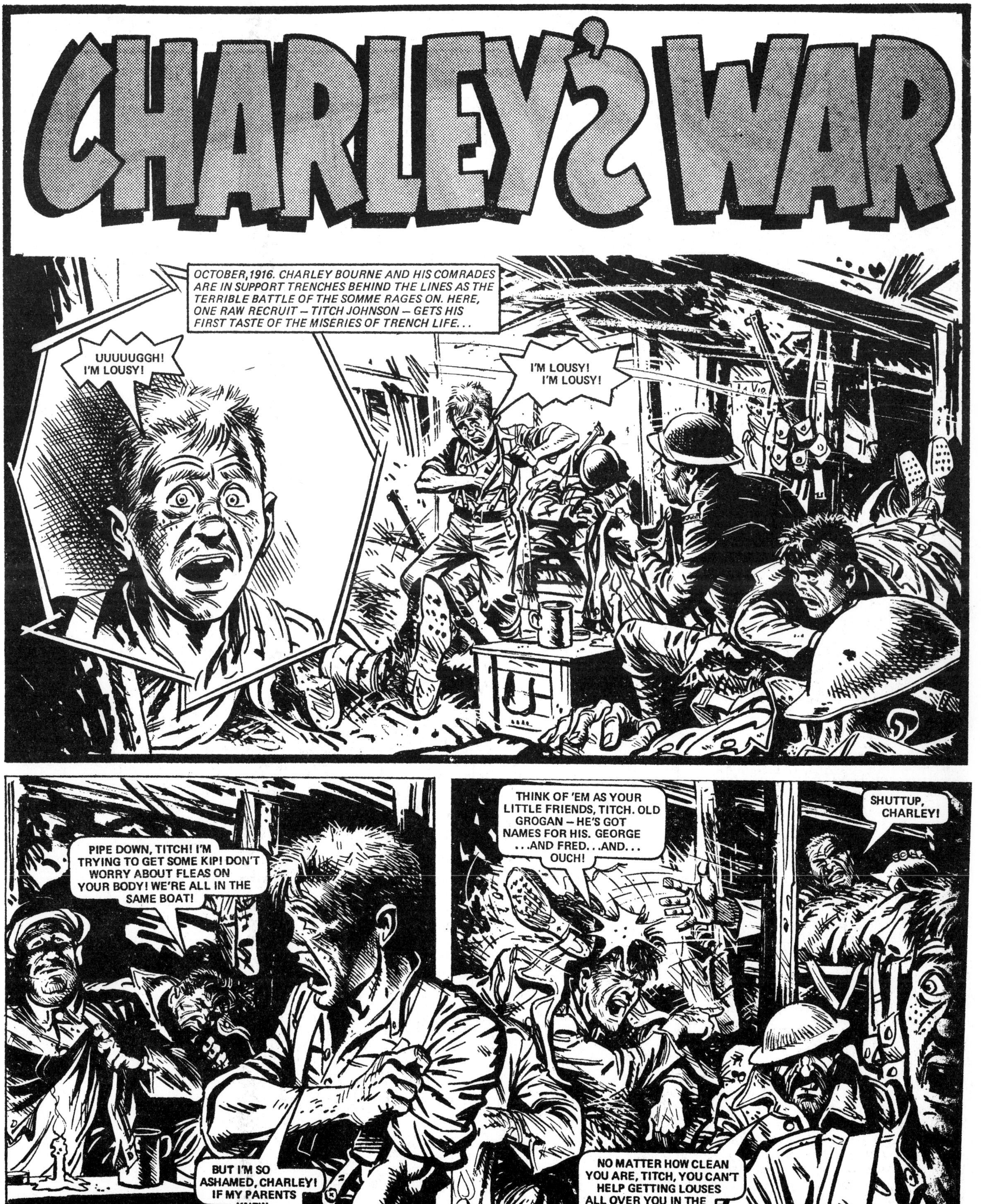
CHARLEY'S WAR
OCTOBER, 1916. CHARLEY BOURNE AND HIS COMRADES ARE IN SUPPORT TRENCHES BEHIND THE LINES AS THE TERRIBLE BATTLE OF THE SOMME RAGES ON. HERE, ONE RAW RECRUIT – TITCH JOHNSON – GETS HIS FIRST TASTE OF THE MISERIES OF TRENCH LIFE...
UUUUUGGH! I'M LOUSY!
I'M LOUSY! I'M LOUSY!
PIPE DOWN, TITCH! I'M TRYING TO GET SOME KIP! DON'T WORRY ABOUT FLEAS ON YOUR BODY! WE'RE ALL IN THE SAME BOAT!
BUT I'M SO ASHAMED, CHARLEY! IF MY PARENTS KNEW...
THINK OF 'EM AS YOUR LITTLE FRIENDS, TITCH. OLD GROGAN – HE'S GOT NAMES FOR HIS. GEORGE ...AND FRED...AND... OUCH!
SHUTTUP, CHARLEY!
NO MATTER HOW CLEAN YOU ARE, TITCH, YOU CAN'T HELP GETTING LOUSES ALL OVER YOU IN THE TRENCHES! NASTY LITTLE INSECTS!

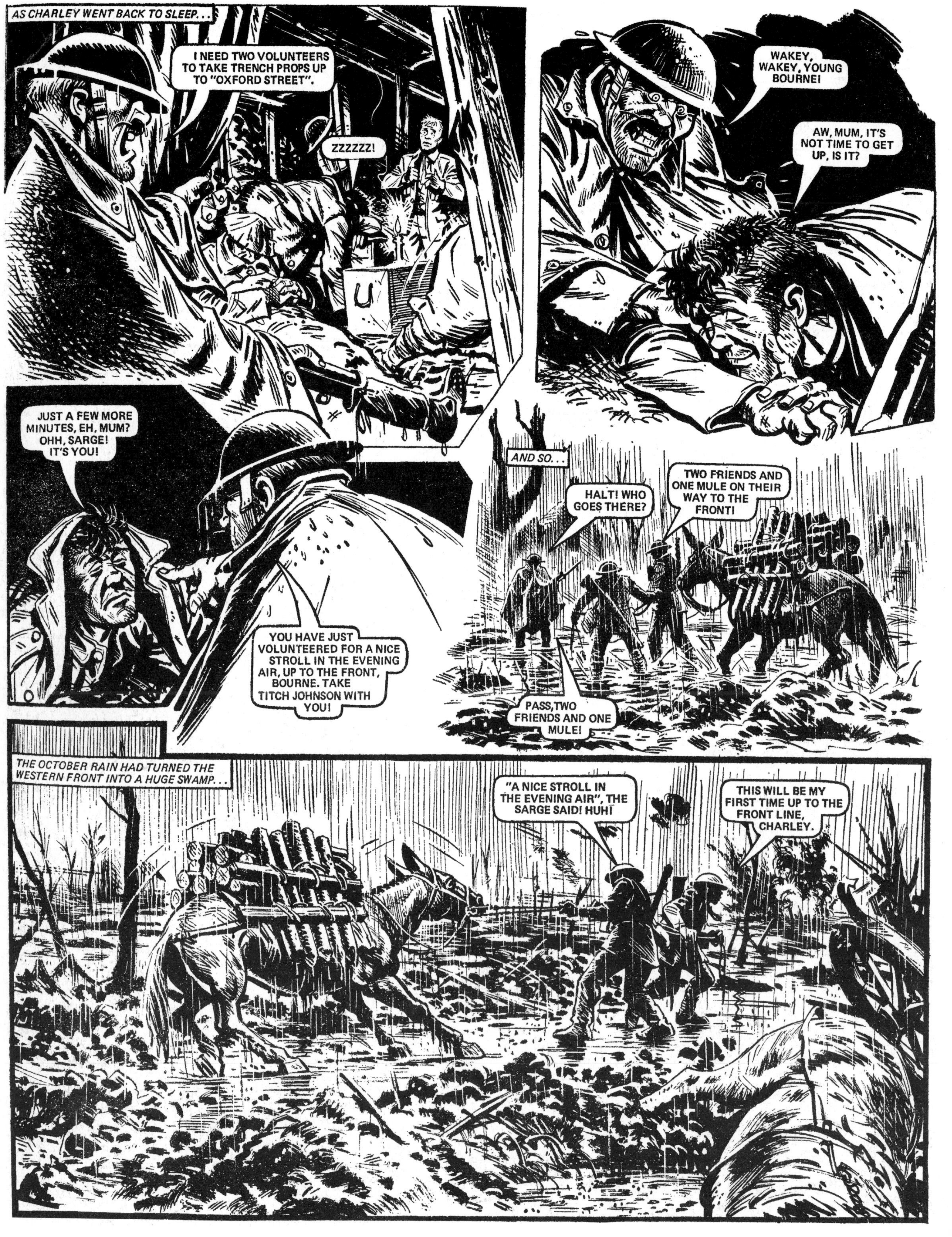

AS CHARLEY WENT BACK TO SLEEP...
I NEED TWO VOLUNTEERS TO TAKE TRENCH PROPS UP TO "OXFORD STREET".
ZZZZZZ!
WAKEY, WAKEY, YOUNG BOURNE!
AW, MUM, IT'S NOT TIME TO GET UP, IS IT?
JUST A FEW MORE MINUTES, EH, MUM? OHH, SARGE! IT'S YOU!
YOU HAVE JUST VOLUNTEERED FOR A NICE STROLL IN THE EVENING AIR, UP TO THE FRONT, BOURNE. TAKE TITCH JOHNSON WITH YOU!
AND SO...
HALT! WHO GOES THERE?
TWO FRIENDS AND ONE MULE ON THEIR WAY TO THE FRONT!
PASS, TWO FRIENDS AND ONE MULE!
THE OCTOBER RAIN HAD TURNED THE WESTERN FRONT INTO A HUGE SWAMP...
"A NICE STROLL IN THE EVENING AIR", THE SARGE SAID! HUH!
THIS WILL BE MY FIRST TIME UP TO THE FRONT LINE, CHARLEY.

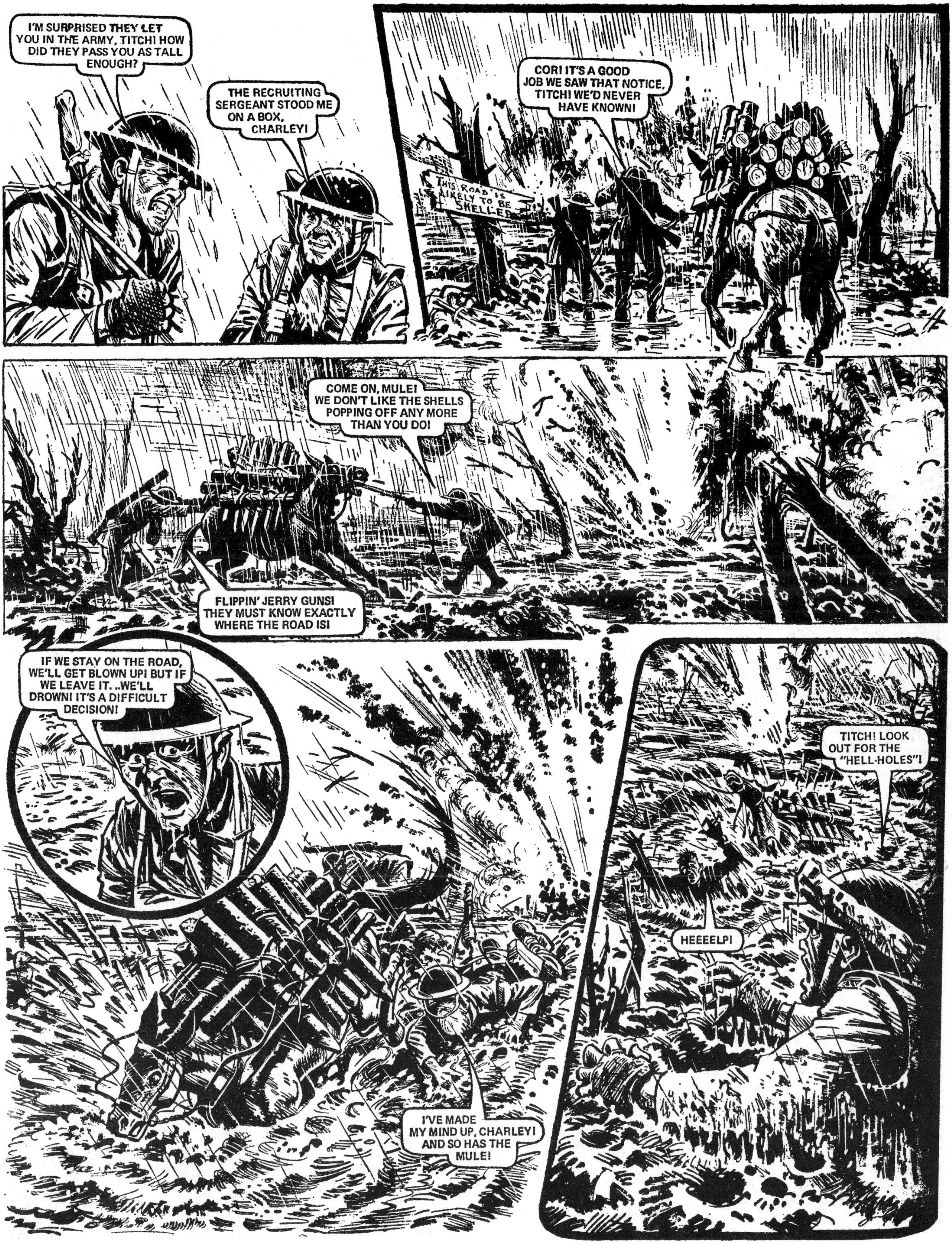
I'M SURPRISED THEY LET YOU IN THE ARMY, TITCH! HOW DID THEY PASS YOU AS TALL ENOUGH?
THE RECRUITING SERGEANT STOOD ME ON A BOX, CHARLEY!
THIS ROAD IS LIKELY TO BE SHELLED
COR! IT'S A GOOD JOB WE SAW THAT NOTICE, TITCH! WE'D NEVER HAVE KNOWN!
COME ON, MULE! WE DON'T LIKE THE SHELLS POPPING OFF ANY MORE THAN YOU DO!
FLIPPIN' JERRY GUNS! THEY MUST KNOW EXACTLY WHERE THE ROAD IS!
IF WE STAY ON THE ROAD, WE'LL GET BLOWN UP! BUT IF WE LEAVE IT. ..WE'LL DROWN! IT'S A DIFFICULT DECISION!
I'VE MADE MY MIND UP, CHARLEY! AND SO HAS THE MULE!
TITCH! LOOK OUT FOR THE "HELL-HOLES"!
HEEEELP!

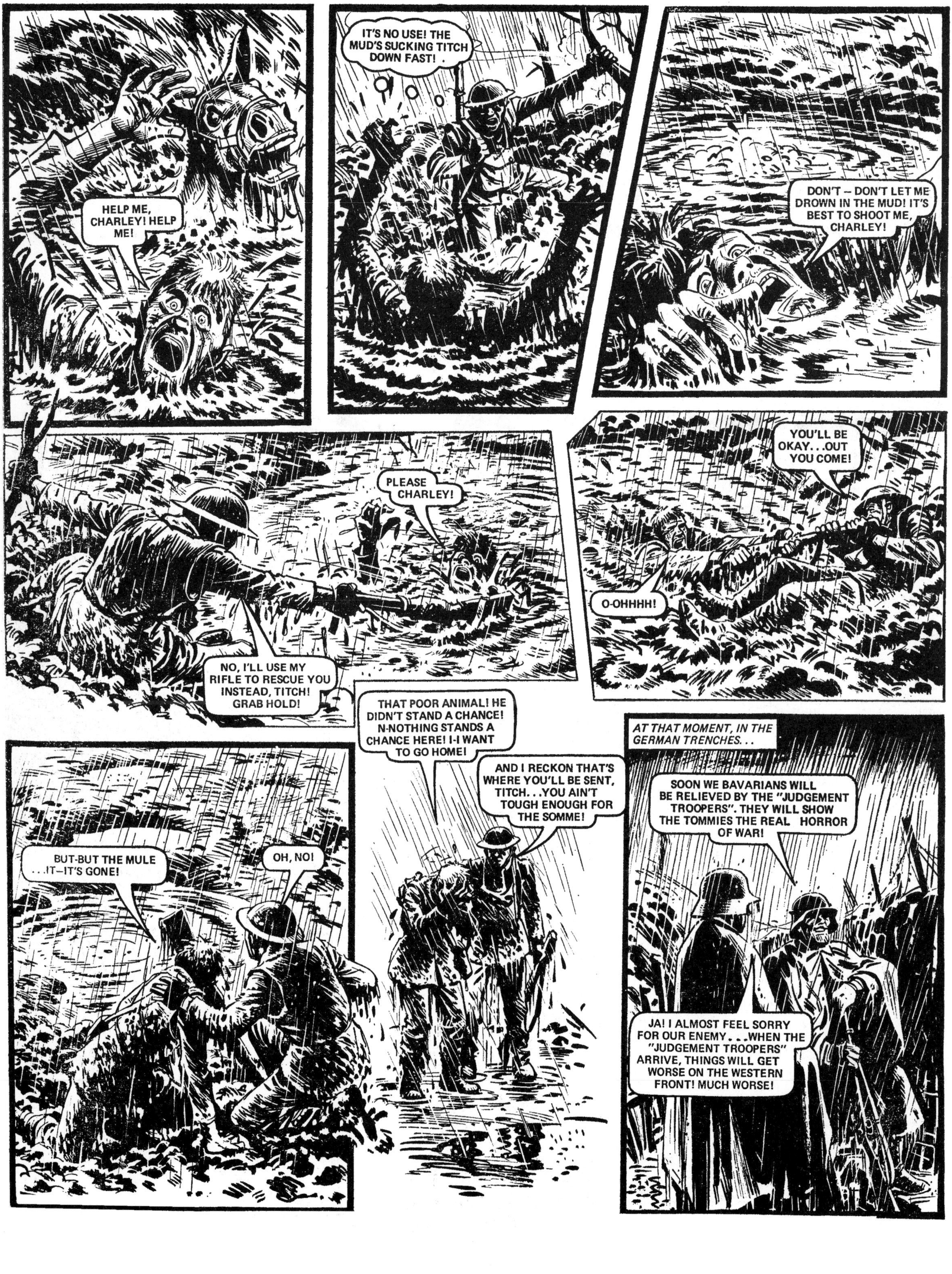
HELP ME, CHARLEY! HELP ME!
IT'S NO USE! THE MUD'S SUCKING TITCH DOWN FAST!
DON'T – DON'T LET ME DROWN IN THE MUD! IT'S BEST TO SHOOT ME, CHARLEY!
PLEASE CHARLEY!
NO, I'LL USE MY RIFLE TO RESCUE YOU INSTEAD, TITCH! GRAB HOLD!
YOU'LL BE OKAY. . .OUT YOU COME!
O-OHHHH!
. . .BUT-BUT THE MULE . . .IT–IT'S GONE!
OH, NO!
THAT POOR ANIMAL! HE DIDN'T STAND A CHANCE! N-NOTHING STANDS A CHANCE HERE! I-I WANT TO GO HOME!
AND I RECKON THAT'S WHERE YOU'LL BE SENT, TITCH. . .YOU AIN'T TOUGH ENOUGH FOR THE SOMME!
AT THAT MOMENT, IN THE GERMAN TRENCHES. . .
SOON WE BAVARIANS WILL BE RELIEVED BY THE "JUDGEMENT TROOPERS". THEY WILL SHOW THE TOMMIES THE REAL HORROR OF WAR!
JA! I ALMOST FEEL SORRY FOR OUR ENEMY. . .WHEN THE "JUDGEMENT TROOPERS" ARRIVE, THINGS WILL GET WORSE ON THE WESTERN FRONT! MUCH WORSE!

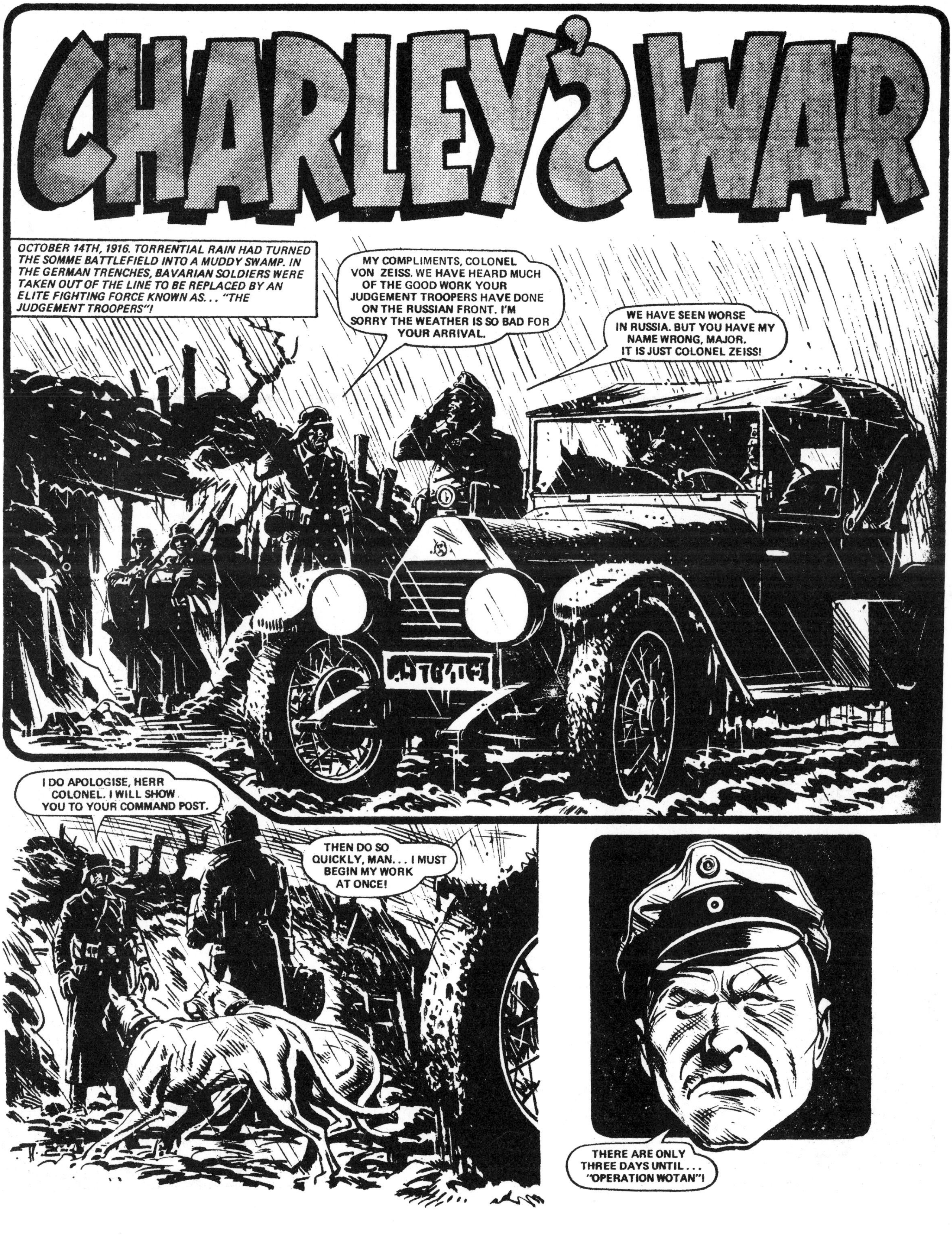
CHARLEY'S WAR
OCTOBER 14TH, 1916. TORRENTIAL RAIN HAD TURNED THE SOMME BATTLEFIELD INTO A MUDDY SWAMP. IN THE GERMAN TRENCHES, BAVARIAN SOLDIERS WERE TAKEN OUT OF THE LINE TO BE REPLACED BY AN ELITE FIGHTING FORCE KNOWN AS. . . "THE JUDGEMENT TROOPERS"!
MY COMPLIMENTS, COLONEL VON ZEISS. WE HAVE HEARD MUCH OF THE GOOD WORK YOUR JUDGEMENT TROOPERS HAVE DONE ON THE RUSSIAN FRONT. I'M SORRY THE WEATHER IS SO BAD FOR YOUR ARRIVAL.
WE HAVE SEEN WORSE IN RUSSIA. BUT YOU HAVE MY NAME WRONG, MAJOR. IT IS JUST COLONEL ZEISS!
I DO APOLOGISE, HERR COLONEL. I WILL SHOW YOU TO YOUR COMMAND POST.
THEN DO SO QUICKLY, MAN. . . I MUST BEGIN MY WORK AT ONCE!
THERE ARE ONLY THREE DAYS UNTIL . . . "OPERATION WOTAN"!

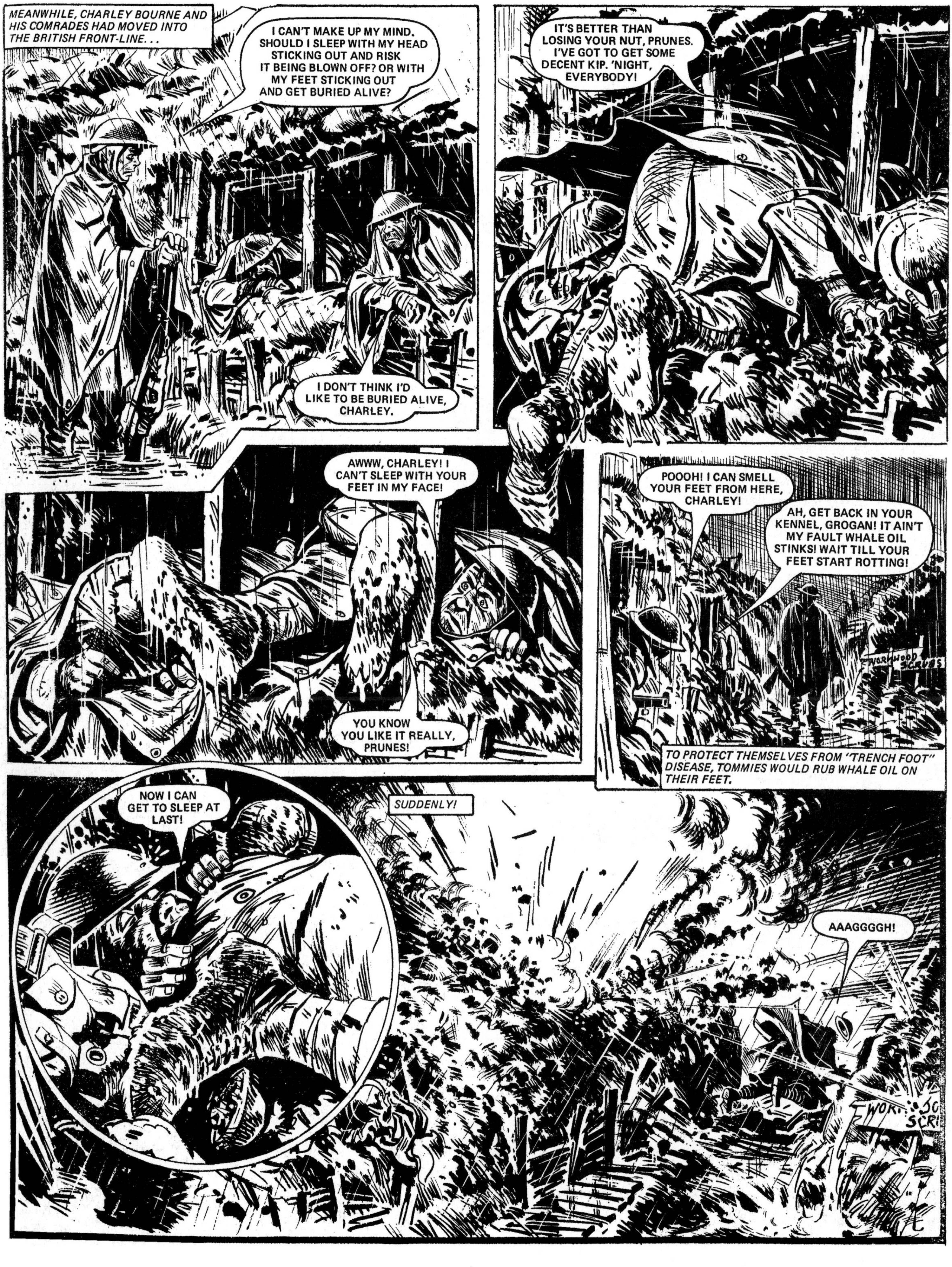
MEANWHILE, CHARLEY BOURNE AND HIS COMRADES HAD MOVED INTO THE BRITISH FRONT-LINE. . .
I CAN'T MAKE UP MY MIND. SHOULD I SLEEP WITH MY HEAD STICKING OUT AND RISK IT BEING BLOWN OFF? OR WITH MY FEET STICKING OUT AND GET BURIED ALIVE?
I DON'T THINK I'D LIKE TO BE BURIED ALIVE, CHARLEY.
IT'S BETTER THAN LOSING YOUR NUT, PRUNES. I'VE GOT TO GET SOME DECENT KIP. 'NIGHT, EVERYBODY!
AWWW, CHARLEY! I CAN'T SLEEP WITH YOUR FEET IN MY FACE!
YOU KNOW YOU LIKE IT REALLY, PRUNES!
POOOH! I CAN SMELL YOUR FEET FROM HERE, CHARLEY!
AH, GET BACK IN YOUR KENNEL, GROGAN! IT AIN'T MY FAULT WHALE OIL STINKS! WAIT TILL YOUR FEET START ROTTING!
TO PROTECT THEMSELVES FROM "TRENCH FOOT" DISEASE, TOMMIES WOULD RUB WHALE OIL ON THEIR FEET.
NOW I CAN GET TO SLEEP AT LAST!
SUDDENLY!
AAAGGGGH!

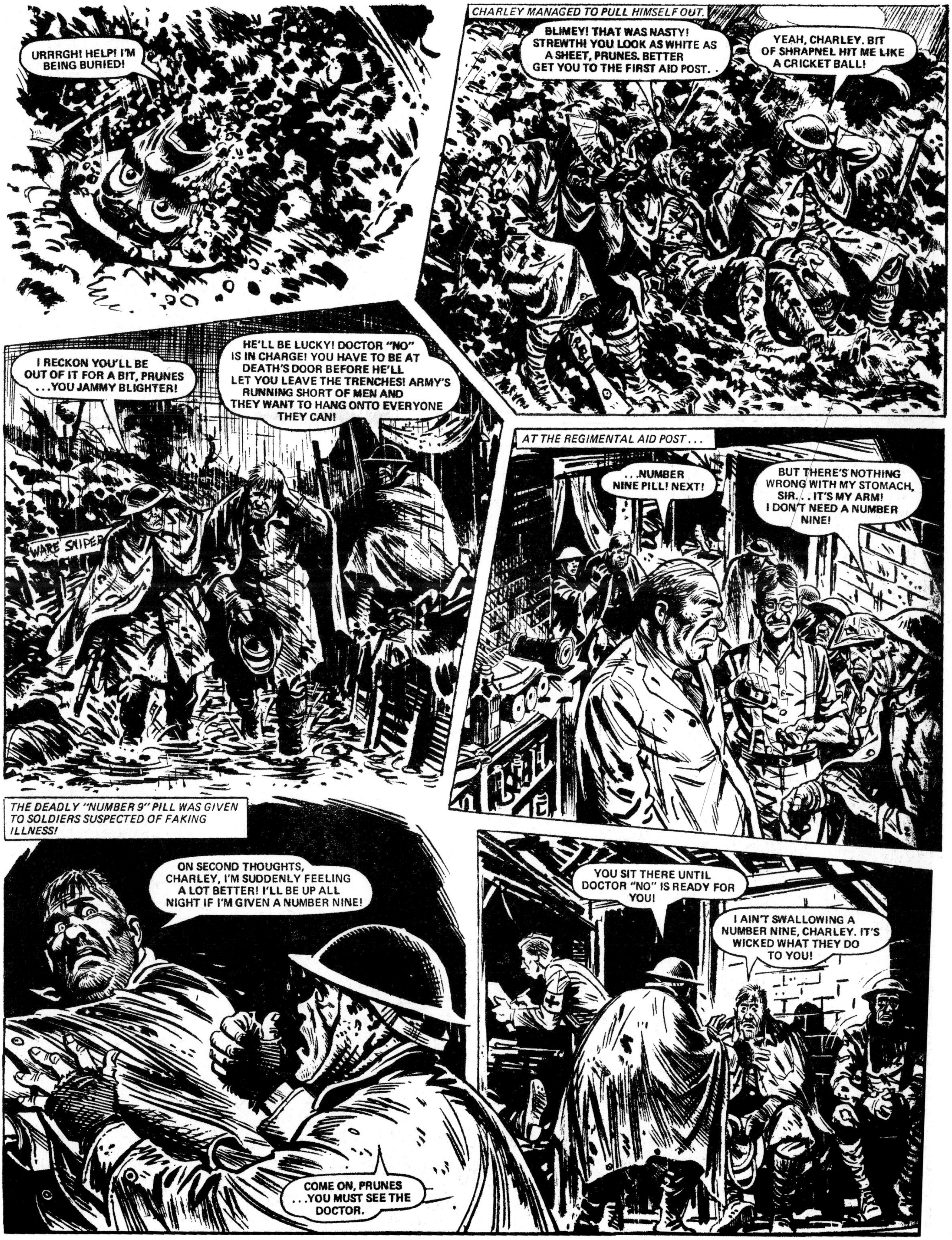
URRRGH! HELP! I'M BEING BURIED!
CHARLEY MANAGED TO PULL HIMSELF OUT.
BLIMEY! THAT WAS NASTY! STREWTH! YOU LOOK AS WHITE AS A SHEET, PRUNES. BETTER GET YOU TO THE FIRST AID POST. .
YEAH, CHARLEY. BIT OF SHRAPNEL HIT ME LIKE A CRICKET BALL!
I RECKON YOU'LL BE OUT OF IT FOR A BIT, PRUNES . . . YOU JAMMY BLIGHTER!
HE'LL BE LUCKY! DOCTOR "NO" IS IN CHARGE! YOU HAVE TO BE AT DEATH'S DOOR BEFORE HE'LL LET YOU LEAVE THE TRENCHES! ARMY'S RUNNING SHORT OF MEN AND THEY WANT TO HANG ONTO EVERYONE THEY CAN!
'WARE SNIPER
AT THE REGIMENTAL AID POST . . .
. . .NUMBER NINE PILL! NEXT!
BUT THERE'S NOTHING WRONG WITH MY STOMACH, SIR. . . IT'S MY ARM! I DON'T NEED A NUMBER NINE!
THE DEADLY "NUMBER 9" PILL WAS GIVEN TO SOLDIERS SUSPECTED OF FAKING ILLNESS!
ON SECOND THOUGHTS, CHARLEY, I'M SUDDENLY FEELING A LOT BETTER! I'LL BE UP ALL NIGHT IF I'M GIVEN A NUMBER NINE!
COME ON, PRUNES . . .YOU MUST SEE THE DOCTOR.
YOU SIT THERE UNTIL DOCTOR "NO" IS READY FOR YOU!
I AIN'T SWALLOWING A NUMBER NINE, CHARLEY. IT'S WICKED WHAT THEY DO TO YOU!

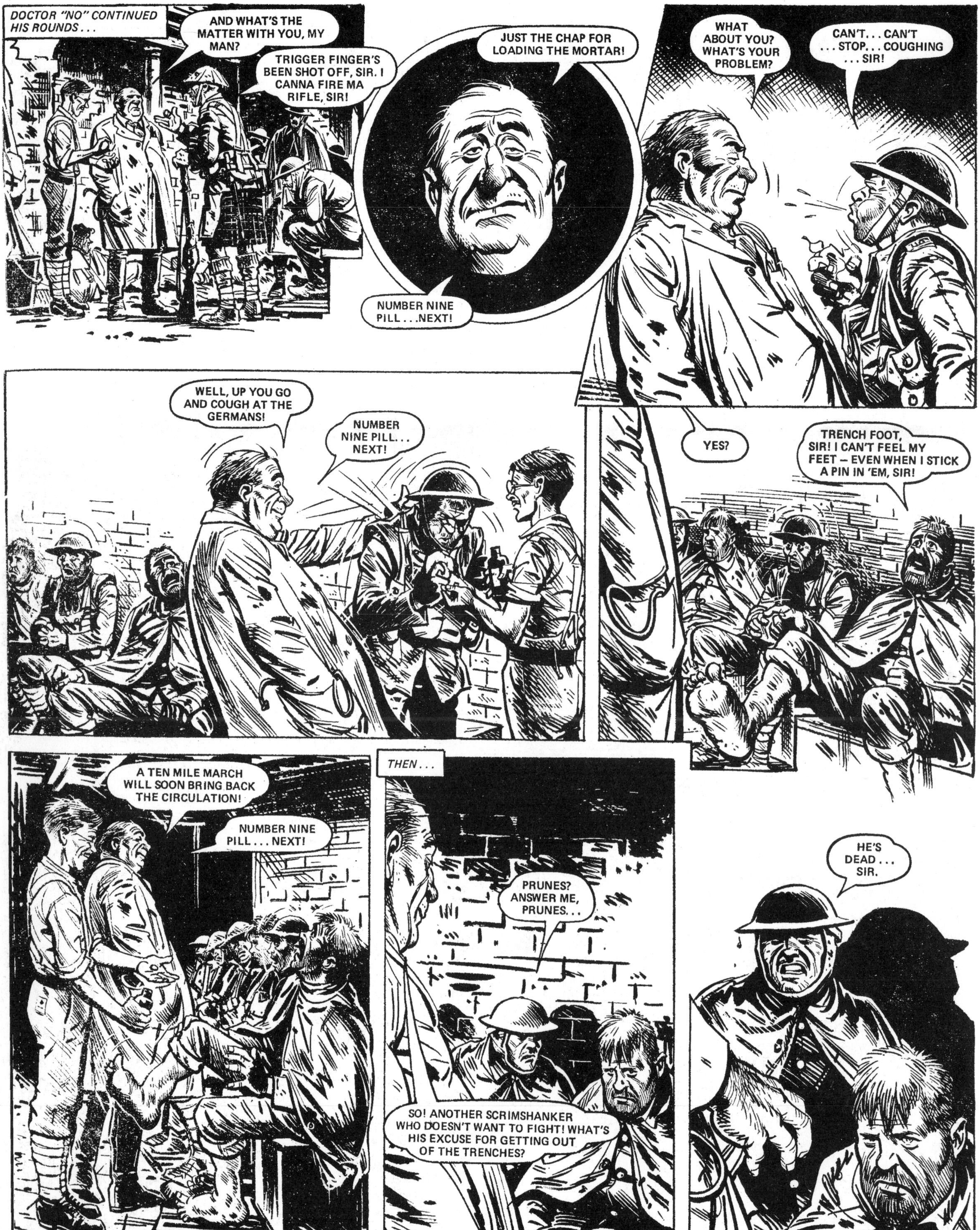
DOCTOR "NO" CONTINUED HIS ROUNDS . . .
AND WHAT'S THE MATTER WITH YOU, MY MAN?
TRIGGER FINGER'S BEEN SHOT OFF, SIR. I CANNA FIRE MA RIFLE, SIR!
JUST THE CHAP FOR LOADING THE MORTAR!
NUMBER NINE PILL . . .NEXT!
WHAT ABOUT YOU? WHAT'S YOUR PROBLEM?
CAN'T. . . CAN'T . . . STOP. . . COUGHING . . . SIR!
WELL, UP YOU GO AND COUGH AT THE GERMANS!
NUMBER NINE PILL. . . NEXT!
YES?
TRENCH FOOT, SIR! I CAN'T FEEL MY FEET – EVEN WHEN I STICK A PIN IN 'EM, SIR!
A TEN MILE MARCH WILL SOON BRING BACK THE CIRCULATION!
NUMBER NINE PILL . . . NEXT!
THEN . . .
SO! ANOTHER SCRIMSHANKER WHO DOESN'T WANT TO FIGHT! WHAT'S HIS EXCUSE FOR GETTING OUT OF THE TRENCHES?
PRUNES? ANSWER ME, PRUNES. . .
HE'S DEAD . . . SIR.

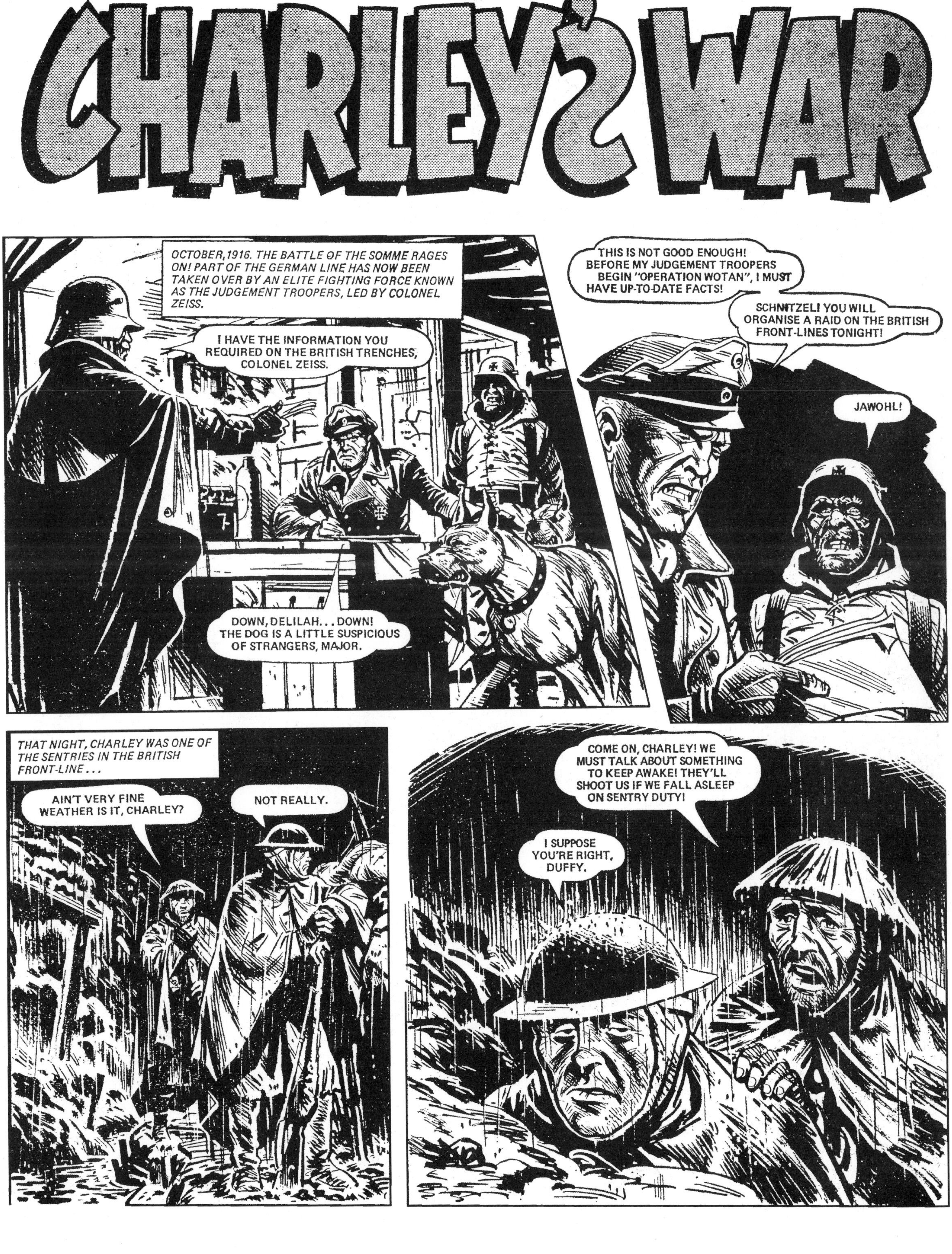
CHARLEY'S WAR
OCTOBER, 1916. THE BATTLE OF THE SOMME RAGES ON! PART OF THE GERMAN LINE HAS NOW BEEN TAKEN OVER BY AN ELITE FIGHTING FORCE KNOWN AS THE JUDGEMENT TROOPERS, LED BY COLONEL ZEISS.
I HAVE THE INFORMATION YOU REQUIRED ON THE BRITISH TRENCHES, COLONEL ZEISS.
DOWN, DELILAH... DOWN! THE DOG IS A LITTLE SUSPICIOUS OF STRANGERS, MAJOR.
THIS IS NOT GOOD ENOUGH! BEFORE MY JUDGEMENT TROOPERS BEGIN "OPERATION WOTAN", I MUST HAVE UP-TO-DATE FACTS!
SCHNITZEL! YOU WILL ORGANISE A RAID ON THE BRITISH FRONT-LINES TONIGHT!
JAWOHL!
THAT NIGHT, CHARLEY WAS ONE OF THE SENTRIES IN THE BRITISH FRONT-LINE...
AIN'T VERY FINE WEATHER IS IT, CHARLEY?
NOT REALLY.
COME ON, CHARLEY! WE MUST TALK ABOUT SOMETHING TO KEEP AWAKE! THEY'LL SHOOT US IF WE FALL ASLEEP ON SENTRY DUTY!
I SUPPOSE YOU'RE RIGHT, DUFFY.

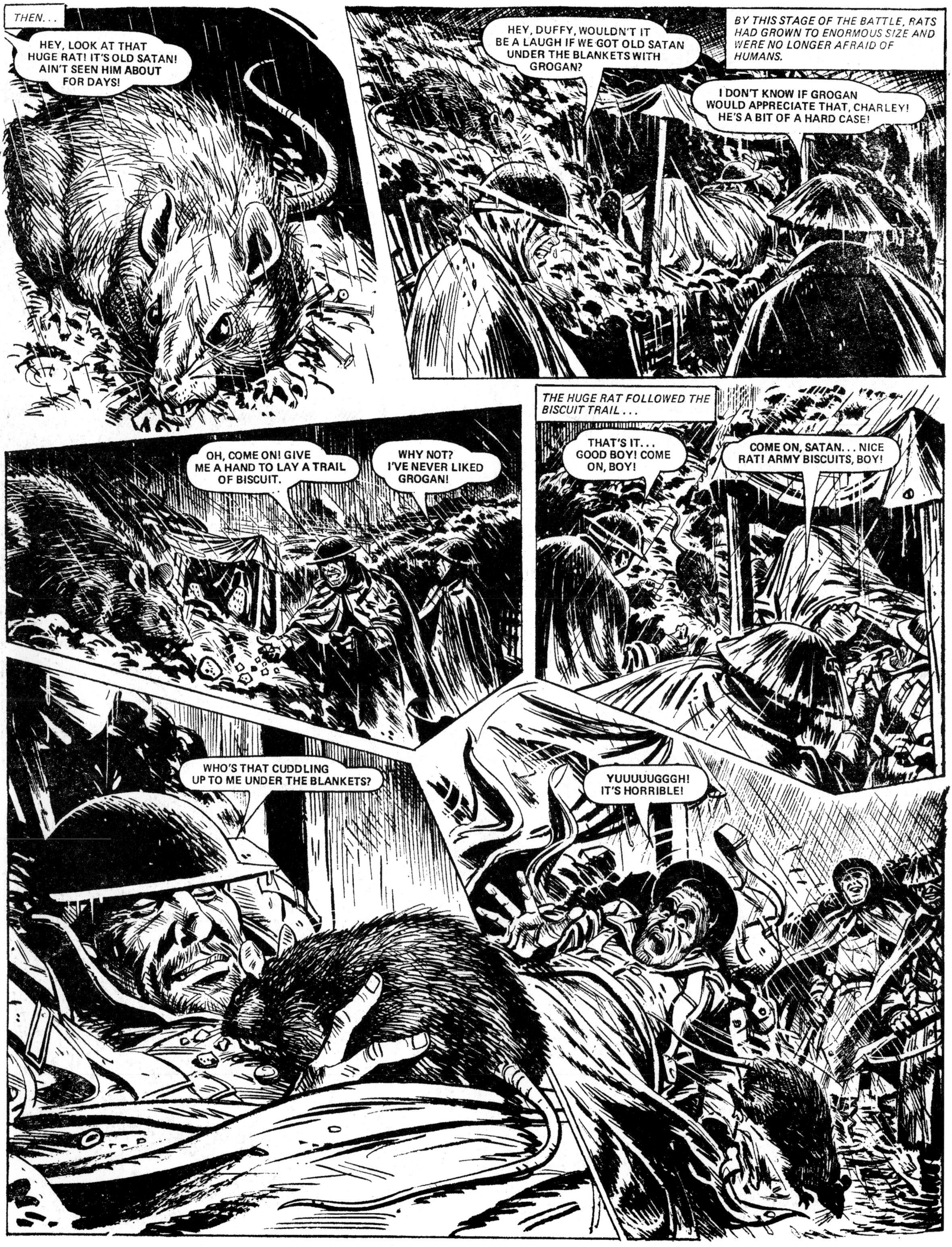
THEN. . .
HEY, LOOK AT THAT HUGE RAT! IT'S OLD SATAN! AIN'T SEEN HIM ABOUT FOR DAYS!
BY THIS STAGE OF THE BATTLE, RATS HAD GROWN TO ENORMOUS SIZE AND WERE NO LONGER AFRAID OF HUMANS.
HEY, DUFFY, WOULDN'T IT BE A LAUGH IF WE GOT OLD SATAN UNDER THE BLANKETS WITH GROGAN?
I DON'T KNOW IF GROGAN WOULD APPRECIATE THAT, CHARLEY! HE'S A BIT OF A HARD CASE!
OH, COME ON! GIVE ME A HAND TO LAY A TRAIL OF BISCUIT.
WHY NOT? I'VE NEVER LIKED GROGAN!
THE HUGE RAT FOLLOWED THE BISCUIT TRAIL . . .
THAT'S IT. . . GOOD BOY! COME ON, BOY!
COME ON, SATAN. . . NICE RAT! ARMY BISCUITS, BOY!
WHO'S THAT CUDDLING UP TO ME UNDER THE BLANKETS?
YUUUUUGGGH! IT'S HORRIBLE!

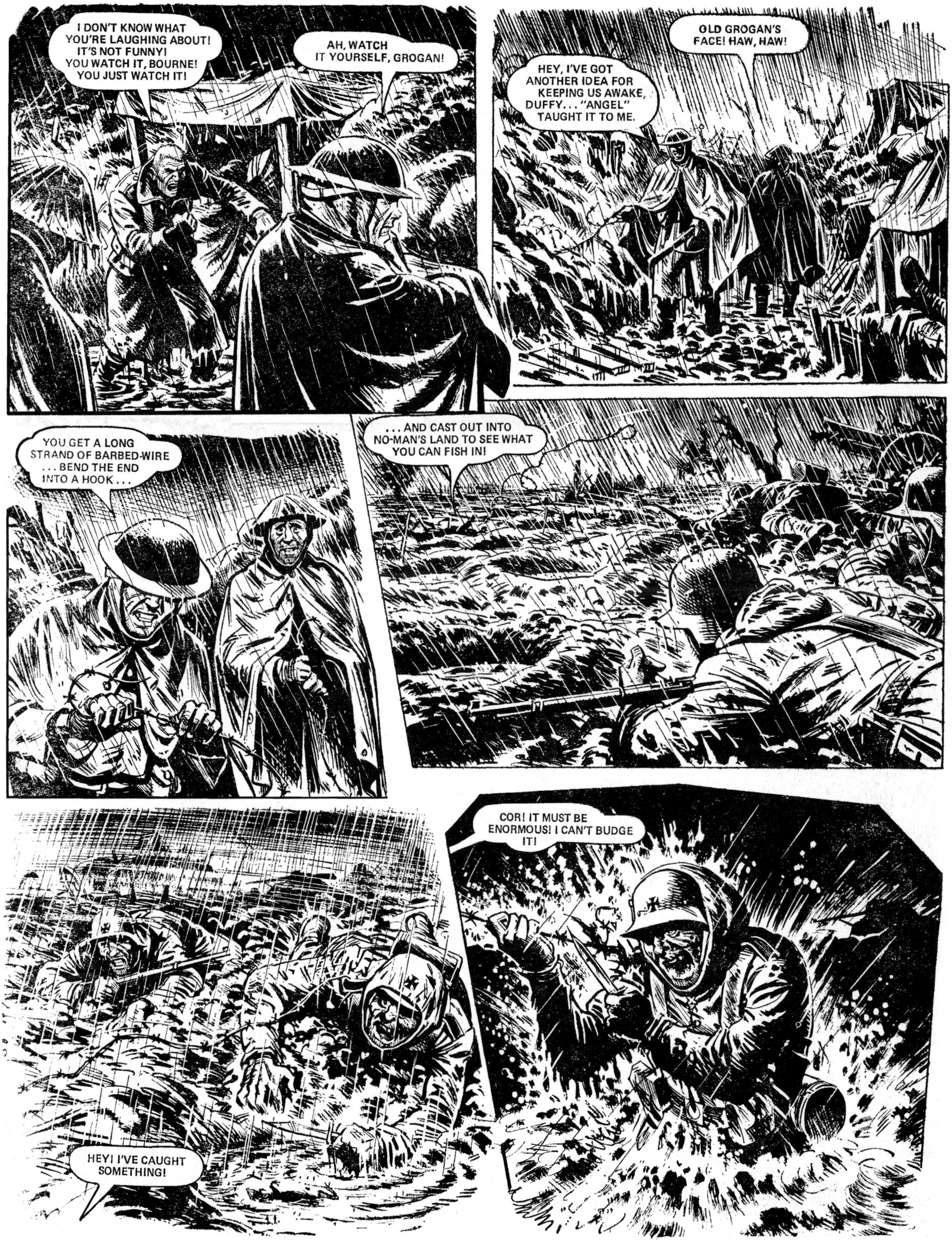
I DON'T KNOW WHAT YOU'RE LAUGHING ABOUT! IT'S NOT FUNNY! YOU WATCH IT, BOURNE! YOU JUST WATCH IT!
AH, WATCH IT YOURSELF, GROGAN!
OLD GROGAN'S FACE! HAW, HAW!
HEY, I'VE GOT ANOTHER IDEA FOR KEEPING US AWAKE, DUFFY... "ANGEL" TAUGHT IT TO ME.
YOU GET A LONG STRAND OF BARBED-WIRE ... BEND THE END INTO A HOOK ...
... AND CAST OUT INTO NO-MAN'S LAND TO SEE WHAT YOU CAN FISH IN!
HEY! I'VE CAUGHT SOMETHING!
COR! IT MUST BE ENORMOUS! I CAN'T BUDGE IT!

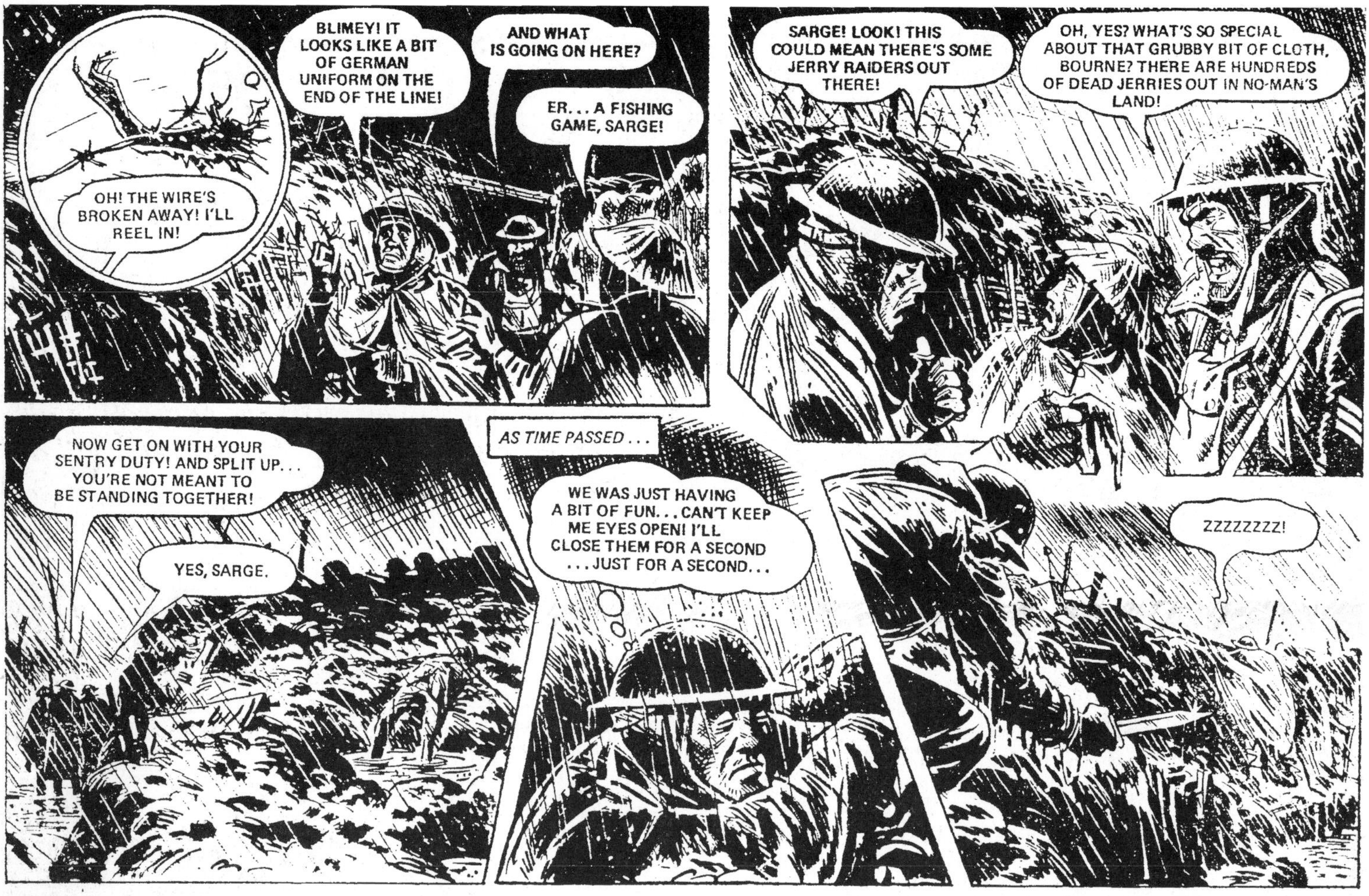
OH! THE WIRE'S BROKEN AWAY! I'LL REEL IN!
BLIMEY! IT LOOKS LIKE A BIT OF GERMAN UNIFORM ON THE END OF THE LINE!
AND WHAT IS GOING ON HERE?
ER. . . A FISHING GAME, SARGE!
SARGE! LOOK! THIS COULD MEAN THERE'S SOME JERRY RAIDERS OUT THERE!
OH, YES? WHAT'S SO SPECIAL ABOUT THAT GRUBBY BIT OF CLOTH, BOURNE? THERE ARE HUNDREDS OF DEAD JERRIES OUT IN NO-MAN'S LAND!
NOW GET ON WITH YOUR SENTRY DUTY! AND SPLIT UP. . . YOU'RE NOT MEANT TO BE STANDING TOGETHER!
YES, SARGE.
AS TIME PASSED . . .
WE WAS JUST HAVING A BIT OF FUN. . . CAN'T KEEP ME EYES OPEN! I'LL CLOSE THEM FOR A SECOND . . . JUST FOR A SECOND . . .
ZZZZZZZZ!

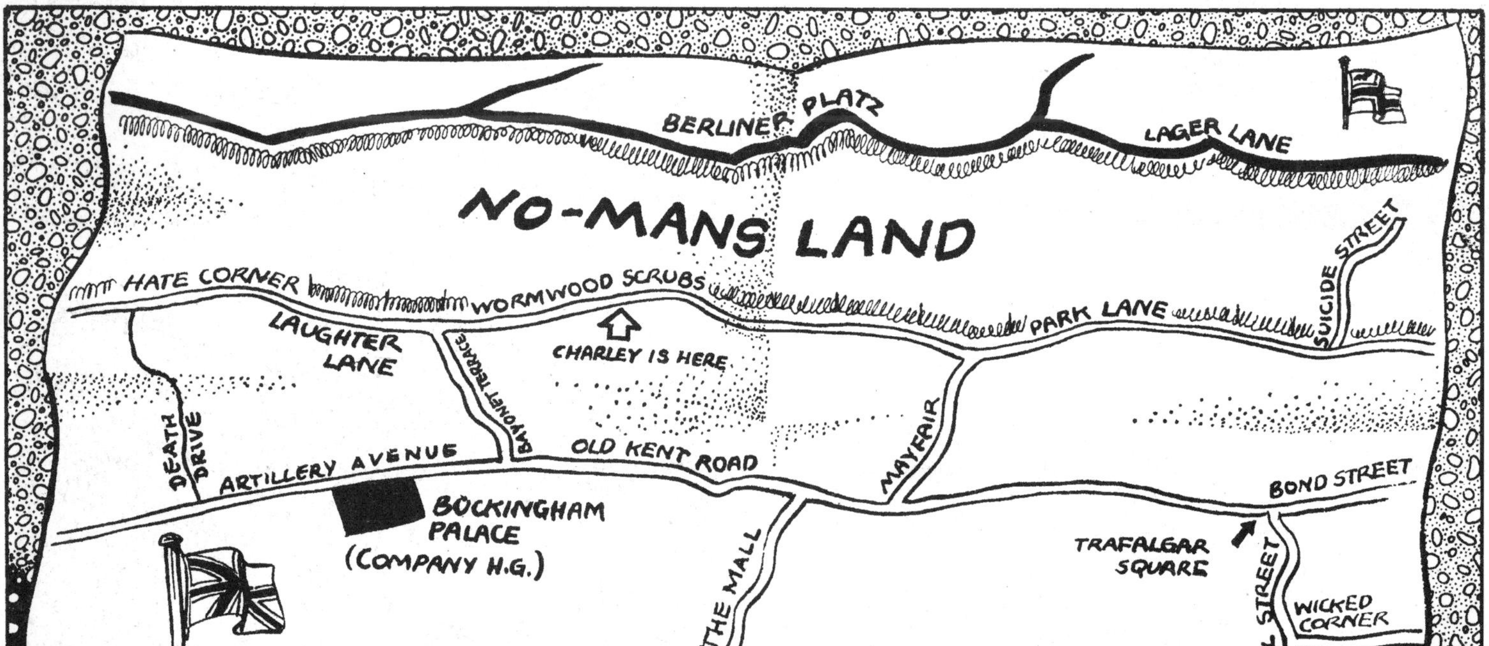
BERLINER PLATZ
LAGER LANE
NO-MANS LAND
HATE CORNER
WORMWOOD SCRUBS
PARK LANE
SUICIDE STREET
LAUGHTER LANE
BAYONET TERRACE
CHARLEY IS HERE
DEATH DRIVE
ARTILLERY AVENUE
OLD KENT ROAD
MAYFAIR
BOND STREET
BUCKINGHAM PALACE
(COMPANY H.Q.)
TRAFALGAR SQUARE
THE MALL
STARSHELL STREET
WICKED CORNER
SAVOY HOTEL
SHRAPNEL VILLA
NUMBER 10
BULLY BEEF BOULEVARD
DOWNING STREET

IMPORTANT: So BATTLE-ACTION readers can follow the movements of British and German troops in the trench warfare of current episodes of "Charley's War", we have devised this map. It will help you to enjoy reading the story all the more. Cut out the map and keep it!

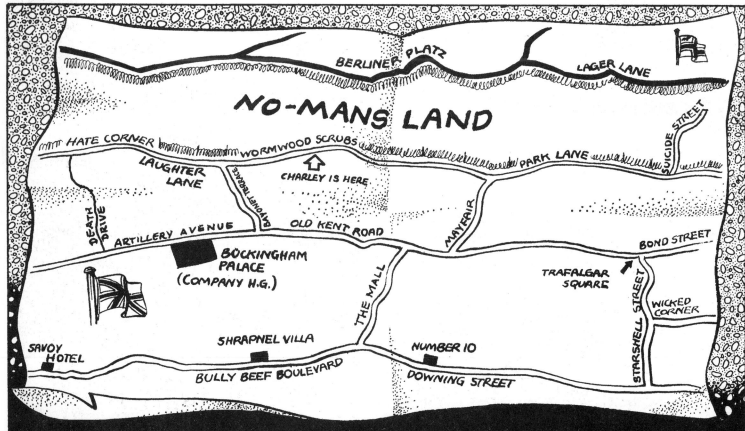

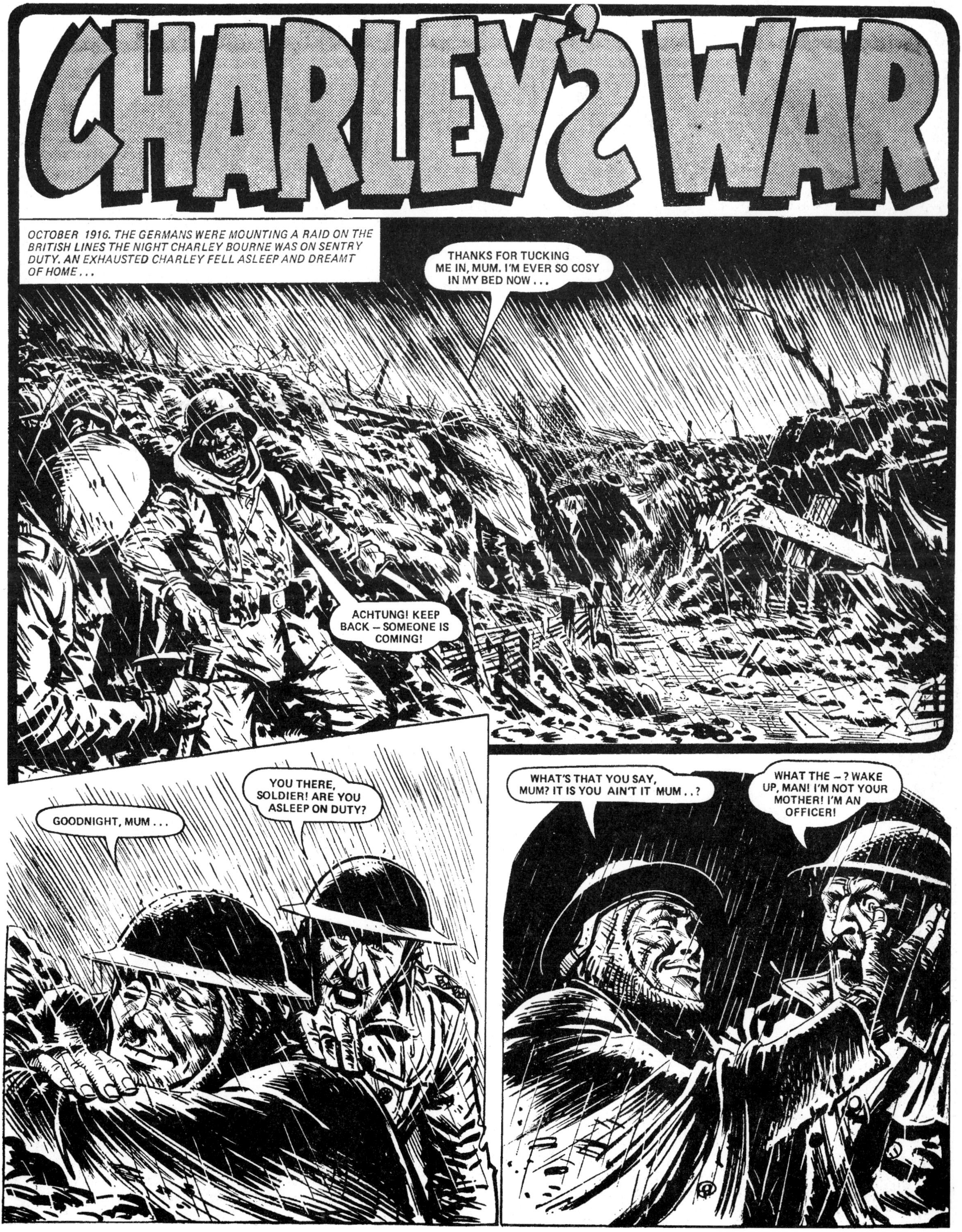
CHARLEY'S WAR
OCTOBER 1916. THE GERMANS WERE MOUNTING A RAID ON THE BRITISH LINES THE NIGHT CHARLEY BOURNE WAS ON SENTRY DUTY. AN EXHAUSTED CHARLEY FELL ASLEEP AND DREAMT OF HOME . . .
THANKS FOR TUCKING ME IN, MUM. I'M EVER SO COSY IN MY BED NOW . . .
ACHTUNG! KEEP BACK – SOMEONE IS COMING!
GOODNIGHT, MUM . . .
YOU THERE, SOLDIER! ARE YOU ASLEEP ON DUTY?
WHAT'S THAT YOU SAY, MUM? IT IS YOU AIN'T IT MUM . . ?
WHAT THE – ? WAKE UP, MAN! I'M NOT YOUR MOTHER! I'M AN OFFICER!

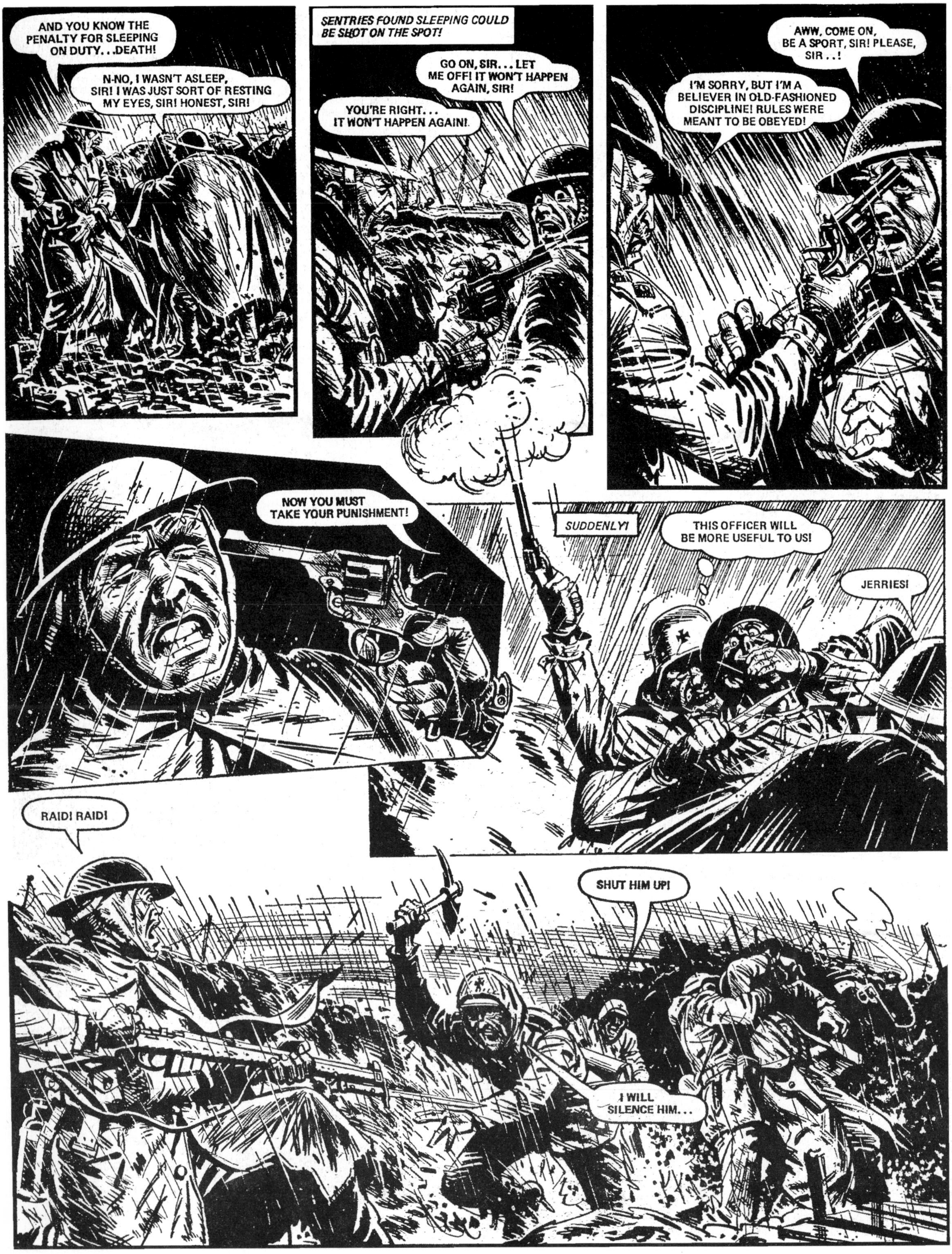
AND YOU KNOW THE PENALTY FOR SLEEPING ON DUTY. . .DEATH!
N-NO, I WASN'T ASLEEP, SIR! I WAS JUST SORT OF RESTING MY EYES, SIR! HONEST, SIR!
SENTRIES FOUND SLEEPING COULD BE SHOT ON THE SPOT!
GO ON, SIR. . . LET ME OFF! IT WON'T HAPPEN AGAIN, SIR!
YOU'RE RIGHT. . . IT WON'T HAPPEN AGAIN!
AWW, COME ON, BE A SPORT, SIR! PLEASE, SIR . .!
I'M SORRY, BUT I'M A BELIEVER IN OLD-FASHIONED DISCIPLINE! RULES WERE MEANT TO BE OBEYED!
NOW YOU MUST TAKE YOUR PUNISHMENT!
SUDDENLY!
THIS OFFICER WILL BE MORE USEFUL TO US!
JERRIES!
RAID! RAID!
SHUT HIM UP!
I WILL SILENCE HIM. . .

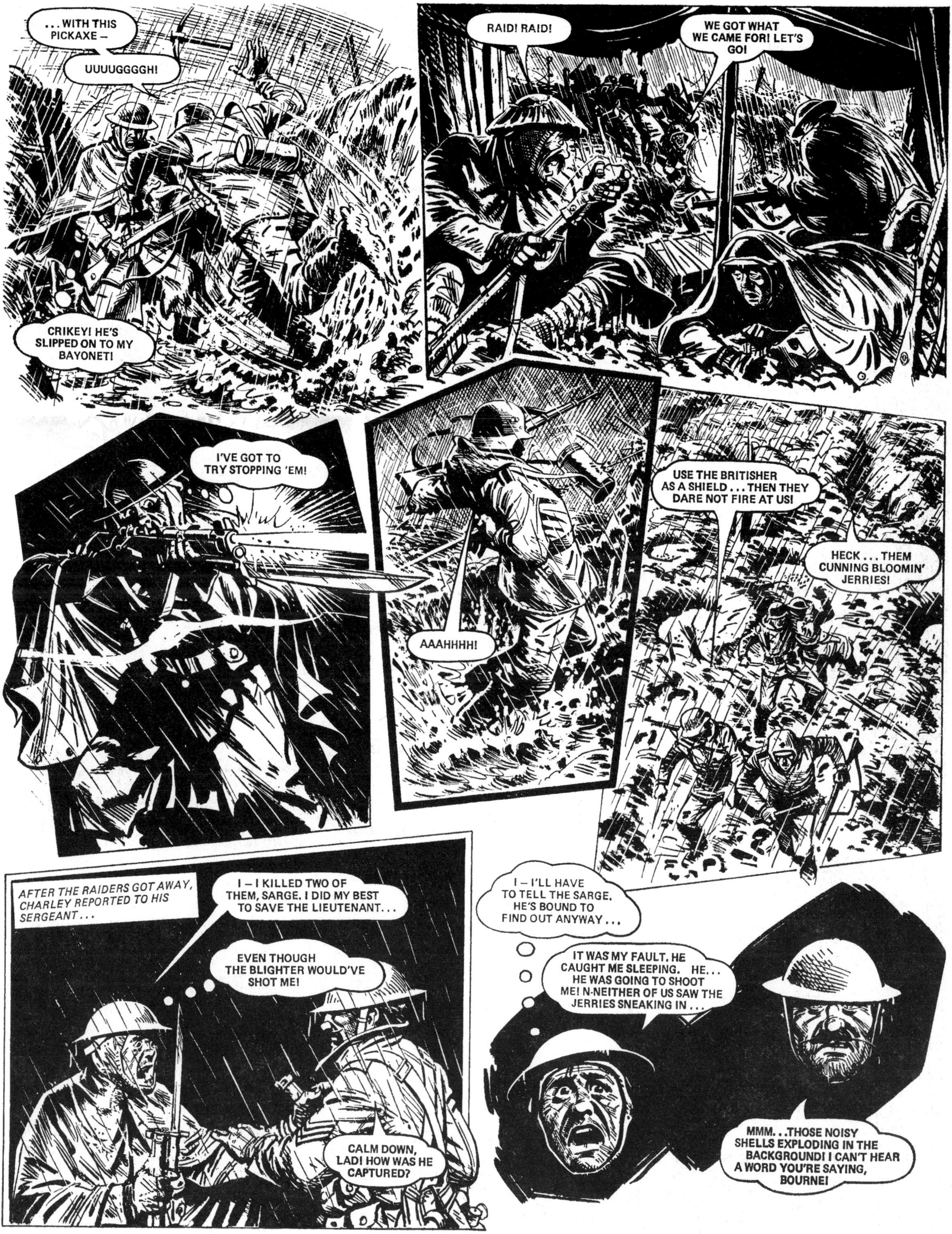
. . . WITH THIS PICKAXE –
UUUUGGGGH!
CRIKEY! HE'S SLIPPED ON TO MY BAYONET!
RAID! RAID!
WE GOT WHAT WE CAME FOR! LET'S GO!
I'VE GOT TO TRY STOPPING 'EM!
AAAHHHH!
USE THE BRITISHER AS A SHIELD . . . THEN THEY DARE NOT FIRE AT US!
HECK . . . THEM CUNNING BLOOMIN' JERRIES!
AFTER THE RAIDERS GOT AWAY, CHARLEY REPORTED TO HIS SERGEANT . . .
I – I KILLED TWO OF THEM, SARGE. I DID MY BEST TO SAVE THE LIEUTENANT . . .
EVEN THOUGH THE BLIGHTER WOULD'VE SHOT ME!
CALM DOWN, LAD! HOW WAS HE CAPTURED?
I – I'LL HAVE TO TELL THE SARGE. HE'S BOUND TO FIND OUT ANYWAY . . .
IT WAS MY FAULT. HE CAUGHT ME SLEEPING. HE . . . HE WAS GOING TO SHOOT ME! N-NEITHER OF US SAW THE JERRIES SNEAKING IN . . .
MMM. . .THOSE NOISY SHELLS EXPLODING IN THE BACKGROUND! I CAN'T HEAR A WORD YOU'RE SAYING, BOURNE!

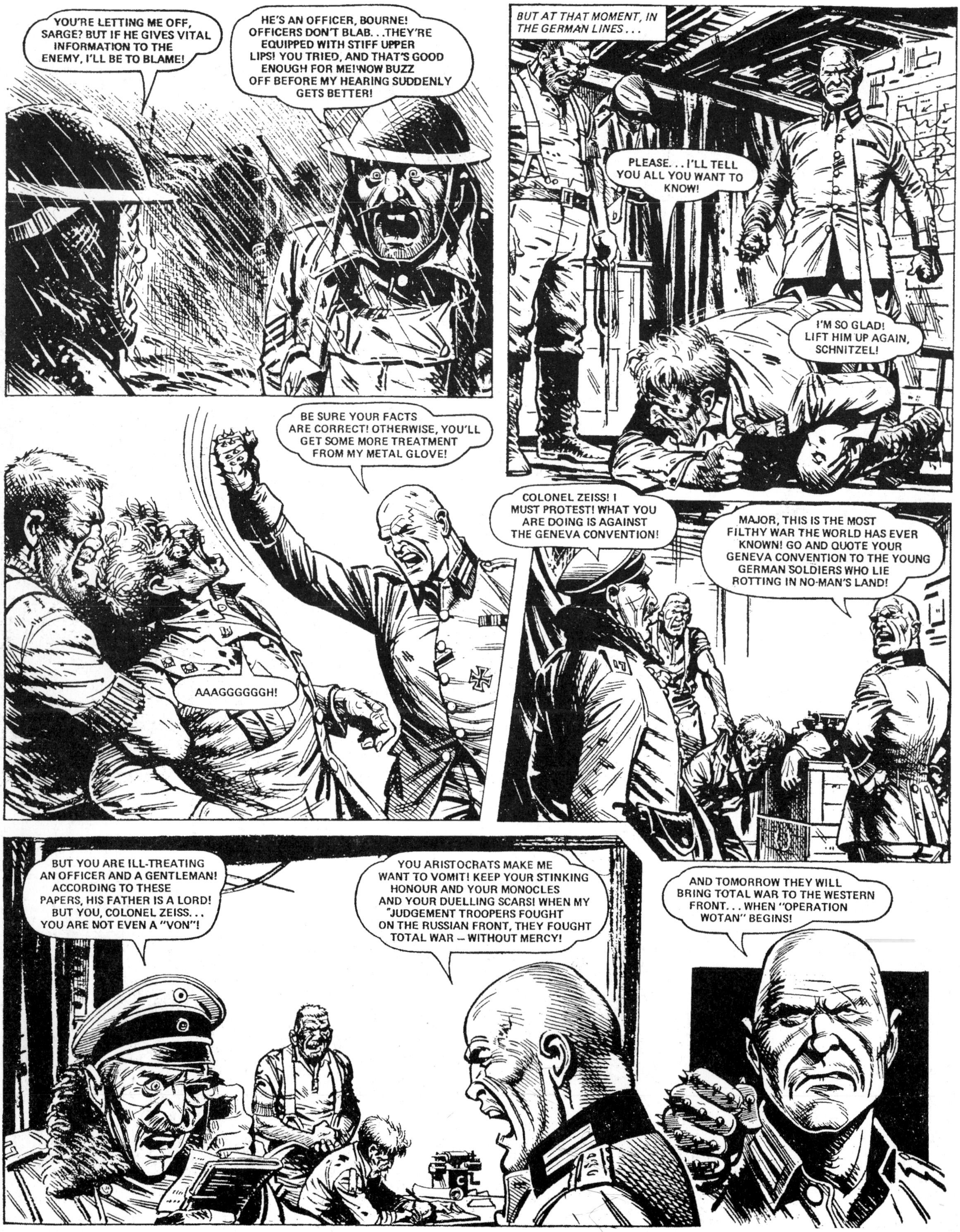
YOU'RE LETTING ME OFF, SARGE? BUT IF HE GIVES VITAL INFORMATION TO THE ENEMY, I'LL BE TO BLAME!
HE'S AN OFFICER, BOURNE! OFFICERS DON'T BLAB. . .THEY'RE EQUIPPED WITH STIFF UPPER LIPS! YOU TRIED, AND THAT'S GOOD ENOUGH FOR ME! NOW BUZZ OFF BEFORE MY HEARING SUDDENLY GETS BETTER!
BUT AT THAT MOMENT, IN THE GERMAN LINES . . .
PLEASE. . . I'LL TELL YOU ALL YOU WANT TO KNOW!
I'M SO GLAD! LIFT HIM UP AGAIN, SCHNITZEL!
BE SURE YOUR FACTS ARE CORRECT! OTHERWISE, YOU'LL GET SOME MORE TREATMENT FROM MY METAL GLOVE!
AAAGGGGGGH!
COLONEL ZEISS! I MUST PROTEST! WHAT YOU ARE DOING IS AGAINST THE GENEVA CONVENTION!
MAJOR, THIS IS THE MOST FILTHY WAR THE WORLD HAS EVER KNOWN! GO AND QUOTE YOUR GENEVA CONVENTION TO THE YOUNG GERMAN SOLDIERS WHO LIE ROTTING IN NO-MAN'S LAND!
BUT YOU ARE ILL-TREATING AN OFFICER AND A GENTLEMAN! ACCORDING TO THESE PAPERS, HIS FATHER IS A LORD! BUT YOU, COLONEL ZEISS. . . YOU ARE NOT EVEN A "VON"!
YOU ARISTOCRATS MAKE ME WANT TO VOMIT! KEEP YOUR STINKING HONOUR AND YOUR MONOCLES AND YOUR DUELLING SCARS! WHEN MY "JUDGEMENT TROOPERS FOUGHT ON THE RUSSIAN FRONT, THEY FOUGHT TOTAL WAR – WITHOUT MERCY!
AND TOMORROW THEY WILL BRING TOTAL WAR TO THE WESTERN FRONT. . . WHEN "OPERATION WOTAN" BEGINS!

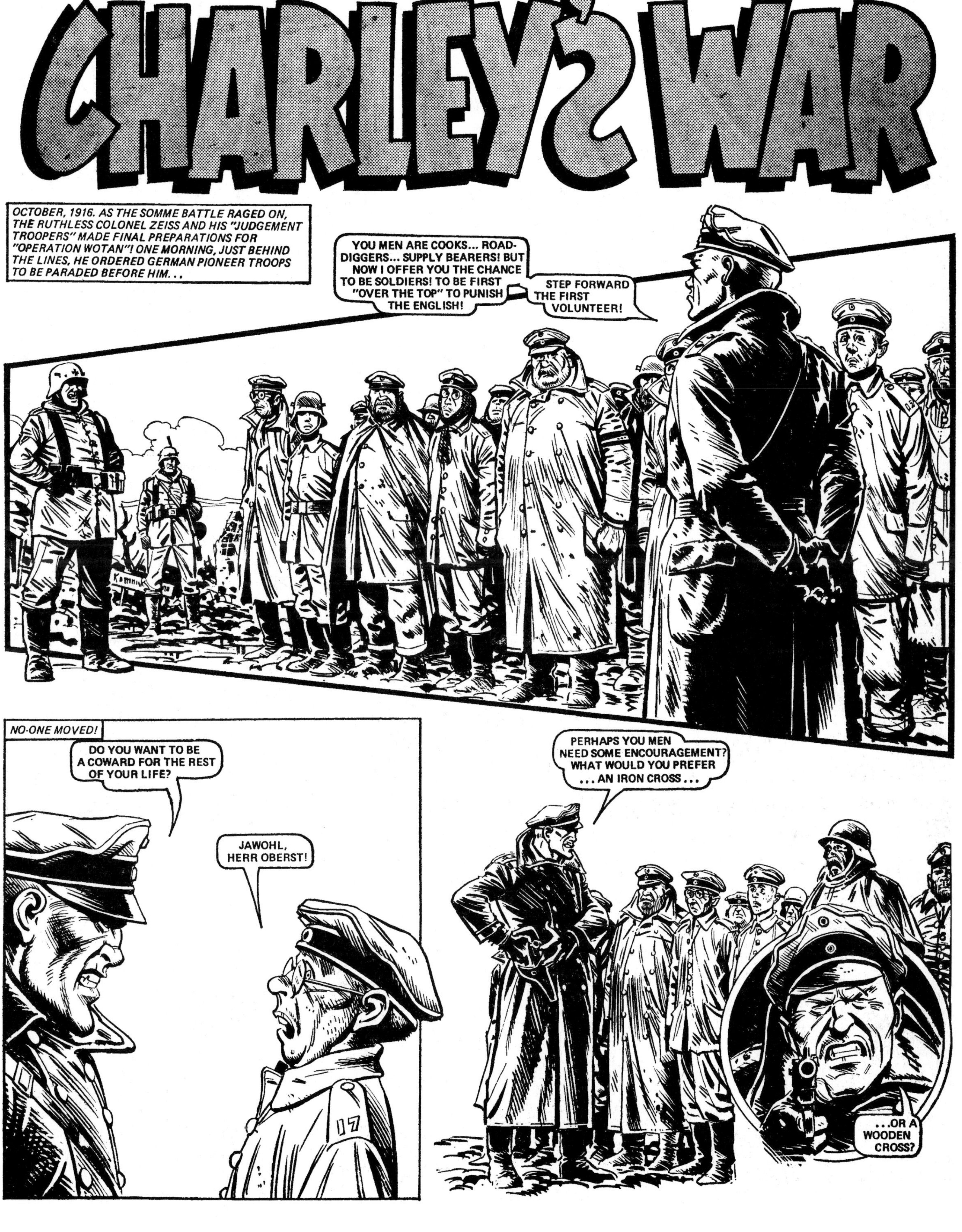
CHARLEY'S WAR
OCTOBER, 1916. AS THE SOMME BATTLE RAGED ON, THE RUTHLESS COLONEL ZEISS AND HIS "JUDGEMENT TROOPERS" MADE FINAL PREPARATIONS FOR "OPERATION WOTAN"! ONE MORNING, JUST BEHIND THE LINES, HE ORDERED GERMAN PIONEER TROOPS TO BE PARADED BEFORE HIM...
YOU MEN ARE COOKS... ROAD-DIGGERS... SUPPLY BEARERS! BUT NOW I OFFER YOU THE CHANCE TO BE SOLDIERS! TO BE FIRST "OVER THE TOP" TO PUNISH THE ENGLISH!
STEP FORWARD THE FIRST VOLUNTEER!
NO-ONE MOVED!
DO YOU WANT TO BE A COWARD FOR THE REST OF YOUR LIFE?
JAWOHL, HERR OBERST!
PERHAPS YOU MEN NEED SOME ENCOURAGEMENT? WHAT WOULD YOU PREFER ... AN IRON CROSS ...
...OR A WOODEN CROSS?

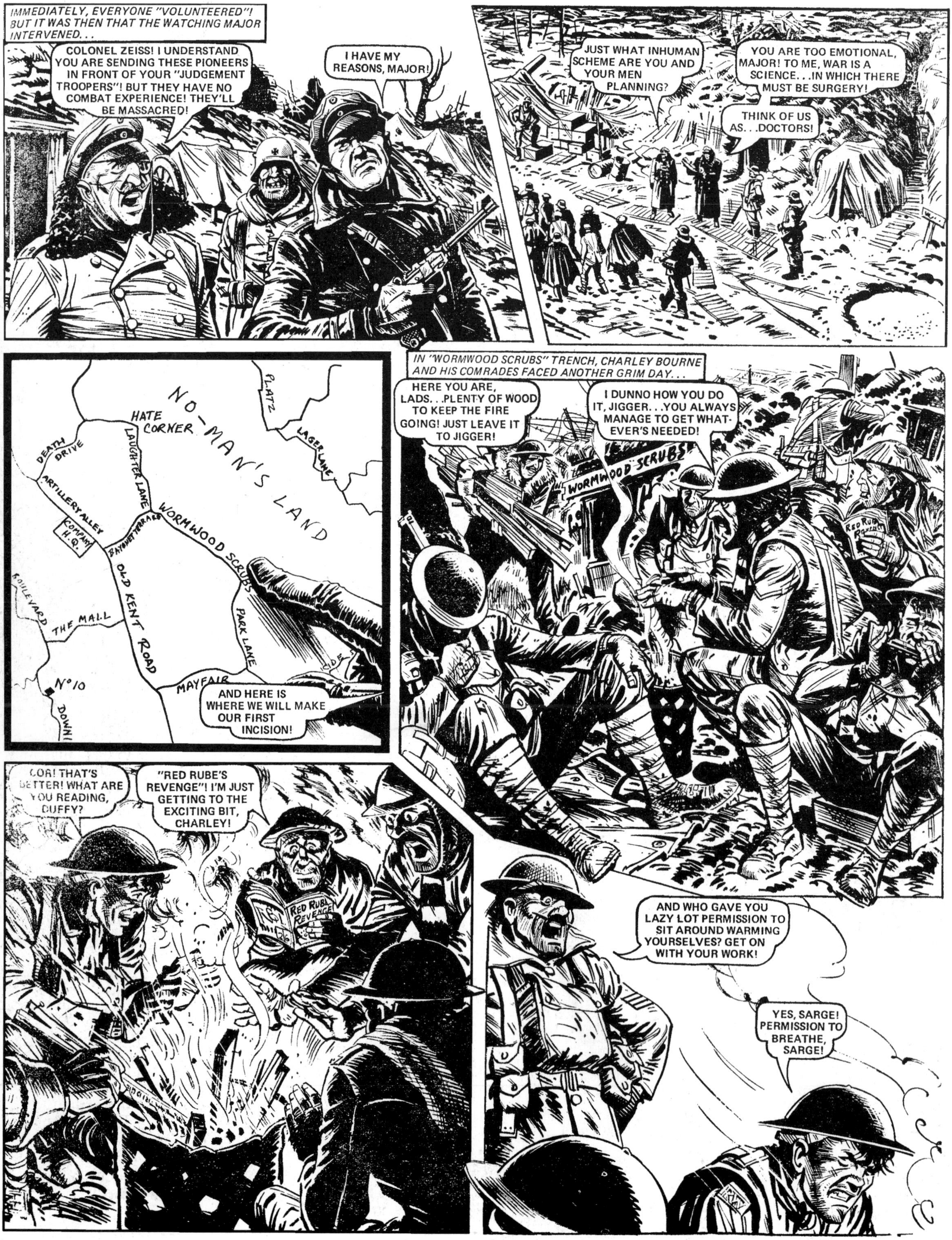
IMMEDIATELY, EVERYONE "VOLUNTEERED"! BUT IT WAS THEN THAT THE WATCHING MAJOR INTERVENED...
COLONEL ZEISS! I UNDERSTAND YOU ARE SENDING THESE PIONEERS IN FRONT OF YOUR "JUDGEMENT TROOPERS"! BUT THEY HAVE NO COMBAT EXPERIENCE! THEY'LL BE MASSACRED!
I HAVE MY REASONS, MAJOR!
JUST WHAT INHUMAN SCHEME ARE YOU AND YOUR MEN PLANNING?
YOU ARE TOO EMOTIONAL, MAJOR! TO ME, WAR IS A SCIENCE... IN WHICH THERE MUST BE SURGERY!
THINK OF US AS...DOCTORS!
NO-MAN'S LAND
HATE CORNER
PLATZ
LAGER LANE
DEATH DRIVE
LAUGHTER LANE
ARTILLERY ALLEY
COMPANY H.Q.
WORMWOOD SCRUBS
BAYONET TERRACE
OLD KENT ROAD
BOULEVARD
THE MALL
PARK LANE
MAYFAIR
Nº10
DOWNI
AND HERE IS WHERE WE WILL MAKE OUR FIRST INCISION!
IN "WORMWOOD SCRUBS" TRENCH, CHARLEY BOURNE AND HIS COMRADES FACED ANOTHER GRIM DAY...
HERE YOU ARE, LADS... PLENTY OF WOOD TO KEEP THE FIRE GOING! JUST LEAVE IT TO JIGGER!
I DUNNO HOW YOU DO IT, JIGGER... YOU ALWAYS MANAGE TO GET WHAT-EVER'S NEEDED!
WORMWOOD SCRUBS
COR! THAT'S BETTER! WHAT ARE YOU READING, DUFFY?
"RED RUBE'S REVENGE"! I'M JUST GETTING TO THE EXCITING BIT, CHARLEY!
RED RUBE REVENGE
AND WHO GAVE YOU LAZY LOT PERMISSION TO SIT AROUND WARMING YOURSELVES? GET ON WITH YOUR WORK!
YES, SARGE! PERMISSION TO BREATHE, SARGE!

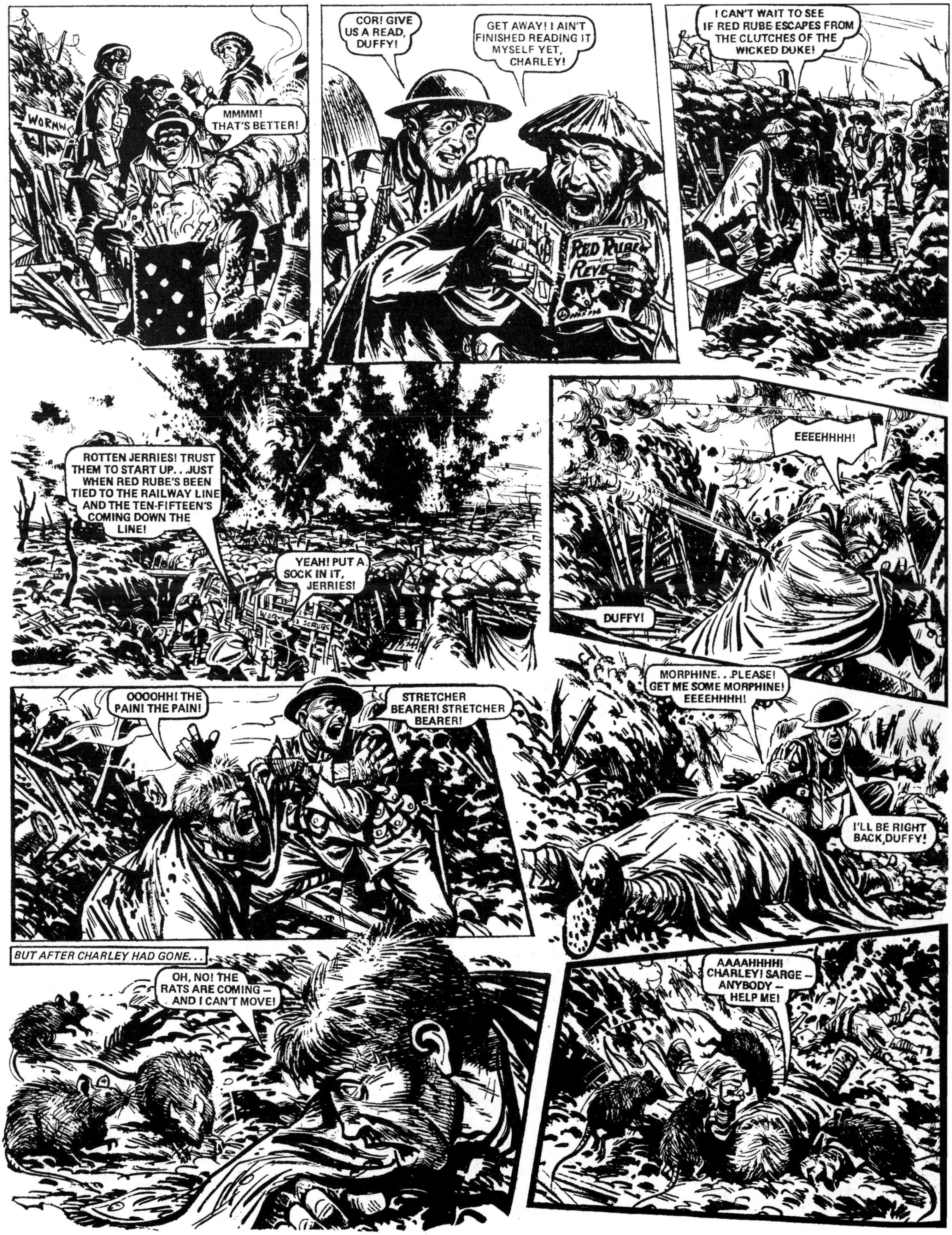

MMMM! THAT'S BETTER!
COR! GIVE US A READ, DUFFY!
GET AWAY! I AIN'T FINISHED READING IT MYSELF YET, CHARLEY!
I CAN'T WAIT TO SEE IF RED RUBE ESCAPES FROM THE CLUTCHES OF THE WICKED DUKE!
ROTTEN JERRIES! TRUST THEM TO START UP.. JUST WHEN RED RUBE'S BEEN TIED TO THE RAILWAY LINE AND THE TEN-FIFTEEN'S COMING DOWN THE LINE!
YEAH! PUT A SOCK IN IT, JERRIES!
EEEEHHHH!
DUFFY!
OOOOHH! THE PAIN! THE PAIN!
STRETCHER BEARER! STRETCHER BEARER!
MORPHINE.. PLEASE! GET ME SOME MORPHINE! EEEEHHHH!
I'LL BE RIGHT BACK, DUFFY!
BUT AFTER CHARLEY HAD GONE...
OH, NO! THE RATS ARE COMING — AND I CAN'T MOVE!
AAAAHHHH! CHARLEY! SARGE — ANYBODY — HELP ME!

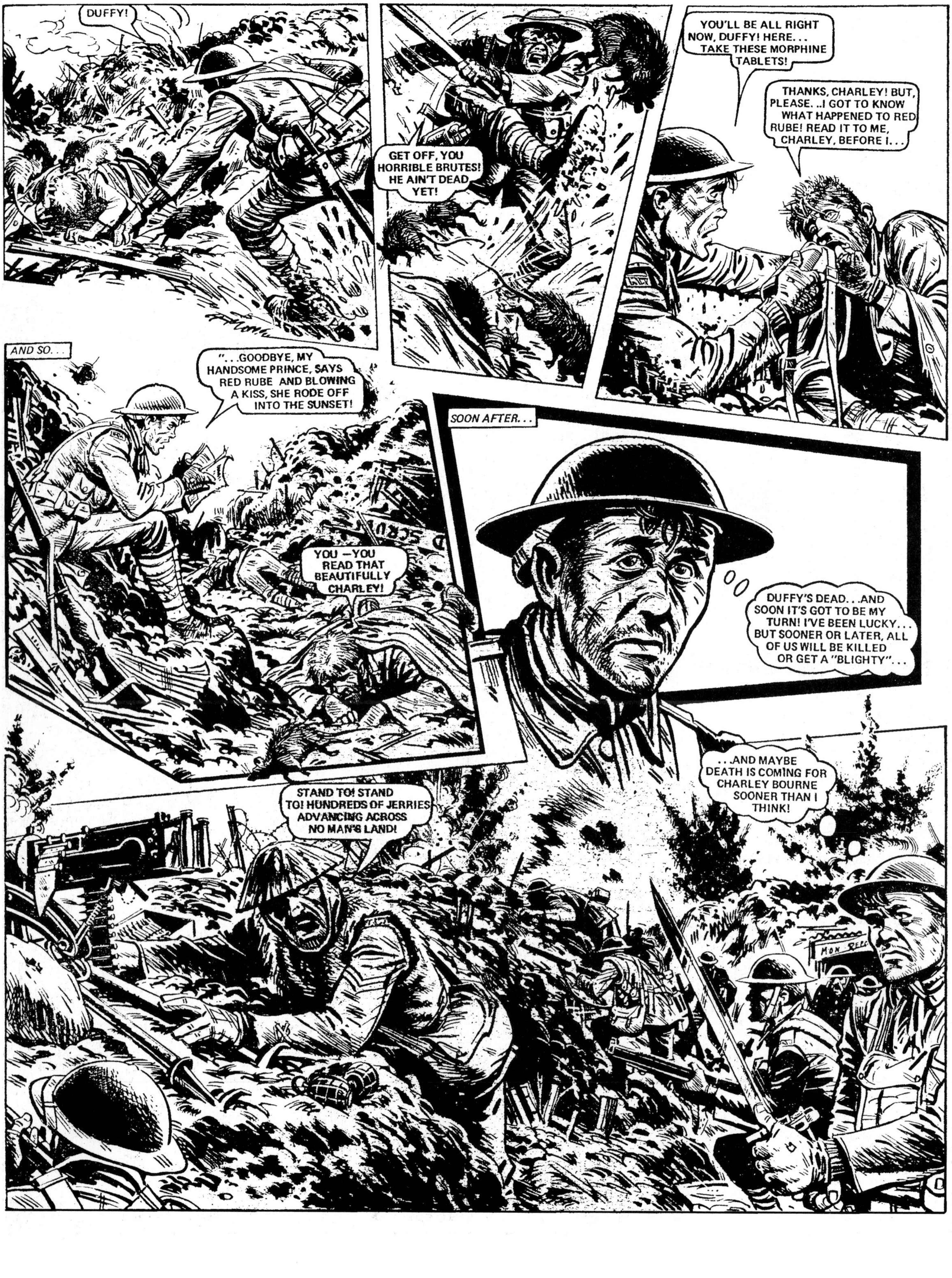
DUFFY!
GET OFF, YOU HORRIBLE BRUTES! HE AIN'T DEAD YET!
YOU'LL BE ALL RIGHT NOW, DUFFY! HERE... TAKE THESE MORPHINE TABLETS!
THANKS, CHARLEY! BUT, PLEASE. ..I GOT TO KNOW WHAT HAPPENED TO RED RUBE! READ IT TO ME, CHARLEY, BEFORE I...
AND SO...
"...GOODBYE, MY HANDSOME PRINCE, SAYS RED RUBE AND BLOWING A KISS, SHE RODE OFF INTO THE SUNSET!
YOU —YOU READ THAT BEAUTIFULLY CHARLEY!
SOON AFTER...
DUFFY'S DEAD...AND SOON IT'S GOT TO BE MY TURN! I'VE BEEN LUCKY... BUT SOONER OR LATER, ALL OF US WILL BE KILLED OR GET A "BLIGHTY"...
...AND MAYBE DEATH IS COMING FOR CHARLEY BOURNE SOONER THAN I THINK!
STAND TO! STAND TO! HUNDREDS OF JERRIES ADVANCING ACROSS NO MAN'S LAND!

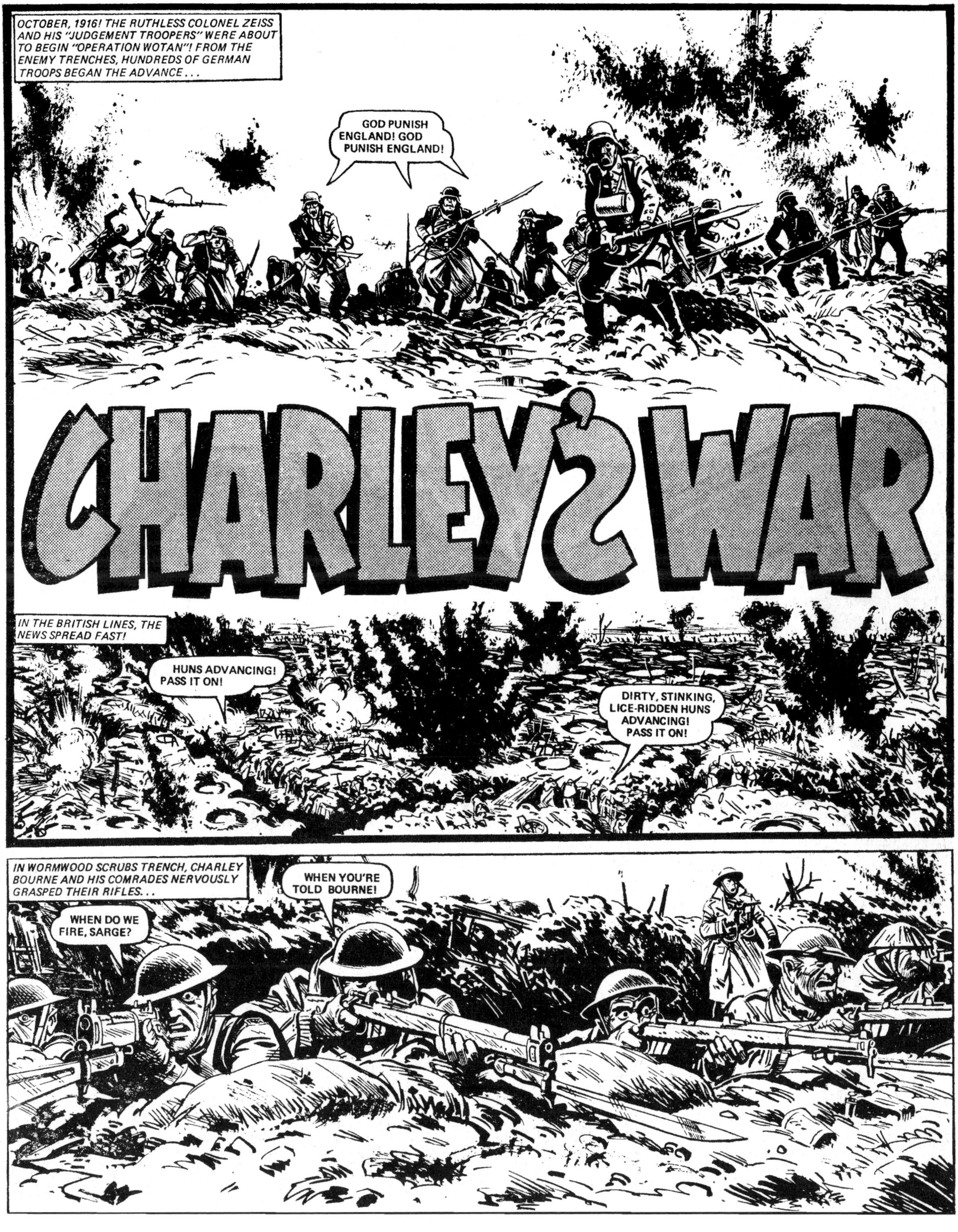
OCTOBER, 1916! THE RUTHLESS COLONEL ZEISS AND HIS "JUDGEMENT TROOPERS" WERE ABOUT TO BEGIN "OPERATION WOTAN"! FROM THE ENEMY TRENCHES, HUNDREDS OF GERMAN TROOPS BEGAN THE ADVANCE . . .
GOD PUNISH ENGLAND! GOD PUNISH ENGLAND!
CHARLEY'S WAR
IN THE BRITISH LINES, THE NEWS SPREAD FAST!
HUNS ADVANCING! PASS IT ON!
DIRTY, STINKING, LICE-RIDDEN HUNS ADVANCING! PASS IT ON!
IN WORMWOOD SCRUBS TRENCH, CHARLEY BOURNE AND HIS COMRADES NERVOUSLY GRASPED THEIR RIFLES...
WHEN DO WE FIRE, SARGE?
WHEN YOU'RE TOLD BOURNE!

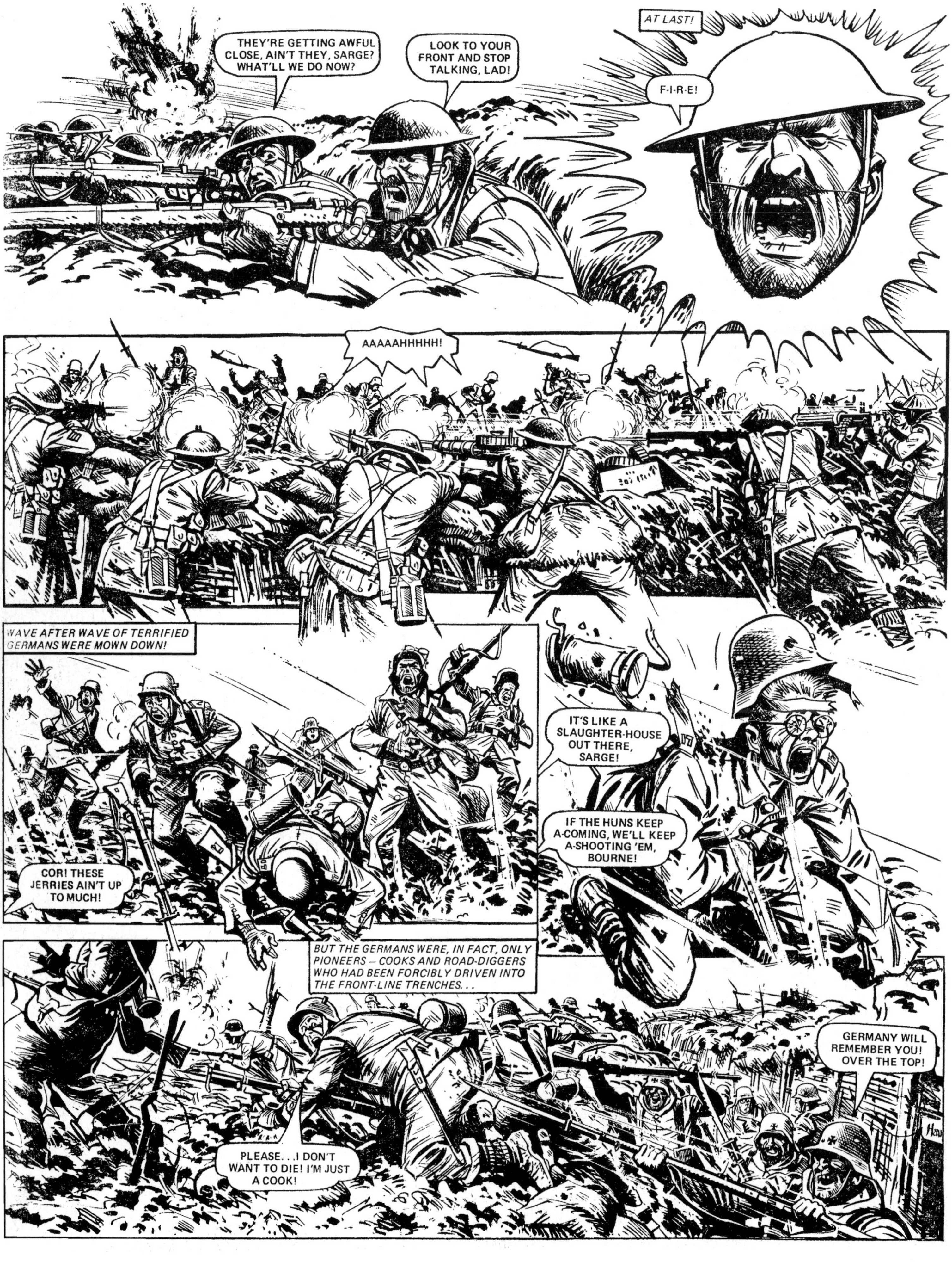
THEY'RE GETTING AWFUL CLOSE, AIN'T THEY, SARGE? WHAT'LL WE DO NOW?
LOOK TO YOUR FRONT AND STOP TALKING, LAD!
AT LAST!
F-I-R-E!
AAAAAHHHHH!
WAVE AFTER WAVE OF TERRIFIED GERMANS WERE MOWN DOWN!
COR! THESE JERRIES AIN'T UP TO MUCH!
IT'S LIKE A SLAUGHTER-HOUSE OUT THERE, SARGE!
IF THE HUNS KEEP A-COMING, WE'LL KEEP A-SHOOTING 'EM, BOURNE!
BUT THE GERMANS WERE, IN FACT, ONLY PIONEERS – COOKS AND ROAD-DIGGERS WHO HAD BEEN FORCIBLY DRIVEN INTO THE FRONT-LINE TRENCHES...
GERMANY WILL REMEMBER YOU! OVER THE TOP!
PLEASE...I DON'T WANT TO DIE! I'M JUST A COOK!

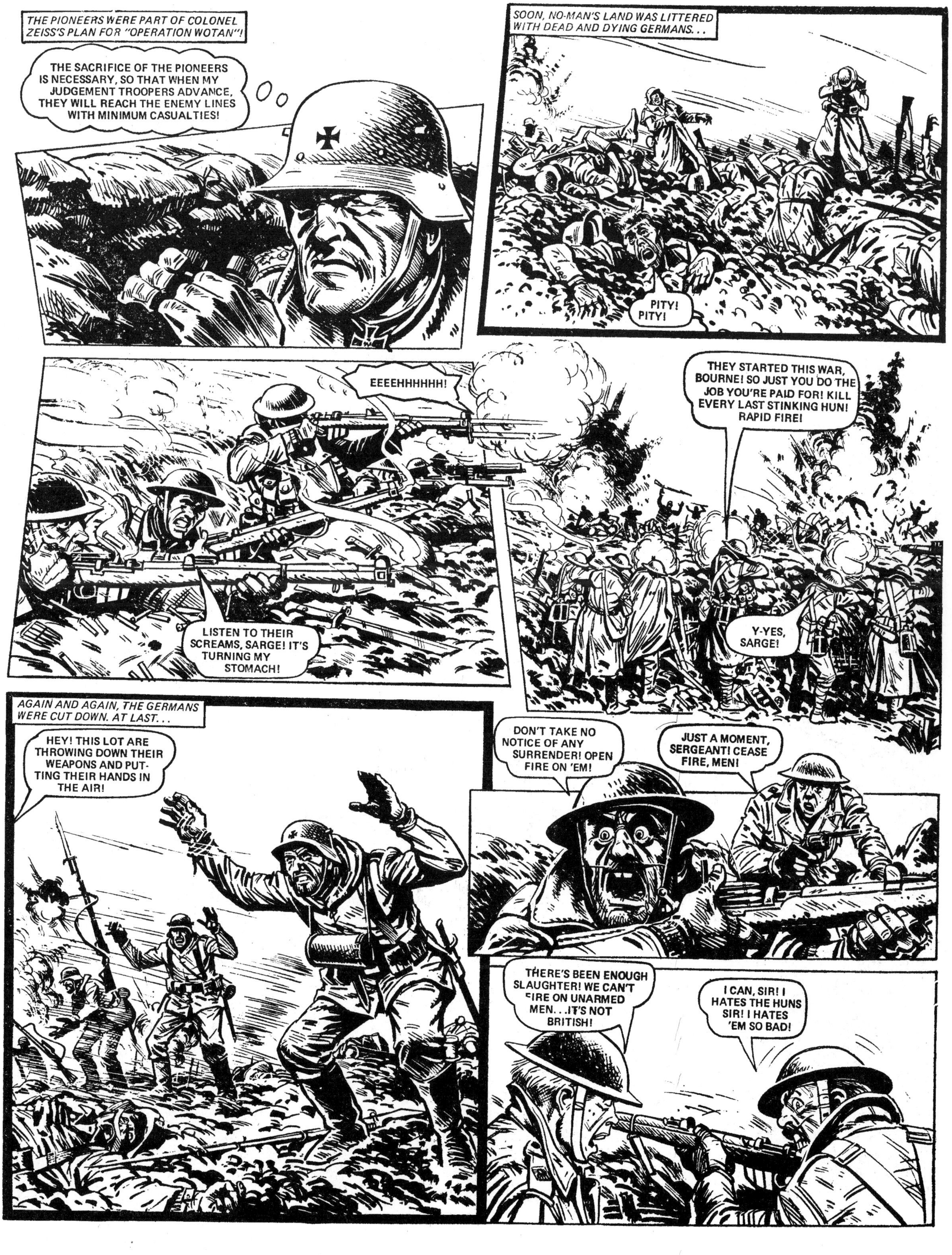
THE PIONEERS WERE PART OF COLONEL ZEISS'S PLAN FOR "OPERATION WOTAN"!
THE SACRIFICE OF THE PIONEERS IS NECESSARY, SO THAT WHEN MY JUDGEMENT TROOPERS ADVANCE, THEY WILL REACH THE ENEMY LINES WITH MINIMUM CASUALTIES!
SOON, NO-MAN'S LAND WAS LITTERED WITH DEAD AND DYING GERMANS...
PITY! PITY!
EEEEHHHHHH!
LISTEN TO THEIR SCREAMS, SARGE! IT'S TURNING MY STOMACH!
THEY STARTED THIS WAR, BOURNE! SO JUST YOU DO THE JOB YOU'RE PAID FOR! KILL EVERY LAST STINKING HUN! RAPID FIRE!
Y-YES, SARGE!
AGAIN AND AGAIN, THE GERMANS WERE CUT DOWN. AT LAST...
HEY! THIS LOT ARE THROWING DOWN THEIR WEAPONS AND PUTTING THEIR HANDS IN THE AIR!
DON'T TAKE NO NOTICE OF ANY SURRENDER! OPEN FIRE ON 'EM!
JUST A MOMENT, SERGEANT! CEASE FIRE, MEN!
THERE'S BEEN ENOUGH SLAUGHTER! WE CAN'T FIRE ON UNARMED MEN... IT'S NOT BRITISH!
I CAN, SIR! I HATES THE HUNS SIR! I HATES 'EM SO BAD!

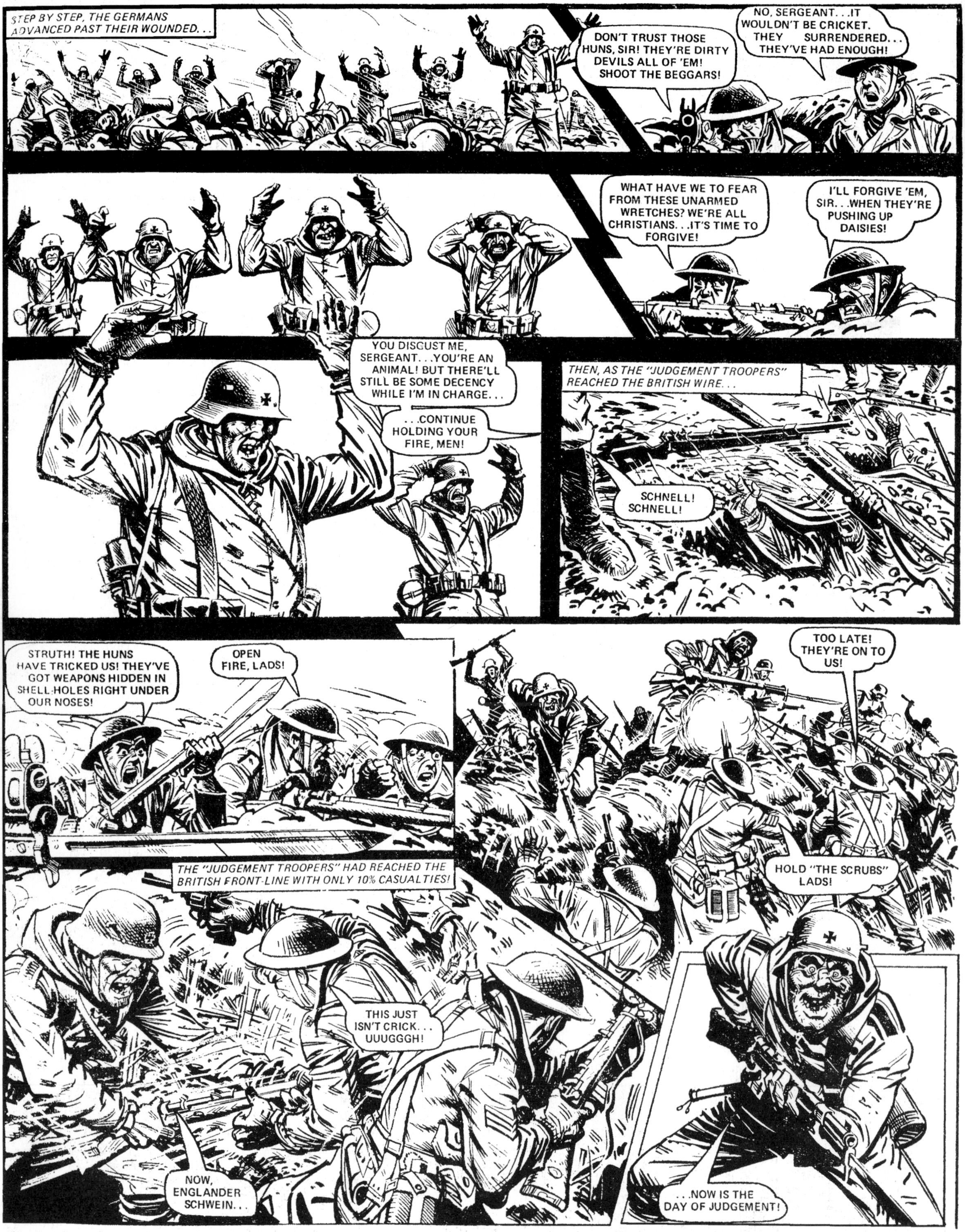
STEP BY STEP, THE GERMANS ADVANCED PAST THEIR WOUNDED...
DON'T TRUST THOSE HUNS, SIR! THEY'RE DIRTY DEVILS ALL OF 'EM! SHOOT THE BEGGARS!
NO, SERGEANT...IT WOULDN'T BE CRICKET. THEY SURRENDERED... THEY'VE HAD ENOUGH!
WHAT HAVE WE TO FEAR FROM THESE UNARMED WRETCHES? WE'RE ALL CHRISTIANS...IT'S TIME TO FORGIVE!
I'LL FORGIVE 'EM, SIR...WHEN THEY'RE PUSHING UP DAISIES!
YOU DISGUST ME, SERGEANT...YOU'RE AN ANIMAL! BUT THERE'LL STILL BE SOME DECENCY WHILE I'M IN CHARGE...
...CONTINUE HOLDING YOUR FIRE, MEN!
THEN, AS THE "JUDGEMENT TROOPERS" REACHED THE BRITISH WIRE...
SCHNELL! SCHNELL!
STRUTH! THE HUNS HAVE TRICKED US! THEY'VE GOT WEAPONS HIDDEN IN SHELL-HOLES RIGHT UNDER OUR NOSES!
OPEN FIRE, LADS!
TOO LATE! THEY'RE ON TO US!
HOLD "THE SCRUBS" LADS!
THE "JUDGEMENT TROOPERS" HAD REACHED THE BRITISH FRONT-LINE WITH ONLY 10% CASUALTIES!
THIS JUST ISN'T CRICK... UUUGGGH!
NOW, ENGLANDER SCHWEIN...
...NOW IS THE DAY OF JUDGEMENT!

STRIP COMMENTARY

by Pat Mills

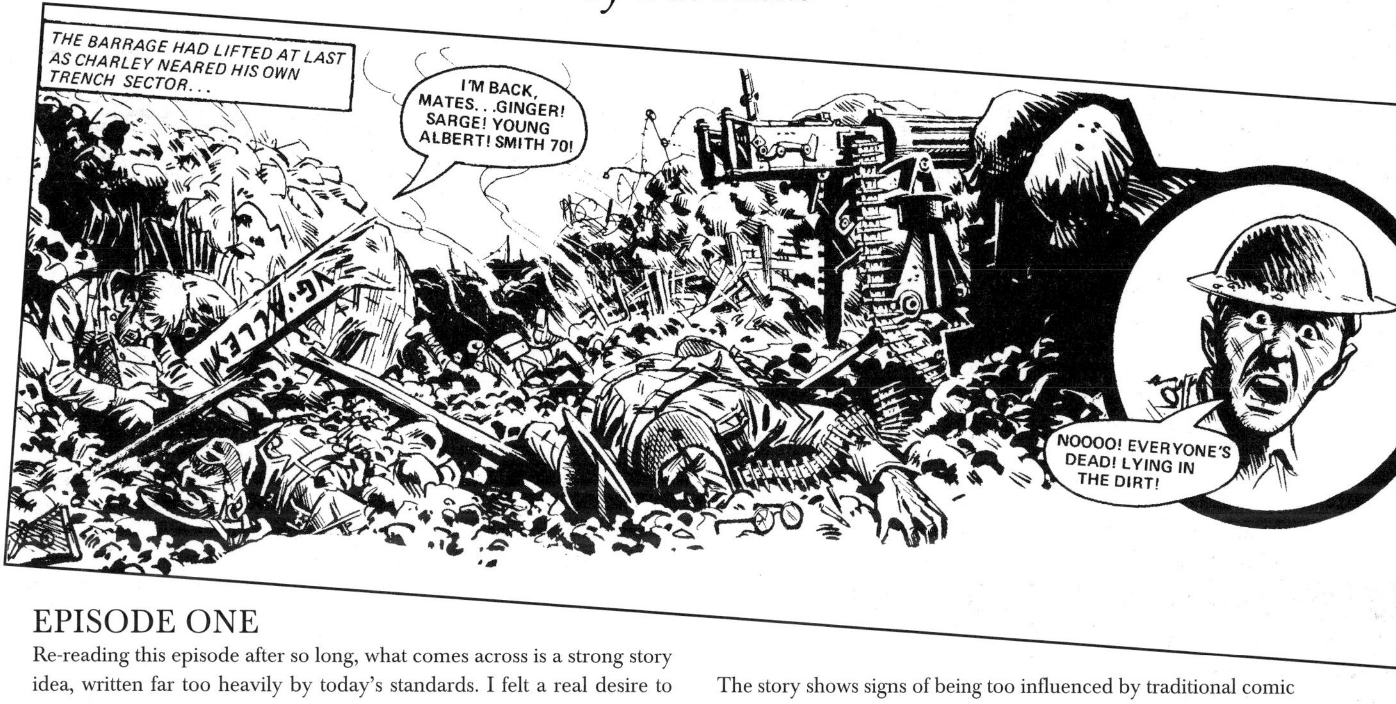
THE BARRAGE HAD LIFTED AT LAST AS CHARLEY NEARED HIS OWN TRENCH SECTOR...
I'M BACK, MATES...GINGER! SARGE! YOUNG ALBERT! SMITH 70!
NOOOO! EVERYONE'S DEAD! LYING IN THE DIRT!

EPISODE ONE

Re-reading this episode after so long, what comes across is a strong story idea, written far too heavily by today's standards. I felt a real desire to edit it after it was drawn; something that wasn't possible in those days, but which I usually insist on now, because a scene that works one way at script stage may come over entirely different once it's drawn. And over-writing becomes glaringly obvious, as it does here.

Heavily editing the final drawn version isn't something artists always approve of, because the writer may alter the story interpretation, and it's by no means common practice even today. You can often tell when a story hasn't been properly edited – the words and the art don't match too well. I think it is necessary to achieve the highest possible standards and I only wish I'd done it here.

But, despite this, the overall sense of trench drama is as powerful as ever and the complexities of the front line are depicted with startling clarity.

EPISODES TWO – THREE

The recreation of the class system in the trenches is authentic and the detail with which Joe depicts it is superb. The image of the dead men lying in the trench on the final page is also powerful.

This episode, too, has some problems from a scripting point of view. The story shows signs of being too influenced by traditional comic writing which can result in unlikely dialogue, for example: "Noooo! Everyone's dead! Lying in the dirt!" Today, I feel, a silent panel would be far more effective. However, you may disagree and if so, it highlights the changing fashions and often subjective nature of writing and editing.

EPISODES FOUR – SEVEN

The execution of British soldiers by our own side is one of the most tragic aspects of World War One. If anyone regards its depiction in *Charley's War* as being over-emotive or pure "comic book", then consider the following: bandleader Victor Sylvester had lied about his age, like Charley, and was serving on the Western Front aged seventeen. He was caught reading a document marked, "For the eyes of officers only", which was a list of soldiers condemned to be shot. As punishment, he was ordered to serve in a firing squad and had to shoot men from his own regiment. During the execution, he shut his eyes, but when he opened them he saw his target was still alive and struggling. An officer finished the man off with a revolver. Sylvester suffered a nervous breakdown as a result.

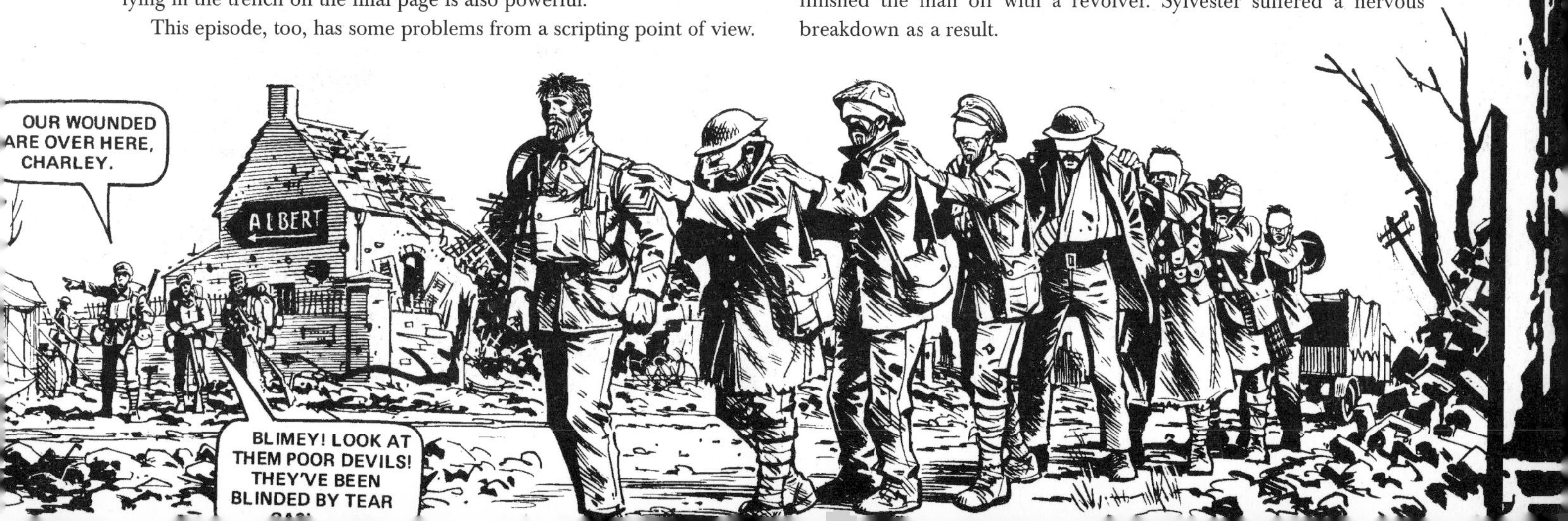
OUR WOUNDED ARE OVER HERE, CHARLEY.
ALBERT
BLIMEY! LOOK AT THEM POOR DEVILS! THEY'VE BEEN BLINDED BY TEAR

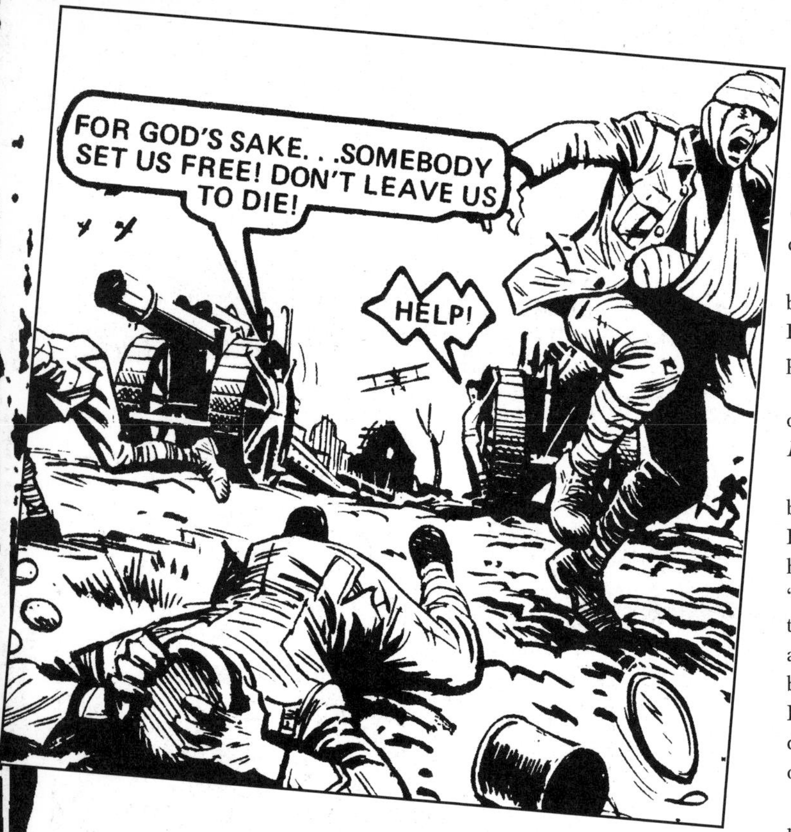
FOR GOD'S SAKE. . .SOMEBODY SET US FREE! DON'T LEAVE US TO DIE!
HELP!

Robert Graves claimed to have seen a secret order that cases of cowardice should *always* be punished by death, no medical evidence being allowed. The doctors, in any event, supported the authorities. As a result, a soldier who was certified mentally defective was executed. Another who was found behind the lines, choking from poison gas, was also shot. Other victims included a seventeen-year-old, a tramp who had been conscripted and went on his travels again, and a nineteen-year-old volunteer who refused to put his cap on. He was shot two days before Christmas. Sometimes if there was a delay, deserters would be sent back into the trenches until the trial could be arranged and then they would removed from the front, tried, sentenced and shot.

307 British soldiers were executed. This figure was far higher than the number of French, Germans or Americans shot for desertion.

EPISODES EIGHT – NINE

Field Punishment Number One was the barbaric punishment used behind the lines and was a key factor in inciting the explosive British mutiny at the Bull Ring in Etaples. This involved 100,000 British soldiers and the full truth about it is still unclear. The mutiny inspired the book and TV series *The Monocled Mutineer*, which today's revisionist World War One historians and Tory MPs have heavily criticised as being inaccurate and unsourced. In fact, the book was very accurate and does quote its sources, even including the full name and address of a mutineer.

EPISODE TEN

The horrors of Field Punishment Number One continue and are graphically drawn by Joe. He was from a wartime generation and had seen action in the navy, so there was nothing "1970s" in his attitudes. The fact that a writer and artist from two very different generations and backgrounds could combine together so effectively strongly suggests we were depicting an objective truth about World War One.

EPISODE ELEVEN

The execution of his commanding officer is still on Charley's mind in this episode – as it is on mine.

Disturbingly, we live in a society where there is a trend by today's historians to rehabilitate the generals responsible for such crimes. For example, *Haig: A Reappraisal 70 Years On*, eds. Brian Bond and Nigel Cave (Leo Cooper, 1999), dispels the "myths" that Haig was callous, cold and indifferent to the horrors his troops were undergoing.

But it's this same Haig who could not visit seriously injured soldiers because it made him physically sick. And who did not just want to execute British soldiers for desertion; he wanted to shoot Australians, too. He promised he would use the death penalty on them "very sparingly".

Similarly, a book on General Kitchener, the originator of concentration camps, has the retro-imperialist title *Kitchener, Architect of Victory, Artisan of Peace* (Carroll & Graf, 2001), which I think tells you all you need to know.

It's worth remembering that, in this same year, the British had just brutally crushed the Easter Rising in Ireland. In May 1916, the Bishop of Limerick wrote to one of these warlords, a General Maxwell, referring to him as the "military dictator" of Ireland. He went on to say to Maxwell, "You took great care that no plea for mercy should interpose on behalf of the poor young fellows who surrendered to you in Dublin. The first announcement we got of their fate was the announcement that they had been shot in cold blood. Personally I regard your action with horror and I believe that it has outraged the conscience of the country. Then the deporting of hundreds and even thousands of poor fellows without a trial of any kind, seems to me an abuse of power as fatuous as it is arbitrary."

There was nothing unique about General Maxwell – he was part of a military class and breed that deserves our condemnation, not approval, and it's shaming for all of us that historians should now attempt to approve or exonerate these individuals of their appalling misdeeds.

EPISODE TWELVE

This is the episode where Charley's popular friend Ginger dies suddenly and without warning, which shocked many readers. I did this deliberately, because I loathe works of fiction where a character is "set up" for death and you can see it coming. I think it's good to challenge the readers' assumptions that a popular sidekick will always be around. We need to maintain a sense of real drama, that anything could happen next…

EPISODE THIRTEEN

We see Charley walking along with the remains of his friend in a bag. I often wonder what would have happened if we had actually showed soldiers torn apart by bombs in comics. I am sure we would have been criticised as being disgusting and horrific and such a comic would be promptly banned. But isn't that the point? The real nature of war would be exposed.

EPISODES FOURTEEN – SIXTEEN

The tanks go into action. They were viewed at the time as "atrocity" weapons: true weapons of mass destruction. I believe our government

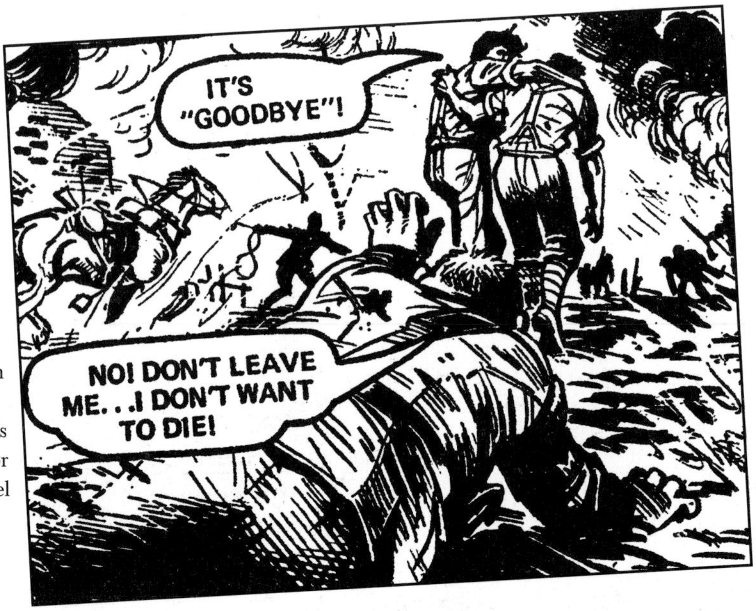
IT'S "GOODBYE"!
NO! DON'T LEAVE ME. . .I DON'T WANT TO DIE!

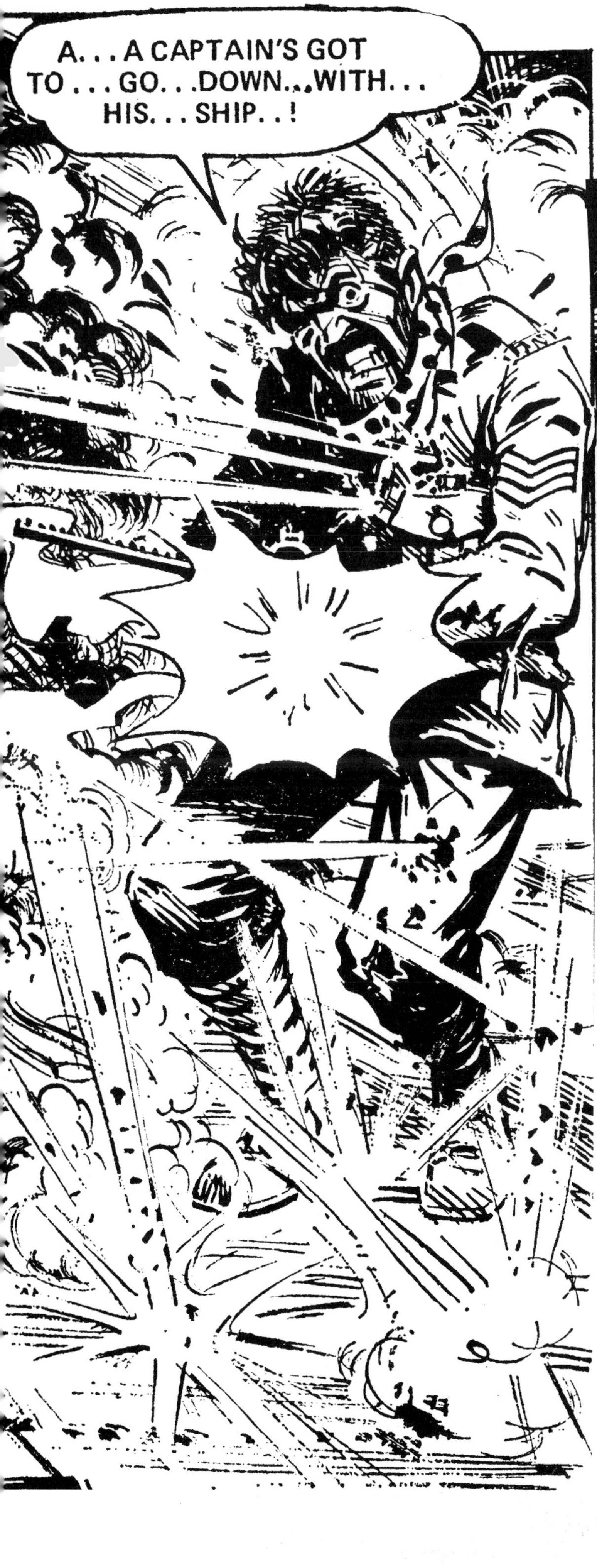
A. . . A CAPTAIN'S GOT TO . . . GO. . .DOWN. . .WITH. . . HIS. . . SHIP. . !

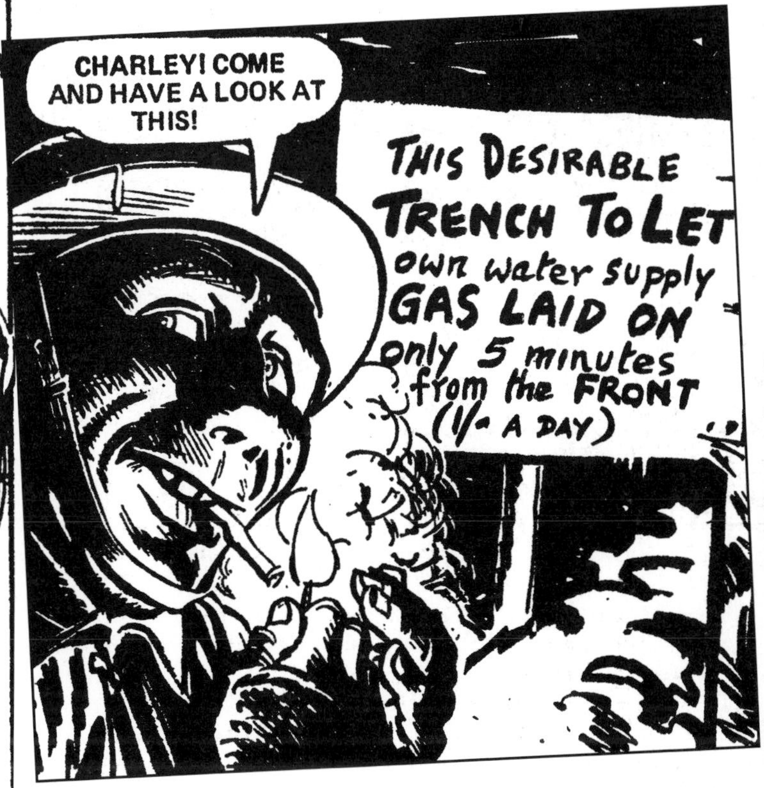
CHARLEY! COME AND HAVE A LOOK AT THIS!
THIS DESIRABLE TRENCH TO LET
own water supply
GAS LAID ON
only 5 minutes from the FRONT
(1/- A DAY)

and media decide what is an atrocity weapon and what isn't and condition the population accordingly. So a World War One tank is rather an amusing ancient contraption, and a modern tank is an impressive military expression of our industrial might. But, basically, a tank is a "good" weapon.

Poison gas, however, is an "atrocity" weapon used by wicked dictators – even though it was used in the 1930s by the RAF on tribesmen in Iraq.

In the recent rehabilitation of General Haig, he is presented as being pro-tank, which is at odds with past accounts. Previously he was presented as a cavalryman who only saw a limited role for the tank. This seems more likely as tanks were only used in a limited way on the Somme.

EPISODES SEVENTEEN – EIGHTEEN

Joe had a special gift – to be able to look at a photo and bring it to life from every angle. This he does with the tanks. The scene where the German soldiers are climbing all over the tank is totally convincing. And the tank interior is amazing. It must have come out of his head because there are no references available and you can almost smell the oil and grease!

By comparison, an image of German soldiers moving a field gun round to shoot the tanks is taken directly from a reference I sent him. Although Joe has done a superb job on it, I still prefer his own vivid imagination.

EPISODES NINETEEN – TWENTY

Steampunk is very popular these days in comics, but to me World War One was the original steampunk war. And the images here would strongly compete with any steampunk comic strip. What could be more fantastic than wearing medieval masks in landships which communicate with each other by semaphore flags? This is pure H. G. Wells!

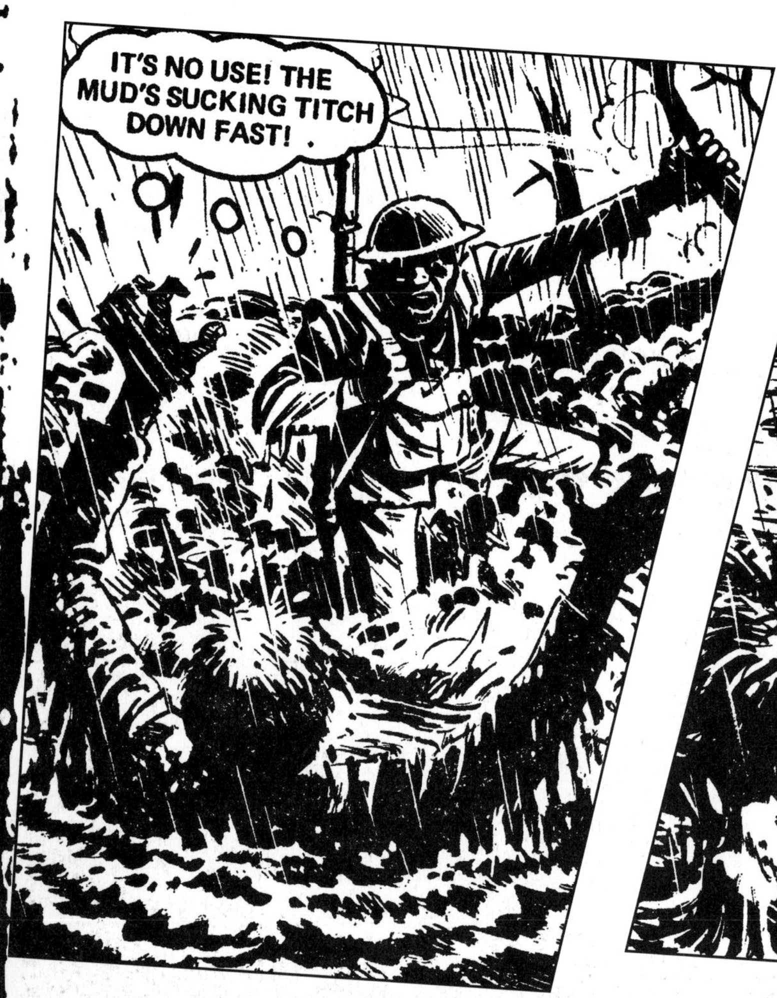
IT'S NO USE! THE MUD'S SUCKING TITCH DOWN FAST!

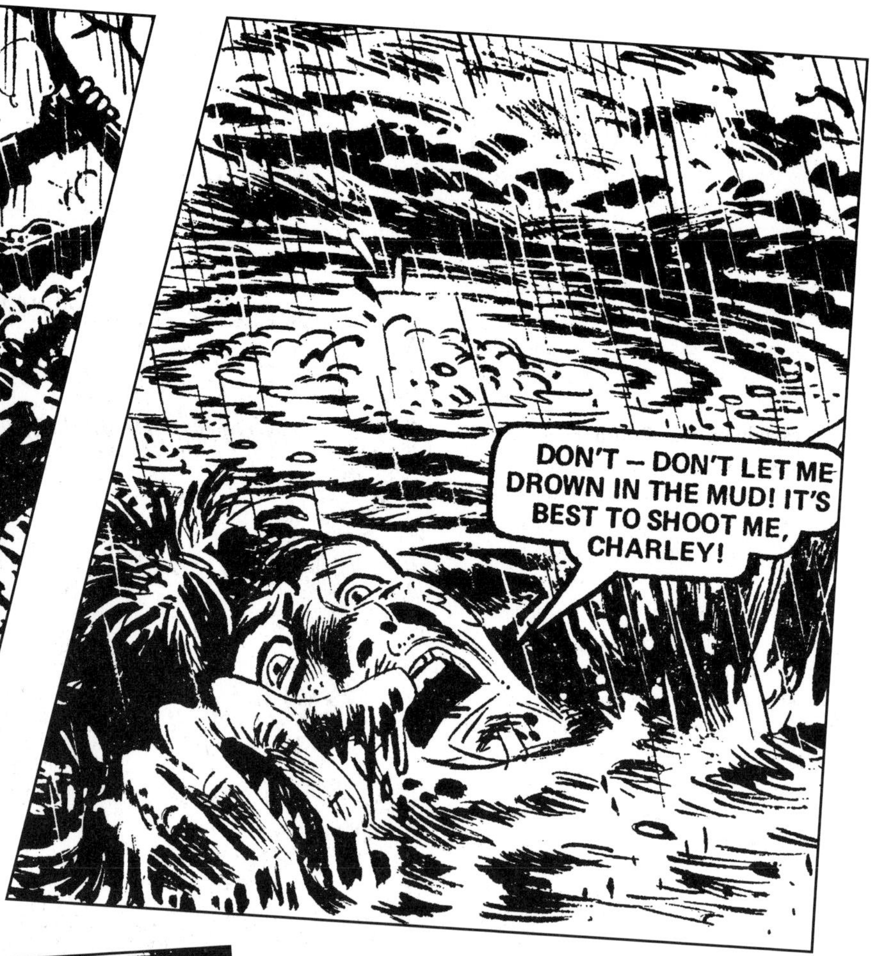
DON'T – DON'T LET ME DROWN IN THE MUD! IT'S BEST TO SHOOT ME, CHARLEY!

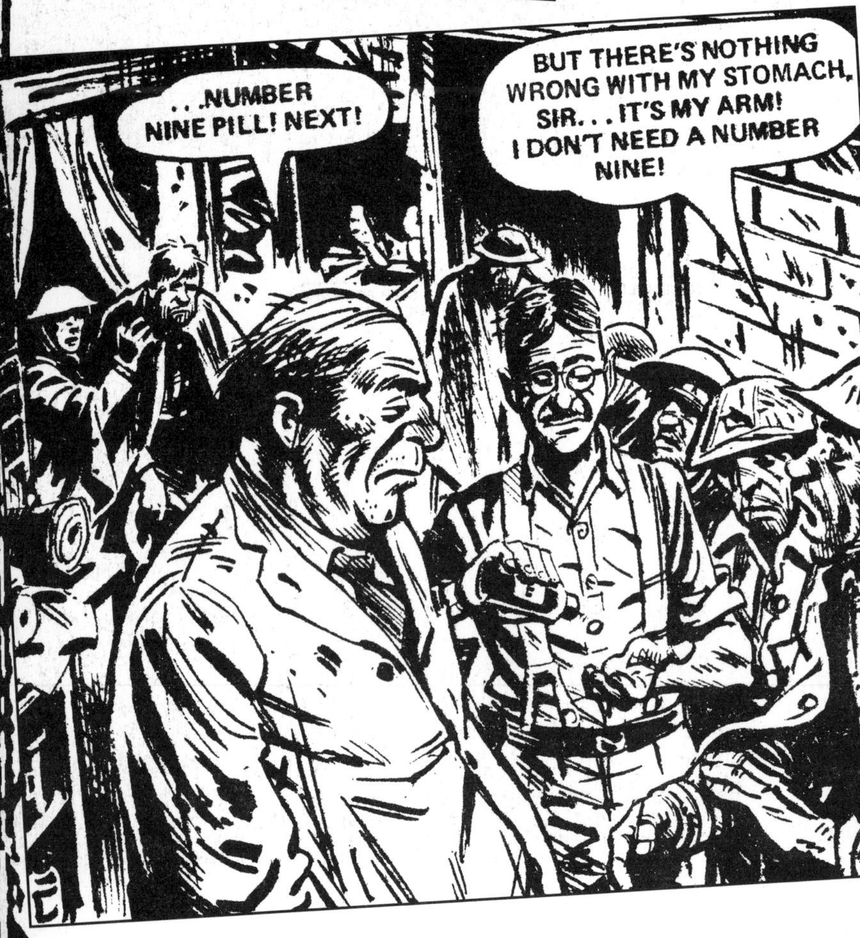
. . .NUMBER NINE PILL! NEXT!
BUT THERE'S NOTHING WRONG WITH MY STOMACH, SIR. . . IT'S MY ARM! I DON'T NEED A NUMBER NINE!

EPISODES TWENTY-ONE – TWENTY-THREE

The sequence where Charley's tank smashes into the church is one of my all-time favourites. There is no such record that it happened so dramatically, but it might have done. And that has always been my criterion.

EPISODES TWENTY-FOUR – TWENTY-FIVE

Episode twenty-four begins the four-page episodes. These give Joe's work the space it deserves. Three pages a week could look a little cramped on occasion. The extra space gives his art comparable stature to French artists who have drawn similar stories about Verdun and the Russian Front. But it was a real strain for him because of his meticulous detail.

Most British artists can produce around six pages a week as it's the only way to economically survive. It's one reason why British artists work for America where backgrounds aren't so important. In fact one American interviewer commented to me recently that, "You really make use of the space behind the characters in your stories."

I understand both points of view, but Joe could never take such short-cuts and I believe it's why he is one of our country's greatest comic artists.

This episode was censored by the new *Battle* editor, Terry Magee. Originally Titch was being sucked down in the mud and Charley had no choice but to agree to Titch's request to shoot him. Instead, the editor wrote in new dialogue with Charley using the rifle to haul him out. And then he arranges for Titch to be sent home. I had to let it go. After all, I was getting away with a lot more…

EPISODE TWENTY-SIX

The Judgement Troopers arrive! This was one of the most popular *Charley's War* stories ever. Not least because Joe now had those four pages to do his art justice. And it's a story I've been asked a lot about. So to answer those queries: the German offensive involving the Judgement Troopers was fictitious, as is the character of Zeiss. But there were lesser German counter-attacks on the Somme and I collected together all the details and combined them into this one powerful assault on the British lines. So the individual incidents are authentic.

Doctor "No" appears here. Needless to say, the dialogue is authentic. It still makes me angry reading his lines. But what a superb visual rendering of him and how well observed. That arrogant and contemptuous attitude towards lesser mortals. The boozer's red nose. His armoured body language. This is the kind of guy who spends most of his time on the golf course, when he isn't in the pub, and has a five-second attention span when we're telling him our health concerns. Only a handful of comic artists – like Kevin O'Neill, Brian Bolland, Dave Gibbons and Charlie Adlard – could draw such a definitive character today.

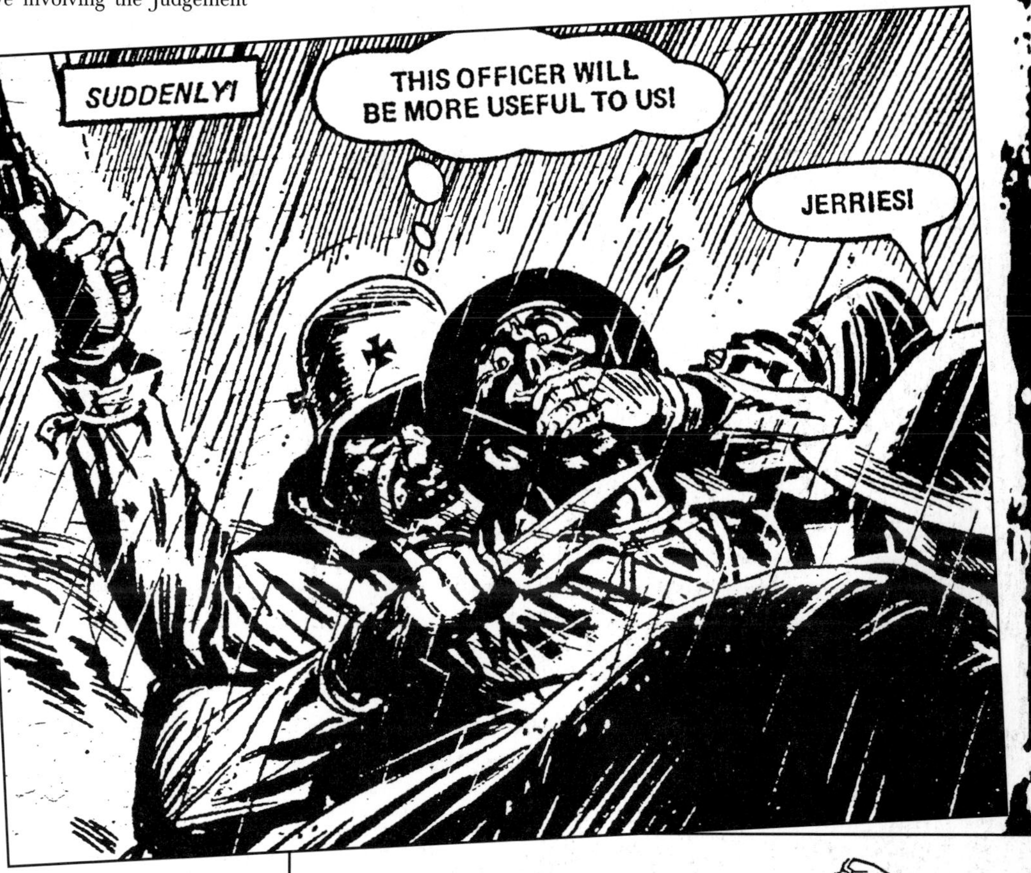
SUDDENLY!
THIS OFFICER WILL BE MORE USEFUL TO US!
JERRIES!

EPISODE TWENTY-SEVEN

A bit more censorship here. Originally they were casting that line out into No Man's Land to fish for rats. The editor thought it was too offensive. But British soldiers did it…

EPISODES TWENTY-EIGHT – TWENTY-NINE

Another of my favourite scenes is this one, where Colonel Zeiss addresses a parade of pioneer troops. Each one is beautifully characterised. Joe really understood human nature and frailty. To do so, must have made him a very warm and special human being. I could stare at scenes like this for hours and have done.

The episode ends with the Judgement Troopers attacking the British lines.

EPISODE THIRTY

The most spectacular sequence ever in *Charley's War* begins. This volume began with an episode which I was less than happy with from a scripting point of view. But it ends with one where I am really pleased with my dialogue and pacing. It feels good to me and I doubt, if I was writing it today, whether I would make any changes. The aristocratic officer might be a little stereotypical and effete for some tastes, but I met a similar character only the other day and I was struck by how little some members of the aristocracy have changed in nearly a century. And there's a reason for this. As actor Peter Cushing once said on television, "I based my life on Tom Merry" – the *Boys' Own* hero. So people do tend to use role models to inspire them, including comic book heroes, a theme Kevin O'Neill and I pursue in our superhero series *Marshal Law*. And they often behave like archetypes they admire or, in this case, a stereotype.

It would be interesting to know which comic book characters today's thirty-somethings may have based their lives on. Charley? Judge Dredd? Slàine? I know of at least one reader who based his life on Judge Dredd…✛

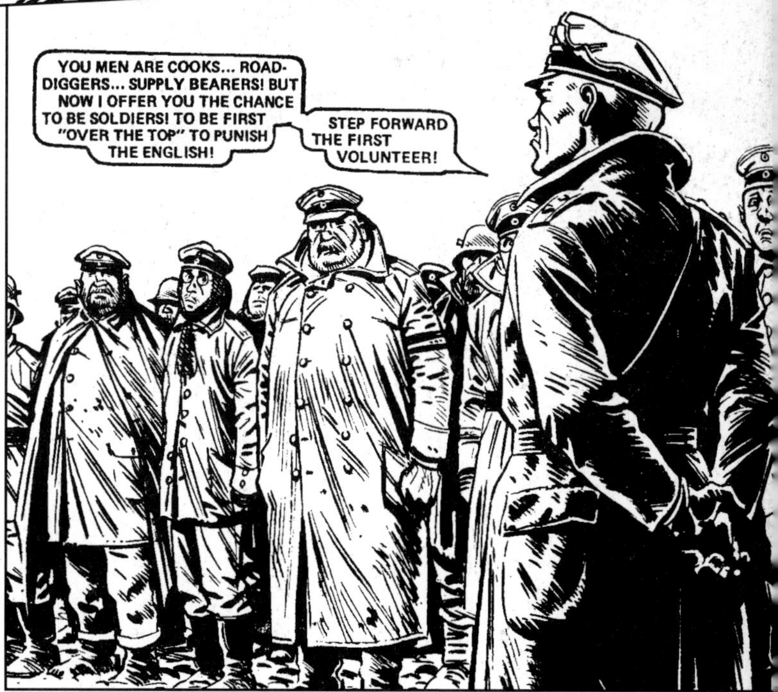
YOU MEN ARE COOKS... ROAD-DIGGERS... SUPPLY BEARERS! BUT NOW I OFFER YOU THE CHANCE TO BE SOLDIERS! TO BE FIRST "OVER THE TOP" TO PUNISH THE ENGLISH!
STEP FORWARD THE FIRST VOLUNTEER!

IN THE AFTERMATH OF *CHARLEY'S WAR*

by Garth Ennis

There's a theory doing the rounds at the moment, expounded in several recent Great War histories, that seeks to lift the burden of guilt from the shoulders of the much-maligned Generals and Field-Marshals. The idea, in essence, is that the mass slaughter of the Flanders battlefields wasn't really their fault. Enough time has passed that we can examine these events with cooler, clearer heads, unclouded by emotional reactions to phrases like, "60,000 killed or wounded in a day". We can acknowledge that the General Staff lacked both the necessary tools to break the deadlock of trench warfare, and the communications to receive up-to-the-minute, accurate intelligence from the front. Given these restrictions, what choice had they but to draw up a plan before each battle, stick to it like glue, and continue feeding men into the line no matter what?

Charley's War first saw print in *Battle*, a weekly war comic published in the UK from 1975 to 1986. The best of the paper's strips combined strong characterisation, intense, direct storytelling, and a heavy dose of realism – some of it extremely harsh. Stories like *Darkie's Mob, H.M.S. Nightshade* and *Johnny Red* showed their readers a world where death was foul and random rather than inspiring, and where long-established characters could be blown away at any moment. *Charley's War*, however, would go even further than that.

Writer Pat Mills' determination to avoid the pitfalls of previous war strips, and his meticulous research into the more obscure aspects of the First World War, are a matter of record now; so is *Battle* Editor Dave Hunt's courageous decision to pull artist Joe Colquhoun from the hugely popular *Johnny Red*, giving the then-untried *Charley's War* the illustrator it deserved. As a regular *Battle* reader in early 1979, I recall a certain amount of, "Huh? *What?*" when I realised my favourite story had lost its regular artist. Once I began reading Colquhoun's new assignment, however, all was swiftly forgiven. *Charley's War* was simply that good.

The art is brilliant. Joe Colquhoun achieved a level of detail in his work that remains unsurpassed to this day; most artists who manage this kind of accuracy do so at the expense of storytelling, their art so static it becomes almost lifeless. Simultaneously, the sheer humanity of the characters he portrayed shone through every panel on every page. "Ole Bill" Tozer, Ginger Jones, Smith 70 and Young Albert, Toots and Pop, the unfailingly decent Lieutenant Thomas and the vile Lieutenant Snell, not to mention Charley himself: these, and the nightmarish locations he captured so completely, remain Colquhoun's legacy.

It was Pat Mills' work, however, that made the story something really special. No one had really tackled the reality of the trenches in comics before, not with the anger that infused Mills' scripts, the fierce determination to show the infantry's miserable lot for what it was. The butchery on the Western Front remains the greatest betrayal of the working class by their "betters"; it was Mills' point-blank refusal to ignore

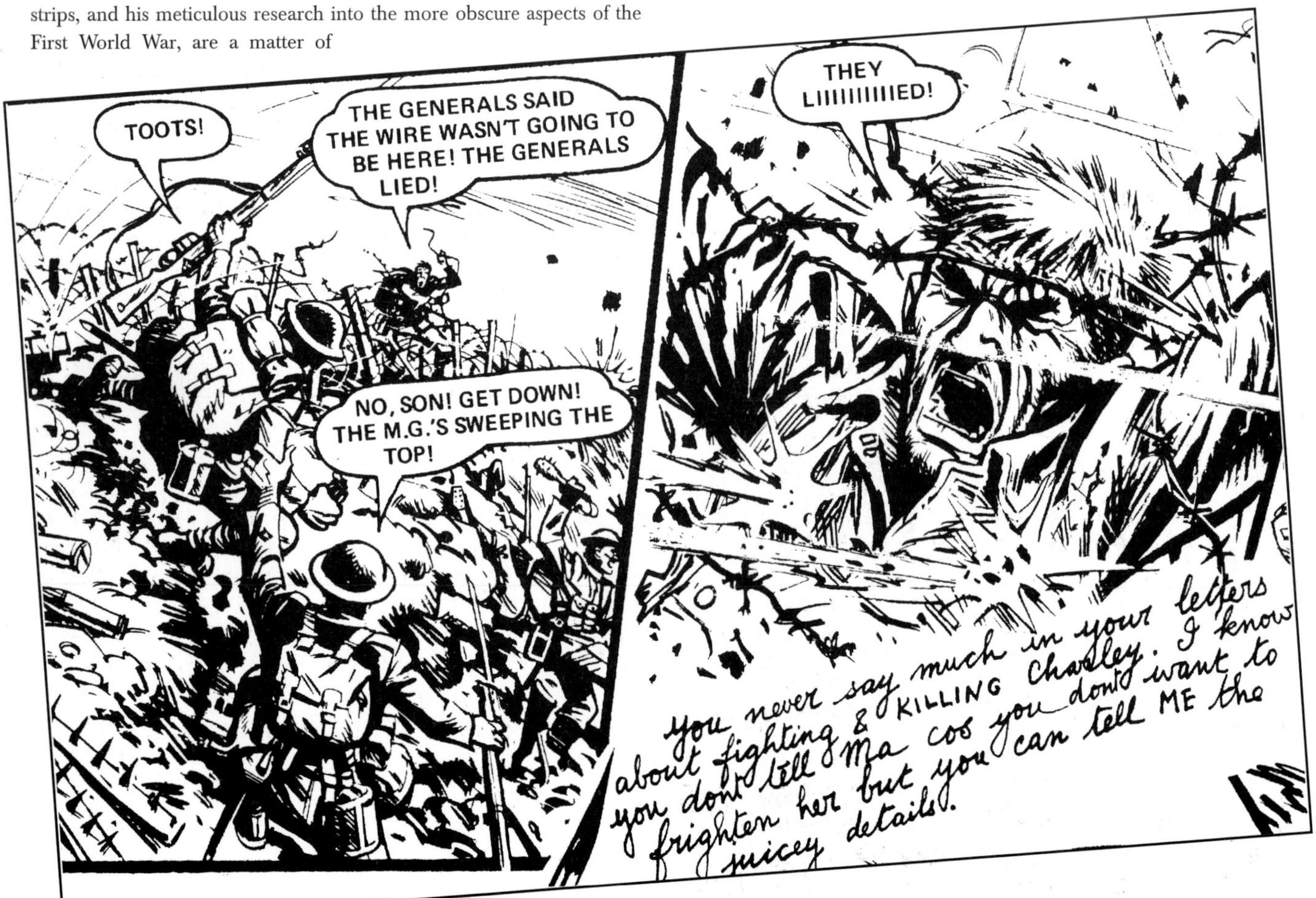
TOOTS!
THE GENERALS SAID THE WIRE WASN'T GOING TO BE HERE! THE GENERALS LIED!
NO, SON! GET DOWN! THE M.G.'S SWEEPING THE TOP!
THEY LIIIIIIIIIED!
You never say much in your letters about fighting & KILLING Charley. I know you don't tell Ma cos you don't want to frighten her but you can tell ME the juicey details.

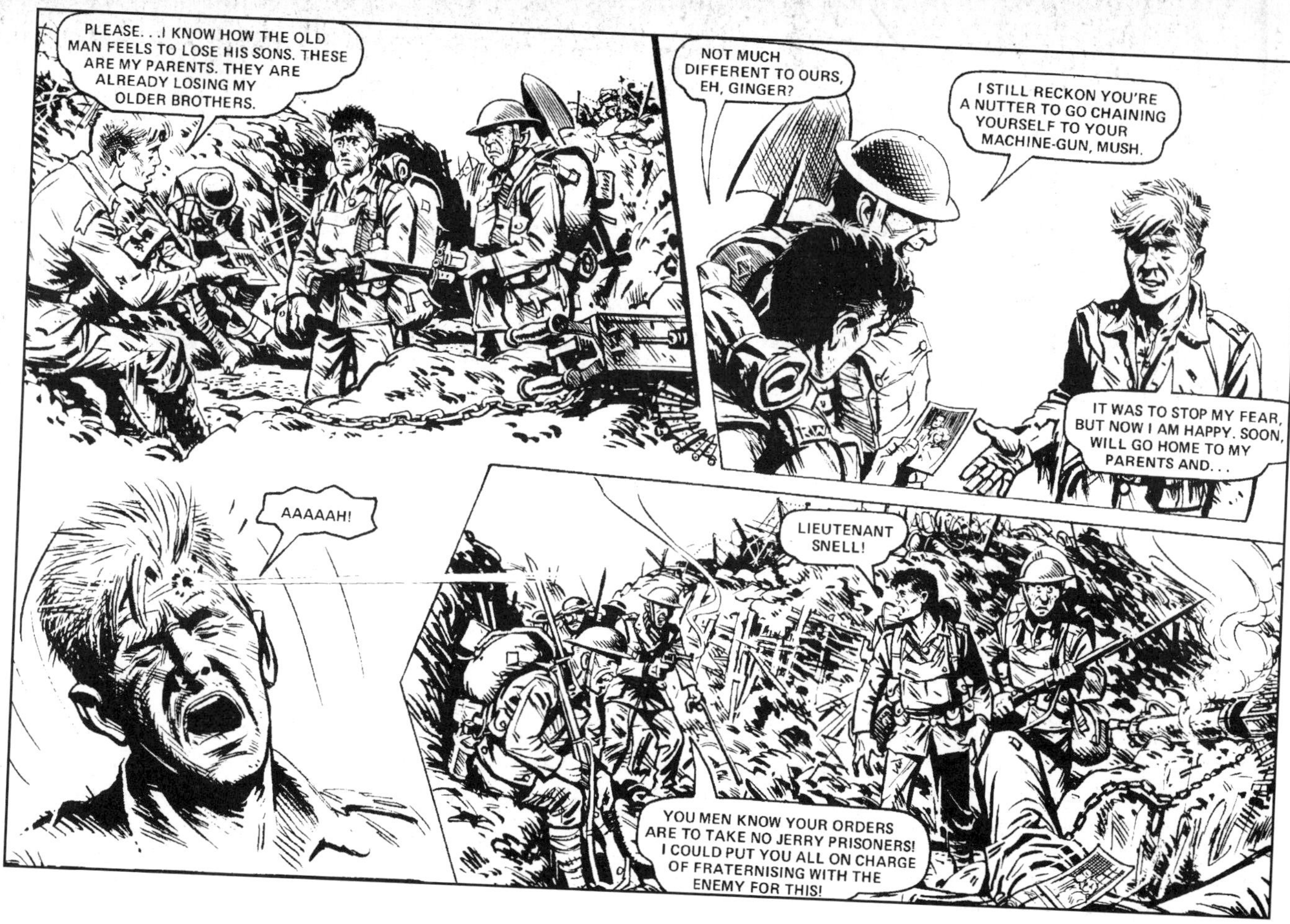
PLEASE. . .I KNOW HOW THE OLD MAN FEELS TO LOSE HIS SONS. THESE ARE MY PARENTS. THEY ARE ALREADY LOSING MY OLDER BROTHERS.
NOT MUCH DIFFERENT TO OURS, EH, GINGER?
I STILL RECKON YOU'RE A NUTTER TO GO CHAINING YOURSELF TO YOUR MACHINE-GUN, MUSH.
IT WAS TO STOP MY FEAR, BUT NOW I AM HAPPY. SOON, WILL GO HOME TO MY PARENTS AND. . .
AAAAAH!
LIEUTENANT SNELL!
YOU MEN KNOW YOUR ORDERS ARE TO TAKE NO JERRY PRISONERS! I COULD PUT YOU ALL ON CHARGE OF FRATERNISING WITH THE ENEMY FOR THIS!

this essential truth that gave the strip its teeth. Long before Norman Tebbit got his knickers in a twist over *The Monocled Mutineer*, *Battle* fans were reading about the British Army mutiny at Etaples in *Charley's War*. The novel *Regeneration* highlighted the shameful discrepancy in the treatment of shell-shock for officers and enlisted men: Mills and Colquhoun had done it first, a good twelve years beforehand.

Mills' greatest triumph, however, was Charley Bourne himself. Creating a successful character whose defining trait is decency is no mean feat; normally, you end up with a dreary goody two-shoes of the kind that infests American superhero comics. Anti-heroes and lovable rogues are much easier to write, quickly overshadowing the straightforward hero. A very basic example: did anyone really care about Luke Skywalker once Han Solo showed up in *Star Wars*? Charley was nothing more than a good young man who struggled to do the right thing, who somehow held onto his humanity in the face of utter Hell – and we loved him for it. He is, quite simply, Pat Mills' greatest creation.

To claim that the men who fought in the trenches of the Western Front were all like Charley would be fantasy; human nature being what it is, there were no doubt as many villains as good guys among their number. The vast majority were merely ordinary. They did their duty as it was explained to them, kept their heads down, and waited for their time "up the sharp end" to be over, one way or another. The point, however, is that they were *there*: volunteers or conscripts, they went to fight for something called their country. Arguments about hindsight and the harsh realities of warfare notwithstanding, they deserved more than to be sent into the German guns by men who could think of nothing better. "What else could they have done?" is just not good enough, whatever spin the current theorists seek to put on horrors like the Somme, Ypres, Verdun, and all the rest.

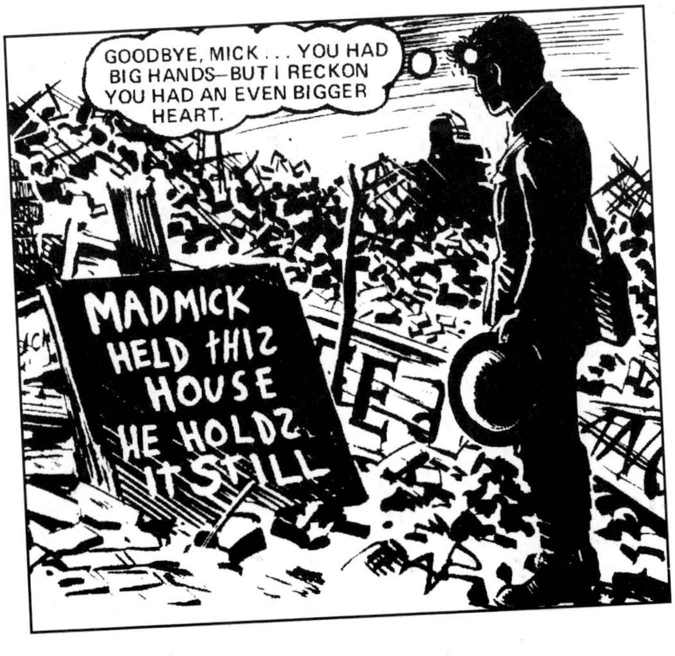
GOODBYE, MICK . . . YOU HAD BIG HANDS—BUT I RECKON YOU HAD AN EVEN BIGGER HEART.
MADMICK HELD THIZ HOUSE HE HOLDZ IT STILL

If you're new to *Charley's War*, I envy you. You've met an unforgettable cast of characters in a story all the more affecting for its basis in reality. Book One related Charley's arrival in the trenches, his exploits on the first terrible day of the Battle of the Somme, and the gruesome secret of the Lost Platoon. This second volume features Weeper and the Beast, the astonishing beginnings of tank warfare, and one of the most memorable sequences in comics' history: "My mate, Sir. My mate Ginger."

The beautiful artwork of Joe Colquhoun and the sheer genius of Pat Mills at his very, very best. The finest comic strip you'll ever read.

Charley's War. ✢

Garth Ennis
New York, August 2005

Garth Ennis is a prolific author of comics. Starting his career on 2000 AD*'s* Judge Dredd*, he has gone on to create some of the most controversial comics of modern times, including* Heartland *and* Preacher*. He has worked extensively in the war comics genre, most recently on the* War Story *series for DC/Vertigo, but also on* Enemy Ace: War in Heaven *and the madcap comedy* Adventures in the Rifle Brigade*. He is currently writing Marvel Comics'* The Punisher *and* Ghost Rider *series, and working on a number of his own projects, including* Back to Brooklyn, Wormwood, *and a new ongoing series,* The Boys.

ALSO AVAILABLE FROM TITAN BOOKS

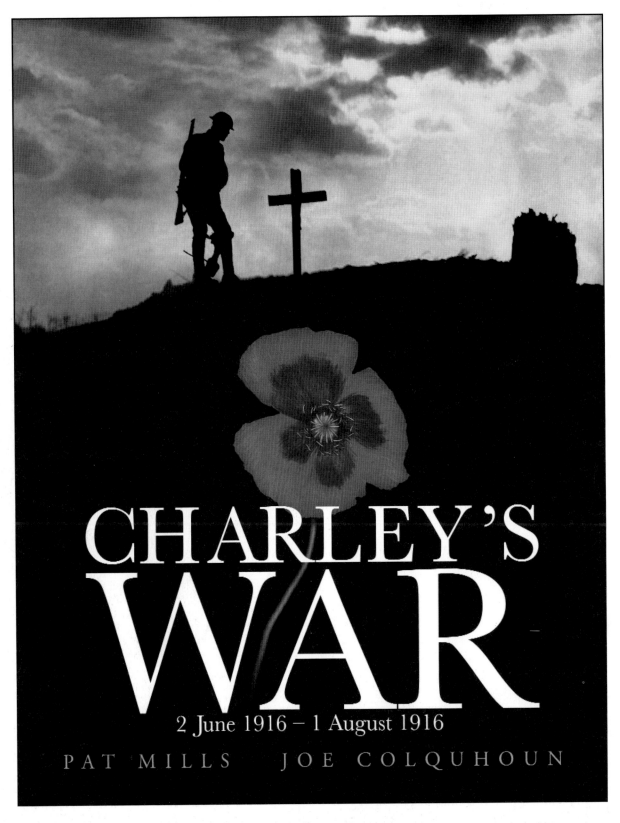